COLIN McPHEE
COMPOSER IN TWO WORLDS

McPhee at work as a writer in
the early 1950s. Photo by Victor Kraft; courtesy of Oliver
Daniel.

COLIN McPHEE

COMPOSER IN TWO WORLDS

CAROL J. OJA

Smithsonian Institution Press

Washington and London

Editor: Gretchen Smith Mui
Production Editor: Duke Johns
Designer: Linda McKnight

Library of Congress Cataloging-in-Publication Data

Oja, Carol J., 1953–
    Colin McPhee : composer in two worlds / Carol J.
Oja.
        p.   cm.
    Includes bibliographical references.
    ISBN 0-87474-732-5 (alk. paper)
    1. McPhee, Colin, 1900–1964.   2. Composers—
United States—Biography.   I. Title.
ML410.M1704   1990
780'.92—dc20
[B]   89-600387

British Library Cataloguing-in-Publication Data
available

Manufactured in the United States of America
97 96 95 94 93 92 91 90   5 4 3 2 1

∞ The paper used in this publication meets the
minimum requirements of the American National
Standard for Permanence of Paper for Printed Library
Materials Z39.48-1984

Unless otherwise indicated in the captions, all photographs in this book are reproduced courtesy of the Colin McPhee Collection, Ethnomusicology Archive, University of California, Los Angeles. For permission to reproduce illustrations, please correspond directly with the owners of the works. The Smithsonian Institution Press does not retain reproduction rights for these illustrations individually or maintain a file of addresses for photo sources.

The iconic figure accompanying the chapter titles is a representation of a traditional Balinese "Rice Mother," a fertility figure made of palm leaves which adorns shrines when rice seeds start to sprout.

To my parents,
Helen and Onni Oja

CONTENTS

PREFACE

Today, in our so-called postmodern era, American composers freely roam the world for inspiration and techniques. The fusion of musical cultures has become the rule rather than the exception. Steve Reich has studied African drumming and Indonesian gamelan, as well as the European classics. La Monte Young is a specialist in Indian traditions and writes incantatory, drone-based compositions. John Zorn constructs deliberately chaotic collages out of sources ranging from Viennese atonality to Vietnamese rock and roll. Songwriter Paul Simon collaborates with a Zulu choral group from South Africa, while "new age" musicians look to Asia for models of meditative serenity.

This musical globe-trotting was not always so prevalent. Only a few decades ago composers were just beginning to peer across Western boundaries into "the whole world of music," as Henry Cowell often put it. Cowell was prominent among them, as were Dane Rudhyar, Harry Partch, and Henry Eichheim. Perhaps the most unusual of these figures was Colin McPhee, a Canadian-born composer making his career in the United States, who in 1931 decided to travel to the island of Bali. He did so in an era when few Balinese gamelans, the island's now-famous percussion orchestras, had been heard in the West. And he did so long before composers such as John Cage or Lou Harrison became disciples of the East.

Unlike his contemporaries, who experienced Asian musics mainly through recordings and those few native performers living in the United States, McPhee journeyed directly to the source of the sounds, living in Bali for nearly a decade and incorporating his experiences into prose and music.

McPhee's achievements are often overlooked today. Few music students come across his name in textbooks, and his works are seldom performed in the United States (they are, however, becoming increasingly popular in Canada and Western Europe). McPhee is remembered primarily by ethnomusicologists and scholars of Southeast Asia. Yet his saga is intriguing not only for his fieldwork but also for his role in integrating the sounds and philosophies of the East into Western composition, especially in his pathbreaking orchestral piece of 1936, *Tabuh-Tabuhan*. His work provides a vital link between Claude Debussy's first encounter with an Indonesian gamelan in Paris in 1889 and the cross-cultural explorations of the late twentieth century. At the same time his story gives an instructive view of the difficulties of surviving as a composer in America. McPhee's status became increasingly precarious as the years passed, and his problems were determined as much by the mechanics of success as by deepening personal distress.

My own attraction to McPhee's work came first through his writings, both in reviews for *Modern Music,* the "little magazine" of American composers, and in his two major books, *A House in Bali* (1946) and *Music in Bali* (1966). He was a skilled stylist, with prose so limpid and evocative that it suggested his subjects as much through assonance as through meaning. Having encountered such a gifted writer, I grew curious about his music and turned to his Concerto for Piano with Wind Octette (1928) and *Tabuh-Tabuhan,* among the few McPhee works to be recorded. Again I felt I had entered a special realm, one of highly developed craftsmanship and inspired invention. After traveling to Bali and experiencing firsthand the legacy of McPhee's work with gamelan musicians during the 1930s, I knew I was facing a career of unusual dimensions, important both for the ways that it broke with convention and for the music and prose it yielded.[1]

If McPhee's career could be represented on a musical score, there would be an opening *sforzando,* followed by erratic highs and lows diminishing into a long, slow *pianissimo.* His life was marked by paradoxes.

While exceptionally talented as both a composer and a writer, he repeatedly lost faith in his abilities. While desiring—even requiring—fame and recognition in order to continue producing, he was unwilling or unable to take the practical steps necessary for achieving them. And while a dedicated artist, driven by the need to express himself in words and music, he would periodically disdain his creativity (even calling it a "burden") by indulging in a hedonistic whim or simply by stopping work.

While these paradoxes were present from the beginning, their negative poles exerted increasingly stronger forces after McPhee composed *Tabuh-Tabuhan,* a work in which he pushed beyond exotic surface effects to reach for an aesthetic union of his Western heritage with Balinese traditions. The piece was written in 1936 and premiered that year in Mexico City. McPhee hung his future on it. But as time passed and the work continued to be unperformed in America, his spirits sank. Other American composers were also suffering neglect. Harold Shapero, a generation younger than McPhee, had a similar experience with his Symphony for Classical Orchestra of 1947, a work ignored for some time after its premiere but now highly respected. Shapero has recalled, "I never wanted to write a big piece after that, and the worst thing that happened was I thought it was all my fault. . . . The hell with [composing], is what I thought." [2] And Joseph Horowitz, in his study of the impact of Arturo Toscanini on American musical taste, has cited McPhee as one of many composers who were victims of Toscanini's "Great Performances" cult, which encouraged worship at the altar of historic European icons. [3]

Rather than seeing his woes as part of conditions within a greater musical community, McPhee took neglect personally. Yet while his individual story may not have been one of steady ascent, his work emanated a distinctive beauty—sensual, often mystical, always richly sonorous. He treated Balinese culture with reverence, and after returning from the island he dedicated himself to conveying that attitude to the Western world.

The complexities of McPhee's personal story and artistic output have affected what materials remain for documenting his life. The Ethnomusicology Archive at the University of California in Los Angeles contains the bulk of his legacy. Its contents are scanty for the early years—the happy and successful ones—and plentiful for the later, darker period. The explanation for this imbalance seems to have two facets: in times of tribulation, McPhee deliberately destroyed memories of happier days, at the same time winnowing his possessions out of practical necessity. Of the more than thirty-five compositions he wrote before the age of twenty-five, only two survive. Perhaps the biggest loss from this early period is the so-called Toronto Piano Concerto. In 1963 he wrote Oliver Daniel, then president of Broadcast Music, Inc., regarding the score: "I'm afraid there is no copy in existence. I took the score to Paris when I went there to study in 1924, but got sick of toting it around after a couple of years, and threw it out with the garbage, if I remember."[4] This may have been a histrionic exaggeration. But such destruction also may have become part of a pattern, for the two remaining early works, as well as McPhee's next extant opus, the Invention for Piano of 1926, survive because they were published. The same is true for much of the rest of his output; the extant works, by and large, are the published ones—those preserved in spite of him.

Together with music manuscripts, McPhee also got rid of many personal documents, especially letters. Writing to his close friend Sidney Cowell in 1945, McPhee acknowledged the drive to obliterate his life story. His letter was inspired by Mrs. Cowell's suggestion that he submit biographical information to David Ewen for *American Composers Today:*

> The other day, . . . I tore up old programs [he lists the contents
> of a Toronto recital from the 1920s] . . . and the reviews after-
> wards. . . . All this, of course, I bury. And I simply can't be
> bothered with old Ewen. It is nobody's business, anyway, what
> I've chosen to make of my life, even if, as you hint, there is a
> legend.[5]

McPhee's destruction of papers was not unique. Other artists—W. H. Auden, Willa Cather, Henry James—have done the same out of a desire for personal privacy. But often that privacy had a special purpose: to conceal homosexuality. Whether this was McPhee's motive can only be guessed at. With the exception of his marriage to Jane Belo, from 1930 to

1938, all his romantic relationships seem to have been with men. Although he was discreet about his sexual liasons, once telling the composer David Diamond that he was "not an exhibitionist,"[6] he did not seem uncomfortable or apologetic when mentioning his relationships in letters. Yet being homosexual in McPhee's day meant keeping an important part of one's self hidden from public view. Secrecy was a way of life.

Some papers exist in spite of McPhee's destructive tendencies. The collection at UCLA contains nearly all his extant compositions, as well as correspondence (mostly from the late 1950s and 1960s), concert programs and newspaper clippings (some of which reach back to his childhood in Toronto), and field notes, transcriptions, and photographs (both movies and still shots) from the years in Bali. No matter how low his mood, McPhee never destroyed any of his Balinese materials.

I have supplemented the collection at UCLA by turning to McPhee's friends and colleagues both for correspondence and for personal memories. Although McPhee did not preserve letters, many of his friends saved the ones he wrote to them. Early on McPhee severed contact with his family in Canada, yet I was able to interview his sister-in-law, Janet McPhee, in Toronto. She, in turn, directed me to one of his childhood friends, Stuart Lawson. Each succeeding period of McPhee's life has been illuminated by other contemporaries. Ann Hull and Sylvan Levin were classmates of his at the Peabody Conservatory in Baltimore from 1918 to 1921. Eric Friedheim knew him in Toronto between 1921 and 1924, when McPhee was a student of Eric's father, Arthur. Aaron Copland, Otto Luening, Hugh Ross, and Louise Varèse remember him from New York in the late 1920s. I Madé Lebah and Anak Agung Gedé Mandera both worked with him in Bali during the 1930s. And Chou Wen-chung, Sidney Cowell, Oliver Daniel, David Diamond, Minna Lederman, and Virgil Thomson came into his life after he returned from Bali in 1939. Ki Mantle Hood and Shirley Hawkins helped him a great deal at UCLA in the early 1960s.

A few details require clarification. Fixing dates in McPhee's life is often difficult not only because documentation is so sparse for certain periods but also because he was quite casual about dating. Often his letters simply say "Monday" or "Thursday," and his field notes frequently give a day and month but no year. To confuse matters further, he made many errors about dates in writing autobiographical statements, including a puzzling change of his birth year, implemented early on. McPhee was skilled, whether intentionally or not, at obscuring the chronology of his life.

Also, discrepancies will be noted between McPhee's spelling of Indonesian terms and my own. During the 1930s, when he was in Bali, a Dutch system of spelling was used; it has since been replaced by a modern Indonesian method in which *u* is used instead of *oe, y* replaces *j, j* replaces *dj,* and *c* replaces *tj.* All Dutch spellings in quotations from McPhee have been kept intact. As much as possible, however, I have used modern spellings within my own text.

Finally, it should be stated that the focus here is on McPhee's life and music. Detailed analysis of his ethnomusicological research awaits future scholars.

ACKNOWLEDGMENTS

Many friends and colleagues, both of Colin McPhee and myself, have helped with this book. Shirley Hawkins, executrix of the McPhee estate, has not only granted access to the McPhee collection; she and her husband Richard Hawkins have also generously given me a place to stay while doing research in California. Sidney Cowell, Oliver Daniel, David Diamond, Minna Lederman, and Janet McPhee, each with a close connection to Colin McPhee, have also freely shared memories and materials. Ann Briegleb, formerly ethnomusicology archivist, and Stephen Fry, formerly music librarian, have eased use of the McPhee papers at the University of California, Los Angeles.

For their many valuable comments, about both the language and the contents of this manuscript, I am grateful to H. Wiley Hitchcock, who generously shared his keen editorial sense and musicianship; to Sherman Van Solkema, who suggested fresh insights into McPhee's music; and to Hildred Geertz and Leo Kraft, who offered much valuable advice. I am also grateful to Kathleen Mason Krotman, Nancy Pardo, and the late Frances Solomon, all on the staff of the Institute for Studies in American Music at Brooklyn College, who transcribed interviews and helped with correspondence, and to the Martha Baird Rockefeller Fund for Music, Inc., the Newberry Library, and the Sinfonia Foundation for research grants.

ACKNOWLEDGMENTS

Thanks as well to Martin Williams at the Smithsonian Institution Press, for taking on this project, and to his colleagues there, Duke Johns and Gretchen Smith Mui, for their impressive editorial precision and general helpfulness. Perhaps the biggest debt is owed my parents, Helen and Onni Oja, for untold generosities over the years, and my husband, Mark Tucker, for his imaginative editorial suggestions and a great deal more.

Many others have contributed to this study, both through correspondence and in person. To all the following I extend my thanks: Judith Becker, University of Michigan; John Beckwith, Institute for Canadian Music, University of Toronto; Michael Blackwood, New York City; Paul Bowles, Tangier, Morocco; Robert Brown, San Diego State University; Maria Calderisi, National Library of Canada, Ottawa; Pino Confessa, Den Pasar, Bali; Mercer Cook, Silver Spring, Maryland; Aaron Copland, Peekskill, New York; Frederick Crane, University of Iowa; Marian Eames, London; James A. Fraser, City of Toronto Archives; Eric Friedheim, New York City; Jose Alvarez Fuentes, Archivo General de la Nacion, Mexico City; Peggy Glanville-Hicks, Sydney, Australia; Emily Good, New York City; Robert Gray, University of Illinois; Victor Carl Guarneri, New York City; Lou Harrison, Aptos, California; Alan Hewitt, New York City; Ki Mantle Hood, University of Maryland–Baltimore County; Audrey Hozack, Hart House, Toronto; Ann Hull, Westport, Connecticut; B. Hunge, New York City; Helmut Kallmann, National Library of Canada; Stuart Lawson, Toronto; I Madé Lebah, Peliatan, Bali; Sylvan Levin, New York City; Otto Luening, New York City; Carolynn Q. McIlnay, registrar, Peabody Conservatory; Bruce MacIntyre, Brooklyn College; Katharane Mershon, Tarzana, California; Rhoda Métraux, Craftsbury, Vermont; Donald Mitchell, London; Paula Morgan, Music Library, Princeton University; Mrs. Allen T. Morrison, Asheville, North Carolina; Alix Moyer, Brooklyn, New York; Joseph Natoli, Niles, Ohio; Jane Olson, Hamden, Connecticut; Don Ott, Ardsley, New York; Edwin A. Quist, Music Library, Peabody Conservatory; Hugh Ross, New York City; William Rueter, Toronto; Beata Sauerlander, New York City; Wayne Shirley, Library of Congress; Louise Spear, Ethnomusicology Archive, UCLA; Ralph Steiner, Thetford Hill, Vermont; William Strickland, Westport, Connecticut; Virgil Thomson, New York City; Andrew Toth, Sanur, Bali; Nadia

Turbide, Westmount, Quebec; Louise Varèse, New York City; David Walker, New York City; William Wallis, Alma Hyslop, and Susan M. S. Gastle, Metropolitan Toronto Library Board; Carol Warren, Murdoch University, Australia; Donald White, Red Bank, New Jersey; and Nora Yeh, Ethnomusicology Archive, UCLA.

In addition, I am grateful to the following sources for their permission to quote from various materials:

For the papers and musical compositions of Colin McPhee: Shirley Hawkins, executrix of the Colin McPhee Collection, Ethnomusicology Archive, University of California, Los Angeles.

For McPhee's Concerto for Wind Orchestra: © 1960 by C. F. Peters Corporation, used by permission.

For McPhee's *Sea Shanty Suite:* © Edwin F. Kalmus & Co., Inc.

For McPhee's *Tabuh-Tabuhan* and *Balinese Ceremonial Music:* © 1960, 1940 G. Schirmer.

For material from McPhee's *Music in Bali:* © 1966 Yale University.

For Colin McPhee's Peabody records: The Archives of the Peabody Institute of the Johns Hopkins University.

For materials from the Margaret Mead Papers, Library of Congress: Courtesy of the Institute for Intercultural Studies, Inc., New York.

For the papers of Benjamin Britten: By permission of the Trustees of the Britten-Pears Foundation and the Britten-Pears Library.

For the papers of Walter Spies: By permission of the Stichting Walter Spiess, Rijksuniversiteit te Leiden.

For the papers of Oliver Daniel: Collection of Oliver Daniel, Ardsley, New York.

For Stravinsky's Piano Sonata: © Boosey & Hawkes, Inc.

LIST OF INSTRUMENT AND PERFORMER ABBREVIATIONS

bcl	bass clarinet		ob	oboe
bsn	bassoon		pic	piccolo
cb	contrabass		pf	piano
cbsn	contrabassoon		sop	soprano
cel	celesta		tamb	tambourine
cl	clarinet		tbn	trombone
E hn	English horn		timp	timpani
fl	flute		tpt	trumpet
glock	glockenspiel		tu	tuba
hn	horn		vcl	violoncello
hp	harp		xyl	xylophone
mrmb	marimba			

Adapted from the BMI Symphonic Catalogue: Supplement #1 (New York: Broadcast Music Inc., 1978)

1

THE EDUCATION OF A PRODIGY

 1900–26

The story of Colin McPhee begins not in Bali or the United States but in Canada, where his family had settled two generations earlier. There he was championed by well-respected musicians and given every opportunity to excel. Several teachers recognized his talent early on, making it possible for him to dream grander-than-average dreams.

McPhee's Old World ancestry was Scottish. His forebears had come to Canada from Islay in the Inner Hebrides, a barren island wide open for sheep grazing. In the early 1830s, as Islayan lands were divided up by a surge of newly arrived mainland Scots, many of the island's residents emigrated to Canada and Australia. Among them was Colin McPhee's paternal great-grandfather John Campbell (1784–1854), who settled about twenty miles southwest of Toronto in an area now called Campbellville. He built a small, stucco-covered log house across from a pond, opened a sawmill, and joined other members of the growing community in founding St. David's Church, a simple structure of now-mellowed red brick on the outskirts of town.[1]

For Colin Carhart McPhee, born in Montreal on March 15, 1900, Campbellville was the family seat.[2] As a boy he often spent summer vacations there, and after his parents moved to Toronto he and his younger brother, Douglas, enjoyed bicycling to the neighboring village. Colin's grandmother, a roughhewn, no-nonsense frontier woman, whom Colin later remembered as wearing boots and smoking a pipe, lived in Campbellville until her death in her nineties.[3] The Campbellville house stayed in the McPhee family through the 1930s.

Years later Colin recalled images of Campbellville and his Canadian church experience when he reviewed Charles Ives's Fourth Violin Sonata. His thoroughly unsentimental reminiscences must have been of St. David's:

> [Ives's Fourth Sonata] has all the nostalgia for Sunday, Moody-and-Sankey, pre-radio peace. Perhaps because of my Presbyterian childhood I remain untouched even by the famous footnotes. I too have sweltered on a hot Sunday afternoon, singing hymns in a red brick church, and I have never cherished the memory, but then, that was in Canada, among log cabins, without the glamor of Alcott.[4]

In Campbellville Colin McPhee's father, Alexander, was born around 1865. Remembered by Colin's sister-in-law, Janet McPhee, as a "rangy, craggy Scot" with "a delightful sense of humor," Alexander was over six feet tall with blue eyes, red hair, and a "dignified" look.[5] He worked in advertising for various newspapers and for the Bell Telephone Company. Colin, whose adult height was a stocky five feet, seven inches, did not resemble his father much in stature, yet the two shared personality traits, especially a facile intelligence. Alexander gained early recognition by devising a version of the Yellow Pages. But according to Janet McPhee, "Later on—well, he made out, but when he retired he was nothing. He had a good mind but without the discipline. It's 'discipline'—that's the whole word. Dougie [Colin's brother] too: brilliant but not disciplined."

Colin took after his mother, Lavinia Carhart, in many more ways. Born of German folk in 1875 in Red Bank, New Jersey, she was "small and round, bright and clever," and she, too had red-gold hair. After marrying Alexander, she settled with him in Montreal. While Janet McPhee has remembered Alexander as perpetually buoyant, "anything but a moody man," Lavinia could be "petulant and demanding . . . expecting everything to come to her," traits that would later emerge in her elder son.

The McPhee family: Alexander, Colin, Douglas, and Lavinia, ca. 1904–5. Reproduced from *Nassagaweya: A History of Campbellville and Surrounding Area* (Campbellville Historical Society, 1982); courtesy of the Metropolitan Toronto Library Board and with the permission of the Campbellville Historical Society.

In 1913 the McPhees moved to Toronto, living in three different houses over the next five years.[6] The last of these still stands at 36 Pacific Avenue. It is a three-story, turn-of-the-century structure in a middle-class neighborhood.

BOYHOOD IN TORONTO

While modern Toronto is a bustling cosmopolitan center with skyscrapers and a large international population, during Colin McPhee's adolescence it was mostly Anglo-Saxon and had a more modest bearing. Like the large midwestern cities in the United States, Toronto was remote and even provincial in some respects, set in the middle of "the cold, clean, remorseless land" described by the Canadian author Robertson Davies.[7] Yet Toronto had a strong cultural life and was growing rapidly. The city's population registered 208,000 in 1901 and increased by more than 80 percent by 1911; within the next ten years it rose to 522,000.[8] Similarly, its boundaries were expanding enormously, and cultural growth kept apace, making Toronto one of Canada's main music centers. Several large concert halls boasted busy performing schedules, especially St. Lawrence Hall, seating five hundred, which had opened in the 1850s, and Massey Hall, seating four thousand, which opened in 1894.[9] Traveling virtuosos stopped off there in both the late nineteenth and early twentieth centuries. In McPhee's day Torontonians could hear Jascha Heifetz or Amelita Galli-Curci and even contemporary composers from the United States, such as Leo Ornstein or Mrs. H. H. A. Beach.[10] Toronto's first orchestra was founded in 1906; it disbanded in 1918 and regrouped in 1923. There were also several schools of music, including the Toronto Conservatory of Music, founded in 1886 and later renamed the Royal Conservatory of Music, the Canadian Academy of Music, and the Hambourg Conservatory, both founded in 1911.

Around the time that the McPhee family moved to Toronto, another boy Colin's age arrived—Stuart Lawson, who has recalled Colin vividly.[11] Both began studying at the Hambourg Conservatory—Lawson in violin, McPhee in piano and composition. Lawson has remembered McPhee as "a person unto himself, . . . a nice lad [who was] very much of a prima donna. . . . Colin and his brother Douglas were very different from one another." Colin was much more "withdrawn" and did not keep in touch with his friends after he left Toronto. "His hands were beautiful, he could stretch tenths so easily. . . . His piano playing was superb."

The Hambourg Conservatory, where McPhee and Lawson both studied, had been started in 1911 by several members of the Hambourg family, Russians who had arrived in Toronto the previous year. In 1913 the conservatory moved to a new location at the corner of Wellesley Street East and Sherbourne Street, a large building that Lawson remembers as a center of musical and cultural activity. The Toronto Symphony practiced there, as did the conservatory's own Hambourg Trio. Many visual artists and writers—such as the painters Arthur Lismer and John Russell and the poets E. J. Pratt, Charles G. D. Roberts, and Arthur Stringer—often met there as well.[12]

One prominent member of the Hambourg Conservatory's faculty was Ernest Farmer (1883–1975), who became McPhee's piano and composition teacher and spurred the young musician's development. An Ontario native, Farmer had followed a pattern typical for Canadian musicians of his day, studying both at home (at the Toronto Conservatory of Music) and abroad (at the Royal Conservatory in Leipzig with Max Reger).

Farmer was well known enough in Toronto to be featured in the February 1916 issue of the *Canadian Journal of Music*. His picture was on the cover, and inside were a profile of his work and an article by him.[13] Farmer believed that composing was essential to the education of all musicians:

> The ability to compose even quite commonplace little pieces, so long as they are correct and pleasing and with a touch of brilliancy or ideal beauty, brings with it so much intimate insight into the nature of music, . . . that no musical education should be considered quite successful without it.

Farmer bemoaned teaching conditions in Toronto: students lacked "suitable" textbooks and suffered under "the delusion that no Canadian, unless he has been to Germany, can possibly compose real music." But he singled out one student, Colin McPhee, whose talent justified "ten times the extra trouble" and set him apart as "the best of four or five decidedly brilliant young composers."

McPhee must have started studying with Farmer right after his family moved to Toronto. With these lessons began a busy music schedule. His first concert review appeared in 1914, when he took part in a recital by pupils of Farmer and his brother Broadus, a violinist. Although the review was short, McPhee and another young fellow were singled out for praise: "The programme included compositions by four pupils of Mr. Ernest Farmer—Douglas Crowe, Sam Sadowski, Gerald Moore [the now-famous accompanist], and Colin McPhee. The two latter, boys of twelve or fourteen, show a constructive skill and poetic feeling which suggest great possibilities."[14]

One year later a Toronto paper published a longer, more detailed account of McPhee's achievements; it was followed by a number of others. Although local Toronto music journals (the *Canadian Journal of Music* and *Musical Canada*) and newspapers (*The Globe, Mail and Empire, Saturday Night*) dutifully reported recitals by many young people, they were especially enthusiastic about McPhee, describing him as a "rising star" or a "specially talented youth."[15] Typical was the following:

> The writer recently had the privilege of hearing the compositions of an unusually gifted young Toronto boy, Colin McFee [*sic*] who has just passed his fifteenth birthday. . . . Young McFee played a Polonaise. . . . The composition was so mature in style that most of the audience assumed that the name of the performer attached to it on the programme was a printer's error. Nevertheless it was an original work by the lad himself, and a very virile and promising work at that. . . . He has a fine feeling for rhythm and an instinct for harmony, with a melodic inspiration surprising for a lad still in knicker-bockers.[16]

McPhee must have been a prolific young composer. Recital programs attest to this, as do his own offhand comments to friends in letters written later in life. The reviewer who described McPhee's *Polonaise* went on to mention other works by the boy: "several 'Album Leaves,'" "Caprices," and "several songs, one of which, a setting of Pauline Johnson's lyric 'The Robin' is particularly delightful." Another Toronto music critic, Hector Charlesworth (1872–1945), recalled *The Robin* years later when he looked back on McPhee's career:

> It does not seem so long ago—though two world cataclysms have happened since—that Ernest Farmer, a Toronto piano teacher, brought to me a little pupil of his, who was not only skilful (for his years) on the piano, but possessed of original gifts as a composer. He was a bright-eyed, fair-haired youngster, and the little pieces he played (one I think had been inspired by the song of a robin) had fresh, ingenuous qualities. The little boy was Colin McPhee. . . . In his 'teens he showed unusual virtuosic ability.[17]

In his article on teaching composition (published in 1916, when McPhee was sixteen), Ernest Farmer claimed that his young pupil had written fifty pages of music.[18]

Only two compositions survive from McPhee's youth: *Four Piano Sketches,* op. 1 (1916), and *Arm, Canadians! March to Glory!* (1917). The former was published by the Empire Music and Travel Club of Toronto, which was affiliated with the Toronto College of Music, and the latter by Whaley, Royce, & Co.[19] The *Sketches* are simple pieces, well-structured, fresh, competently written. With titles reminiscent of nineteenth-century album leaves, each captures a single mood or image: "April," "Prelude," "Water Nymph," and "Silhouette." Such pianistic impressions were the stuff of the day, judging from the regular "New Music" column of the *Canadian Journal of Music.* The pieces were written under Farmer's tutelage, and he singled out "Water Nymph" as a successful product of his pedagogical method.[20]

McPhee's *Sketches* attracted considerable attention in Toronto. Farmer taught them to his piano pupils and performed them at one of the Hambourg Conservatory's regular Saturday recitals.[21] A single sketch, "Water Nymph," was published separately in the *Canadian Journal of Music* in February 1916 as part of a series begun the previous fall.

The second of McPhee's two early publications was *Arm, Canadians! March to Glory!,* subtitled "Canadian War Song" and dedicated to "Canada's Heroic Army." It bore a weighty endorsement: "Highly commended by Gen. Sir Douglas Haig, Commander-in-Chief of the British Army in France." Patriotic fever ran high in Canada during World War I and must have hit young Colin as hard as it did many of his countrymen. His song was one of more than three hundred such pieces published in Canada between 1914 and 1918.[22] *Arm, Canadians!* (ex. 1) is a rousing call to battle. The text, by Victor Wyldes, has bold sounds and melodramatic images:

> Sons of Heroes! Heirs of Empire!
> Bred to dare and fear no fate,
> Set ablaze our freedom's watchfire:
> Arm to war on Hosts of Hate.
> Loud the foe's defiant fanfare
> Sounds across the ocean deep:
> On the lurid fields of warfare
> Ghouls of Death their harvest reap [verse 1].

EXAMPLE I   *Arm, Canadians! March to Glory!* chorus.

McPhee's verse-chorus setting has a vigorous chordal accompaniment filled with left-hand octaves. It speaks the language of such rousing hymns of praise as Handel's "Thine Is the Glory" (from *Judas Maccabaeus*) and Oliver Holden's "All Hail the Power of Jesus' Name."

Whaley, Royce, & Co., which printed the song "for the author," was an old Toronto firm founded in 1888; from 1890 to 1920 it published more music than any other Canadian house.[23] Even its imprint, however, was not enough to make the work a success among the sea of other patriotic ditties. Janet McPhee remembers there were "stacks" of *Arm, Canadians!* stored in the basement of the McPhees' Pacific Avenue home.

A CONSERVATORY STUDENT

Colin McPhee left Canada in the fall of 1918 to further his musical education. Instead of Europe, which would have been the usual route for an ambitious young Canadian, he went to the Peabody Conservatory in Baltimore, the oldest such institution in the United States. These were the waning days of World War I—no time to sail for France or Germany. McPhee would have that experience later.

At Peabody McPhee concentrated equally on piano and composition, and as in Toronto he immediately made a strong impression, winning the three-year O. R. Boise Memorial Harmony Scholarship. His striking talent set him apart from his contemporaries, or so two of them remember.[24] Ann Hull, a student slightly older than McPhee, has said he "became quite famous among all of us because he was so gifted." Sylvan Levin, another fellow Peabody student, has concurred.

McPhee's two principal teachers at Peabody were Gustav Strube in composition and Harold Randolph in piano. Both were powerful presences at the conservatory. A 1944 article about Randolph for the *Musical Quarterly* conveyed reverential respect for the man; it was written by Denoe Leedy, who appears to have been a Randolph pupil, and it tells something of the teacher's background.[25] Randolph was educated in the United States, at Peabody, and directed the conservatory from 1898 until his death in 1927. Through Randolph, McPhee first touched the Liszt lineage, for Randolph's own Peabody piano teacher had been Carl Faelten, a Liszt pupil. Randolph attained modest stature as a virtuoso, performing with Theodore Thomas in the late 1880s and with the Boston Symphony Orchestra beginning in 1897; he also gave recitals with Fritz Kreisler and Maud Powell. According to Leedy, Randolph radiated virtue:

> a veritable symbol of musical and personal distinction. . . . The sum total of his qualities as man and artist had its ethical value. It taught one to cultivate self-discipline, to appraise all experience in terms of the highest standards, and to be both courageous and fastidious in shaping one's way of life.[26]

Gustav Strube also was someone to reckon with—a solid musician with an uncompromising professional manner. As conductor of the Baltimore Symphony Orchestra, he was described by an acquaintance as "a hard taskmaster" whose "language [could] be direct and sharp. . . . He frightened nearly everybody except those who refused to run up the white flag at his first gruff bark; if they stood their ground, the Old Man was ready to meet them on it." [27] His praise to students was "charily given." Strube came to Peabody in 1913 after playing first violin with the Boston Symphony Orchestra for twenty-three years. He had also conducted the Boston Pops from 1898 to 1912 and was associate conductor of the Worcester (Massachusetts) Festival from 1909 to 1916. Strube circulated among Baltimore's intelligentsia, especially the Saturday Night Club, a group of literary figures and musicians that included H. L. Mencken. He was an active composer whose newest works were occasionally featured in *Musical America* in the early years of the century. Despite a German heritage (or perhaps because of it), Strube was something of a musical Francophile. As a *Musical America* reporter put it in 1911, Strube tried "to beat the modern French man at his own game." [28] He admired the music of Debussy: "Never an ugliness, never a forced effect foreign to the nature of the instrument. Only beautiful sounds." And he found Vincent d'Indy to have "a great intellect and tremendous technic."

Under the supervision of these two men, McPhee grew enormously. As a pianist he appeared in twenty-two recitals in his three years at

Colin in the early 1920s.

Peabody. While his repertory drew upon standard literature, from Bach to Debussy, he also featured his own works on six of those programs. Among the highlights were performances of three piano concertos (Beethoven's Fourth, Saint-Saëns's Fourth, and McPhee's own First, the last two with the Peabody Orchestra), a solo piano recital, and a shared recital of his own compositions.[29] Ann Hull has remembered: "He could do anything at the piano. He could play two tunes at once—things like that." And Wallingford Riegger later claimed McPhee had told him that "his teachers wondered at his gift for improvising."[30]

In 1919 McPhee earned a teacher's certificate in piano and in 1921 a diploma in composition. He received no diploma in piano, and Harold Randolph's yearly evaluations of his pupil gave some clue why. Randolph concurred in part with McPhee's fellow students, such as Hull, when he described the young man as "an extraordinarily promising pupil" and "a talent of very nearly the first order." He pronounced McPhee's piano

hands "magnificent." [31] Yet his evaluations, which show careful considera-
tion of McPhee's aptitude and achievement, pinpointed a significant short-
coming from the outset: although McPhee was "very industrious," he was
"lacking in method." In 1918–19 Randolph observed, "Very marked piano
talent, but thro' either nervousness or lack of proper preparation always
disappoints in performance," and added, "considerable facility in and
understanding of modern music—almost none of classics." The next year
Randolph made a related judgment: "[McPhee] loves to be always exploring new fields instead of *completing* any undertaking. . . . [There is] still
much to desire considering his immense possibilities." Perhaps it is not
surprising, then, that Randolph's last evaluation (1920–21) began with the
words "Failed for Piano Diploma." After once again describing McPhee as
"extraordinarily" gifted and "quite unusually intelligent" and noting that
"his Examination Recital was about the best concert playing he ever did
here," Randolph went on to explain his verdict:

> Can't be certain whether his shortcomings are due to lack of real
> piano talent or inability to do the necessary intensive, thoughtful
> study. Certain it is that he has never played anything to my
> entire satisfaction. Makes excellent beginnings, but easy things
> get no further than the most difficult—in fact not so far.

That year, like the previous one, Randolph put a question mark under
"diligence." Perhaps McPhee was already showing signs of the "un-
disciplined brilliance" that his sister-in-law has described as a family trait.

McPhee seemed to have had more consistent success as a composer.
At Peabody he wrote some twenty works, including songs, short piano
pieces, two piano sonatas, and a piano concerto, *Le Mort d'Arthur,* which he
premiered with the Peabody Student Orchestra on May 26, 1920. None of
these is extant, yet they must have pleased McPhee's composition teacher
because he gave his young student strong evaluations. In 1919–20 and
1920–21 Strube filled out the same forms as had Randolph, awarding
McPhee 8s and 10s for diligence and progress and As for overall
achievement. [32]

McPhee had fun at Peabody, too. While at least one of his Toronto friends had characterized him as "withdrawn," in Baltimore he seemed to open up and was more than willing to leave the practice room for zany student antics. According to reports in the *Peabody Bulletin,* he was a cutup in skits at annual alumni dinners and plunged into a whirl of extracurricular activities. A mimed spoof of a piano recital was presented at a banquet in December 1919; one of the actors was "See See McPhee," cast in the role of "A Critic." C. C. presented a "delicate portrayal of the Critic's profound and interested attitude." [33]

Ann Hull has fondly remembered McPhee's Peabody pranks: "He was extremely personable and a lot of fun to be with." Already a budding gourmet, he once gave a luncheon in his apartment for Harold Randolph, as Hull has recalled:

> The apartment consisted of one room where he had a gas stove,
> and he cooked the meal on that. It was a complete luncheon
> featuring a chicken dish. . . . At the end Mr. Randolph said,
> 'What are you going to do with the bones, Colin?' And Colin
> said, 'Let me show you; it's very easy because this is a convenient
> apartment.' And with that he moved the stove over to the side,
> and there was a hole in the floor to the cellar. Colin simply threw
> the bones down the hole.

McPhee's final Peabody performance was not in the kitchen or concert hall but in the back pages of the *Peabody Bulletin,* where he published four of his caricatures. [34] With that he graduated and returned to Toronto, not just to be with family but to begin another critical leg of his musical journey.

TORONTO REVISITED

> He seems to have hands that can do anything on the keyboard
> and a brain that never forgets. And over both there is a tempera-
> ment that literally burns . . . a genius. [35]

These are extravagant words, but they became common in descriptions of McPhee's keyboard panache after his return to Toronto in 1921. Even the most idealistic expectations seemed to be coming true. His concerts were well publicized and their reviews stunning.

McPhee's move back to Toronto coincided with the arrival of the famed pianist Arthur Friedheim (1859–1932) at the Canadian Academy of Music. To Canadians Friedheim was a returning celebrity, and to McPhee he became an important teacher. In 1894, while touring North America to champion the music of Franz Liszt, Friedheim had been the featured soloist at the opening of Toronto's largest concert facility, Massey Hall. In fact, he was renowned in Canada as a whole, where "reviewers and audiences reacted with . . . unusual warmth in a country which was notoriously critical and unenthusiastic." [36] In 1914 he began a tour of one hundred Canadian cities, sponsored by the piano firm of Heintzman, which was to include "towns where no great performer had ever been heard." The tour had to be canceled soon after it began, however, because of the hostility that Friedheim's German name aroused as World War I got underway.

Friedheim's decision to begin teaching at the Canadian Academy in 1921 was a major event in Toronto, announced with a feature article in the July issue of *Musical Canada* and his picture on the magazine's September cover. He was hailed as "one of the greatest living exponents of Liszt." [37] Friedheim had studied first with Anton Rubinstein and then with Liszt during the last eight years of the composer's life, also serving as Liszt's secretary for a time in Rome and Weimar. The title of Friedheim's memoirs—*Life and Liszt*—suggests how much his self-image revolved around the old abbé.

With Friedheim by his side, McPhee focused on piano performance during the next three years in Toronto. He composed, but not as pro-lifically as at Peabody, and he also taught at the Canadian Academy. [38] He seemed to be preoccupied with building a strong keyboard technique and a personal interpretative voice. Friedheim and the music of Liszt guided the way.

McPhee developed a good relationship with his teacher, one that endured long beyond the Toronto years. Friedheim's son Eric has recalled, "Colin was very close to the Friedheim family in Toronto between 1921 and 1923, frequently dining with us at our resident hotel. My father considered Colin among his outstanding pupils." [39] In a short chapter of *Life and Liszt* titled "I Am Content," Arthur Friedheim later wrote of McPhee with admiration:

> [Today] I have received from far-off Java a letter from a former
> Toronto pupil, Colin McPhee, perhaps the most gifted pupil I
> ever had. His innate musical sense, his sturdy application and a
> striking personality marked him out for a brilliant career on the
> concert platform. I felt a sense of personal loss when, after I left
> Canada, he gave up the piano altogether and applied himself
> entirely to composition. [40]

Inspired by Friedheim, McPhee began to devote himself to the music of Liszt. His first solo recital under Friedheim's tutelage took place on February 16, 1922, at the Canadian Academy of Music and featured two Liszt works, *Harmonies du soir* and *Waldesrauschen*. [41] That May McPhee played the Liszt Second Piano Concerto at a recital of Friedheim's postgraduate students; Friedheim was at the second piano.

By December 1922, when McPhee made his official Toronto debut outside the sponsorship of any teacher or institution, a substantial Liszt group became a hallmark of his concerts and his own transcription of the *Rákoczy March* a staple. One critic—Hector Charlesworth, who had followed McPhee since childhood—was impressed with the young pianist's technical prowess: "He has an execution which dazzles by its masterful insouciance, backed by a youthful energy that is almost rampant. . . . His feats in glisando [*sic*], arpeggio, trilling and staccato passages were captivating." [42]

Another critic, Augustus Bridle, was less partisan, perhaps because he was just beginning a career at the *Toronto Daily Star* and had no connection to McPhee's past. Bridle depicted a hesitant young man, slightly awkward on stage. With this review Bridle began a series of pieces about McPhee that tell a great deal about the young musician's keyboard style, as well as his compositions: "With a mixture of nervous anxiety and studied nonchalance this youth who always leaves the stage with his left hand in his trousers pocket, flung out furies of triumphant sound that made the little theatre pulsate with unaccustomed energy." [43] But beneath this burst of brilliance Bridle looked for more sensitivity, more softness and lyrical relief:

> Sustained gusto, often rising to a brilliant bravour [*sic*], was the keynote. Only two or three times did he play cantabile with perfect ease; and even then he seemed impatient to begin some more dynamics. . . . His Beethoven Sonata was crisply and cleverly played. The player seemed to feel the tones and the rhythms rather than the piece.

For Bridle and others, it was with Liszt that McPhee soared: "The Liszt group McPhee seemed to enjoy rather [more] than most; no doubt because most of them are wild, big and daring and suitable to the prodigious ecstasy of youth." Bridle was enthusiastic about McPhee's rendition of the *Rákóczy March,* "which he has made one of his recent hobbies."

This recital at the Hart House Theatre was to be the first of three programs given there during the 1922–23 season. The series was highly publicized in Toronto, appearing in *The Globe*'s weekly list of important events for the 1922–23 season. McPhee was hailed alongside the likes of Paderewski, Hofmann, and Galli-Curci as "the brilliant Toronto pianist." [44]

The Hart House was a recent Toronto addition, having opened in November 1919 on the University of Toronto's St. George campus. Membership was limited to male students, graduates, and faculty members. A series of recitals and concerts, which eventually became a long-standing Hart House tradition, began on November 12, 1922, in an event featuring the pianists Reginald Stewart and McPhee, a thirty-voice choir, and a six-piece instrumental group conducted by J. Campbell-McInnes. [45]

The opening of Hart House made an impact on other young intellectuals in Toronto, such as Morley Callaghan (b. 1903), a Toronto native who was to have a successful career as a fiction writer. In his memoir, *That Summer in Paris,* Callaghan recalled how much the Hart House Library affected his intellectual development, for there he discovered authors such as F. Scott Fitzgerald. [46]

In addition to giving recitals in the Hart House concert hall, McPhee wrote music for two stage presentations in its theater. Neither score survives. The first was incidental music for a 1922 production of Hippo-lytus's *Euripides*. The music was scored for soprano solo, women's chorus, string trio, oboe, flute, and harp and seems to have been difficult: "Re-hearsals for this [production] have been going on for some time; [they have been] not less strenuous because the incidental music is one of the features of the presentation."[47] McPhee's second work was the accompaniment for a melodrama based on Matthew Arnold's *The Forsaken Merman,* given by Bertram Forsyth in the early twenties.[48]

McPhee composed other music in Toronto, although his own works appeared on only a few recitals. On February 16, 1922, at the Canadian Academy of Music he performed his *Elegy* and on the second Hart House program his *Improvisation* and *Sea Legend*. All are lost, and no reviewers appear to have commented on them.

Perhaps the most important of McPhee's Toronto compositions was his Second Piano Concerto, premiered by the Toronto Symphony Or-chestra on January 15, 1924.[49] This score, too, is no longer extant. Luigi von Kunits conducted, and McPhee was the soloist. The work had three movements: Allegro moderato, Scherzo vivace, and Finale. According to the program notes, "the Concerto No. 2 . . . is written somewhat in the style of a Symphony, the orchestra playing an equally important part with the piano." McPhee began composing the work in June 1923 and finished it by November. His recital appearances dwindled and then stopped entirely as he worked on the piece. Bridle billed the work as "the first time on record that a Canadian concerto has been played by a Canadian artist with a Canadian orchestra" and went on to boast that McPhee "copied out all the orchestral parts himself. The thing is entirely his own creation."[50]

Another reviewer depicted the work as adventuresome, even bois-terous. Listeners were bewildered: "The audience was large and very keen, but it is safe to say that a great many people left the hall more than a little puzzled, and others slightly amazed."[51] The absence of a recurring, lyrical melody jarred the audience, and several critics, such as the one quoted here, dubbed McPhee an experimenter. The style of the piece must have been new to Toronto.

In his preview of the concert, Bridle grasped a characteristic that was to become dominant in McPhee's later work: exploitation of timbre. Bridle suspected that the work's thematic fragmentation might be problematic for the audience, but he seemed to perceive McPhee's goal: "When you hear it you will feel instinctively for some rope of melody; but it is not there. Themes instead; just a few notes in a line on which the composer hangs a whole lot of dazzling orchestration and brilliant pianism." [52]

After the premiere, Bridle had even more to say about the orchestration:

> The composer filled up the gaps with color and storm and
> dissonance. He combined instruments defiantly. He created new
> alignments of polyphonic noise. Once for example the tam-
> bourine shook, the brasses blared, the tympani shot off a slavo
> and the double basses carried on after the echo with some
> tempestuous jigsawings in decrescendo—and suddenly the piano
> crept in and took up all that looked like a plain theme, crushed
> one pack of semitones against another and led off into another
> heyday of pandemoniums. There were many episodes like this. [53]

Equally as brilliant and flamboyant was McPhee's final recital in Toronto, given at Foresters' Hall on March 29, 1924. A large, handsome photograph of him announced the event in *Saturday Night*, [54] and the concert was billed as a "Farewell Recital." It had some grandiose touches. The stage at Foresters' Hall was fitted with a small Japanese screen against a "great dark green [back]drop; twelve thick red candles [stood] on an arboreal stan-dard." The setting was "posteresque," and in the audience were "a great many local music lovers who with warrant believe that a distinguished career awaits [McPhee]." [55] It was a splendid send-off.

McPhee played a substantial program, opening with the "Moon-light" Sonata and closing with his motto piece, the *Rákoczy March*. [56] There was also McPhee's *Three Moods,* with subtitles reminiscent of his published teenage pieces: "Prelude," "Spring Afternoon," and "Death Music." These, too, are lost. Critics said a little about the first and third pieces—that the "Prelude" was "thoughtful" and that "Death Music" "seemed more of a thematic exercise than an expression of profound emotion." [57]

Energized by this outpouring of hometown support, McPhee soon left Toronto for study in Paris. On the eve of McPhee's departure, Bridle wistfully mused about the young man's future relationship to his country:

> McPhee is one of the poets of whom with such ecstasy and intel-
> lectual imagination we have all too few and as a rule dispense
> with those that we have. . . . We hope he will come back ten
> times as big as now to a country ten times better able to appre-
> ciate him.[58]

That hope was never realized, for in the years ahead McPhee returned seldom, becoming an exile from his native land. The American writer Edmund Wilson, a contemporary of McPhee, has described the fugitive as a recurring character type in Canadian fiction, whether in the novels of Morley Callaghan, whose "principal characters . . . [often] find themselves at odds with society," or in those of Hugh MacLennan, whose wanderers "return but . . . have to recognize that their instincts are quite out of tune with the correctitude they had left behind."[59] McPhee too must have had conflicting emotions about leaving Toronto. While he had been nurtured there and given every chance to grow as a musician, he may have also felt restricted by the place, with little room for his imagination to roam. If McPhee's family shared the ideals of other Scottish Presbyterians, they valued dedication to commerce and strict morals and were probably suspicious of the creative life. Wilson recalled a young painter in Toronto saying that "to be an artist in Canada was regarded as 'a kind of sin, and to be a good artist makes it worse.'"[60]

Callaghan, who was reaching adulthood in Toronto at the same time as McPhee, told in his memoirs of meeting Hemingway during the writer's brief tenure on the *Toronto Star* in the early twenties. For Callaghan, Toronto placed tight limits on a person:

> I think I saw . . . why Hemingway wanted to get out of Toronto
> like a bat out of hell. He had a kind of frantic pride, and though
> he had good friends among his colleagues in Toronto, they
> couldn't imagine they were in the presence of a man who was
> writing the best prose that had been written in the last forty

years. Was that why he said to me so firmly, "Whatever you do, don't let anyone around here tell you anything"?[61]

Whether or not McPhee listened to his fellow Torontonians, he did decide to leave. His first goal was Paris, where he sought personal and artistic freedom along with many other young talents from both Canada and the United States. Arthur Friedheim, the Canadian Academy of Music, Massey Hall, and his family were all left behind. A life of rootlessness had begun.

PARIS PILGRIMAGE

McPhee's time in Paris is lean in documentation. Few letters survive, and press coverage was modest. In Toronto, where he was a treasured part of a bustling music community, his every musical move had been followed with devoted regularity. But in Paris the papers were overwhelmed by aspiring artists who sought attention. Other young composers from the New World faced the same problem; the only one who received anything approaching significant coverage in the Paris press was George Antheil.

Whatever his attitude toward Toronto, McPhee must have realized that he had come to France through the generosity of some of his home-town's most prominent citizens. Augustus Bridle acknowledged the difficulty in obtaining such support: "Many young artists yearn to be gone tomorrow; not all of them, not many of them, go. . . . To migrate to Europe for post-graduate instruction means money; more than is usually available. As a rule musical talent does not thrive in homes where bridge parties abound."[62]

McPhee was among the lucky ones. His "farewell recital," designed to raise funds for the trip, must have brought some cash. But money flowed in from other coffers as well. The Imperial Order of the Daughters of the Empire had hoped to give him a scholarship, but in February 1924 that plan fell through.[63] However, McPhee received substantial support from Sir Albert Gooderham, president of Gooderham and Worts, a Toronto liquor company. Gooderham's patronage of McPhee seems logical; he was founder and president of the Canadian Academy of Music, and he served as president of the Toronto Symphony Orchestra when it premiered McPhee's concerto in 1924.[64]

When McPhee settled in Paris, probably sometime in the summer or fall of 1924, he took lodgings on the rue Visconti, located on the edge of the artistic community of the Latin Quarter, not far from Saint-Germain-des-Prés. While there, he studied piano with Isidor Philipp (1863–1958) and composition with Paul Le Flem (1881–1984). Philipp was an especially renowned pedagogue. He gave lessons at the Conservatoire and was a demanding teacher of keyboard technique (his edition of Pischna's exercises has been called "knuckle-breaking").[65] Perhaps his many two-piano arrangements of Bach, Mendelssohn, and other composers had some influence on young McPhee, who would later write so many two-piano scores.

Paul Le Flem was himself a student of Albert Roussel and Vincent d'Indy and in 1921 succeeded Roussel as professor of counterpoint at the Schola Cantorum. He was also a choral conductor and music critic. Le Flem's own works were greatly influenced by the neoclassical concision of Roussel. Why McPhee studied with Le Flem and not with Nadia Boulanger, who was attracting so many of his North American contemporaries, is not known.

McPhee first received public notice in Paris during the spring of 1925, when one of Philipp's favorite pupils, Clara Rabinowitch, premiered McPhee's *Sarabande* at the Salle Erard.[66] Rabinowitch's program also included *Feux follets* by Philipp and *Pres d'un lac dans le Wisconsin* by the expatriate American composer Blair Fairchild. The *Sarabande* won McPhee substantial notice in the Paris edition of the *Chicago Tribune* as part of a regular column by Paul Shinkman titled "Latin Quarter Notes":

> Should you be strolling along the serene rue Visconte [*sic*] on the left Bank one of these afternoons, and hear a mighty crash of chords overhead—you will know that Colin McPhee, the young Canadian composer, is at his Steinway, perhaps tossing off a concerto or two. . . . There is a strange harmonic glow about the McPhee compositions . . . particularly his recently completed *Sarabande*.[67]

McPhee's Paris debut took place on May 6, 1925, in a concert that included his *Sarabande* as well as his Toronto composition "Spring Afternoon."[68] Although there seem to have been no Paris reviews and the music is lost, news of the event reached Augustus Bridle at the *Toronto Daily Star:*

> Colin McPhee made his Paris debut as pianist in a spangling recital at the Salle Malakoff, playing Chopin Etudes . . . and his own Sarabande and Spring Afternoon that he played here. A number of distinguished people, Canadians and others, were present. Hon. Philippe Roy and Prince Oblensky, as well as musicians, authors, painters, clergy and mesdames of the opera. The affair was a brilliant success; though McPhee has sent nothing about it.[69]

One week before the concert, McPhee had written Irving Schwerké, the music critic for the Paris edition of the *Chicago Tribune,* inviting him to attend. His letter gives a unique firsthand glimpse of his youthful aspirations: "I know it's the night of Heifetz and I don't suppose you could come. Do you think for even twenty minutes—anyway here are two tickets." He included a list of his compositions and ended exuberantly:

> I intend to remain in Paris more or less next year studying with Philipp, but hope to get a few engagements here and there. In the meantime I am looking for money, and hope to make my debut in New York in a year's time, playing a new piano concerto of my own. Dreams, but all mine seem to realize lately![70]

During the 1925–26 season McPhee gave two recitals in Paris, both at the Salle des Agriculteurs. The first occurred on November 9, 1925; the second on February 10.[71] His repertory was broadening. Works by nineteenth-century romantics—especially Liszt—were ever-present. Yet there were important additions: the third Prokofiev piano sonata, performed in February, and especially two Scarlatti sonatas, performed in November. McPhee's curiosity was stretching to both the nearer present and the further past.

The audience at McPhee's November performance was large and

enthusiastic, and press coverage was substantial. *Le Ménestrel, Le Figaro, Paris-Soir,* and the Paris edition of the *Chicago Tribune* evaluated the event variously. While the critic for *Paris-Soir* was complimentary, the writer for *Le Ménestrel* acknowledged McPhee's sincerity and expert technique but questioned the depth of his interpretations, a complaint similar to that voiced by Toronto critics.[72] Schwerké, whom McPhee had invited to the May concert, reviewed the November event instead. His opinion was mixed. In keeping with his attitude toward other young composers, Schwerké criticized McPhee's own works but praised his keyboard gifts: "He has a facile technic, is well-poised and plays without descending to the cheap mannerisms and affectations which so many of the modern crop of pianists deem essential to the health of art. He has no small amount of singing quality in his touch." Like other reviewers, however, Schwerké was troubled by McPhee's emotional distance from the music:

> In spite of technical attainments and his apparent musicalness,
> Mr. McPhee's interpretation of the pieces . . . left the feelings
> quite unperturbed. . . . If he knows what is hidden in the music
> he plays, he has not yet mastered the art of telling a hall full of
> people about it and sharing his knowledge with them.[73]

Unfortunately, little else remains of McPhee's Paris pilgrimage. Years later he wrote that some of his songs had been performed there in 1926 by Jane Bathori, with himself at the piano, and he seems to have done other accompanying as well.[74]

McPhee lived near the Latin Quarter in its heyday. Literary figures such as Gertrude Stein, Ernest Hemingway, and James Joyce, as well as Hart Crane, e. e. cummings, George Davis, and Glenway Wescott, were all around him. Stravinsky, the Ballets Russes, Erik Satie were names of the day. And during the same decade young Americans, including Marc Blitzstein, Aaron Copland, Roy Harris, Walter Piston, and Virgil Thomson, were arriving at Nadia Boulanger's studio. The intellectual and musical stimulation must have been intoxicating. McPhee's reaction to it, however, remains unknown.

2

A YOUNG PROFESSIONAL IN NEW YORK

 1926–31

During the summer of 1926 Colin McPhee arrived in New York to find a city alive with new music. Riding a wave of post–World War I prosperity and self-confidence, American composers were joining other creative artists in an effort to gain acceptance both at home and abroad. With modernism as the rallying cry and innovation as its essential ingredient, the newest art seemed most possible in a country unburdened by age-old cultural traditions. Societies such as the International Composers' Guild and the League of Composers had been founded to perform the most recent music; publishing enterprises such as Henry Cowell's *New Music* and the Cos Cob Press began expediting access to scores; and the journal *Modern Music* appeared to provide a forum for experimental ideas. In an environment so vigorously charged, an ambitious young composer could find both the inspiration and the means for advancing his career.

And so McPhee did.[1] He immediately became involved in the new music community in several capacities. His works were performed on programs by the Guild, the Copland-Sessions Concerts, the Pan American Association, and Howard Hanson's "American Composers" series at Eastman, and he in turn played piano on these same concert series.[2] The first publisher of his mature compositions was the *New Music Quarterly,* and he also served as a board member of the New Music Society and the Pan American Association. McPhee's years in Paris gave him a background similar to that of his contemporaries, and the friendships he formed abroad must have helped ease entry into the United States. Even though McPhee did not officially become an American citizen until the early 1940s, from 1926 on his work is part of the history of music in the United States.

In the 1920s McPhee was viewed as an important figure among a new generation of American composers. As Henry Cowell put it some years later, "Colin McPhee seemed to me when I first knew him in the mid-twenties one of the most gifted of the young composers about, one worth watching and sure to make himself an expanding career."[3] While not enjoying the status of Cowell or Aaron Copland, who by late in the decade had emerged as leaders, McPhee was on a par with Marc Blitzstein and Roy Harris, composers not yet firmly established but showing significant promise. By the early thirties, when assessments were being made of the rising American school, McPhee's name figured prominently. In *American Composers on American Music* (1933), Henry Cowell placed him in the first of eight groups of contemporary composers, comprised of "Americans who have developed indigenous materials or are specially interested in expressing some phase of the American spirit in their works." Cowell gathered kindred souls in this category, including also Charles Ives, Carl Ruggles, Charles Seeger, Roy Harris, Henry Brant, and Ruth Crawford. He wrote:

> I (Henry Cowell) belong to this group also, as I have initiated
> independently various new sorts of harmony, rhythm, counter-
> point, and other musical mediums. Colin McPhee, Canadian,
> follows to some extent the modern French style of clever music
> but treats it in a personal manner. His music forms a sort of
> bridge between the more characteristic Americans and those
> who are somewhat Europeanized.[4]

McPhee was also among the select group of composers given special treatment in the body of Cowell's book in an essay written by Wallingford Riegger.[5]

In 1933 another major summary of musical achievements was published, this one by Aaron Copland in *Modern Music.* There Copland cited
McPhee among those who had formed "an entirely new generation" of
"the American school of composers of our own day."[6]

McPhee officially entered this new music arena on November 28,
1926, with the performance of his *Pastorale and Rondino* at a concert
presented by Edgard Varèse's International Composers' Guild in Aeolian
Hall.[7] The Guild had been founded in 1921 to perform contemporary
compositions. Among its high points had been the American premieres of
landmark European works, especially Schoenberg's *Pierrot lunaire* (performed by the Guild in 1923), as well as numerous presentations of
important American products, such as Carl Ruggles's *Men and Mountains*
(1924) and Varèse's *Hyperprism* (1923). McPhee's *Pastorale and Rondino* appeared on the first program of the Guild's final season, together with *Three
Pagan Hymns,* by Eugene Goossens, *Darker America,* by William Grant Still,
Trio in A for Piano and Strings, by Ildebrando Pizzetti, *H. P.,* by Carlos
Chávez, and *Five Sacred Songs,* by Anton Webern. McPhee's work was
subtitled "Sonatina for two flutes, clarinet, trumpet and piano," and at
least part of it, the "Pastorale," had been composed in Paris and performed
by a chamber ensemble there.[8]

This score, too, is lost. But McPhee wrote program notes for it that
give some sense of the music. McPhee's language in describing the piece
showed that the nascent modernism of his Toronto piano concerto had
been further developed in Paris and that he was now steeped in neoclassicism—an innovative, often irreverent reshaping of historic idioms
that was popular at the time.[9] He wrote of using ground basses and
contrapuntal techniques, as well as "vigorous" rhythmic changes, the
incorporation of a "fox trot," several tonalities "combined in different
planes," and many "angles and shrill sounds." Gone are the poetic fancies
of his youth. In their place is the dispassionate analysis so typical of the
1920s, with its images of science and mechanics.

McPhee's description of *Pastorale and Rondino* shows contact not only
with neoclassicism but also with the experimental ideas of Varèse, with
whom he was then studying. Years later Varèse's wife Louise would look

back on McPhee as "Varèse's talented pupil," who was taken on at a time when the Frenchman was trying to establish himself as a teacher: "In spite of the militant concern of Varèse's friends, there was not sufficient response to form the classes Varèse had envisioned. He had two or three new pupils that winter [1926–27]. . . . Besides Colin McPhee, there were three or four of Salzedo's young harp pupils."[10] For at least a year during the late twenties, McPhee rented an apartment in the Varèses' house on Sullivan Street in Greenwich Village. Most likely, McPhee's Paris composition teacher, Paul Le Flem, had recommended him to Varèse. Le Flem and Varèse had studied together at the Schola Cantorum under Albert Roussel, and during the late twenties Le Flem boosted Varèse's Paris concerts through favorable reviews in *Comoedia.*

In writing that the *Rondino* should be "heard as one sees objects through a prism," McPhee may have been recalling Varèse's 1922 work *Hyperprism* or a related image often used by his teacher—that of a crystal. And in using the word "planes" to describe his use of tonality, McPhee was adopting a term that for Varèse was part of a complex vision:

> When new instruments will allow me to write music as I conceive it . . . the movement of sound-masses, of shifting planes, will be clearly perceived. . . . Certain transmutations taking place on certain planes will seem to be projected onto other planes, moving at different speeds and at different angles.[11]

Judging from McPhee's extant pieces, there was no real musical link between him and a sonic adventurer such as Varèse; McPhee would remain loyal to traditional techniques and sound resources. But for a brief time he adopted the descriptive vocabulary of his teacher.

As was typical of new works by young composers performed in New York during this period, McPhee's *Pastorale and Rondino* received only brief critical notices. New music did not gain easy acceptance by the establishment. W. J. Henderson of the *New York Sun* called McPhee a "young American futurist [with] a talent not yet ripe but promising," and Olin Downes of the *New York Times* was vague: "'Pastorale and Rondino' impressed as a mixture of musical conventionalities, oddly harmonized and instrumentated [sic], and a bit of jazz, which came in handily for a change, but did not raise the piece from the ground."[12] Another critic dismissed the piece as "pleasant but inconsequential."[13] Since no score of the *Pastorale and Rondino* is known to exist, the scantiness of the critics' comments is especially unfortunate.

After this debut McPhee spent the next several years in New York working to gain status as both a performer and a composer. He still had hopes of a concert career, and on March 13, 1927, he strode forth optimistically, presenting a solo recital at the Greenwich Village Theatre. The program was strikingly different from previous ones in Toronto and Paris: no Liszt or Beethoven and less nineteenth-century repertory in general. Instead McPhee turned to two baroque works (Vivaldi's "Aria" and a Scarlatti sonata) and a modern reworking of another (Galilei-Respighi's "Gagliarda")—all of which were significant choices, given the neoclassical aspects of his *Pastorale and Rondino*.[14] In addition, he included one group each of nineteenth- and early twentieth-century pieces and also performed three of his own compositions: the *Sarabande* of 1923, a Nocturne, and an arrangement of Gershwin's *The Man I Love*. The last was also a sign of the times, as concert artists reached out to "jazz" (or so they called popular songs of the day). Jascha Heifetz, Fritz Kreisler, and Efrem Zimbalist had all recently added "jazz" tunes to their recitals, as had Eva Gauthier, whose career would soon intersect with McPhee's.

This seems to have been McPhee's first and last solo recital in New York. As a concert career became less desirable (or perhaps less possible), he increasingly focused on composition, giving piano performances largely within the context of new music events. On April 10, 1927, he participated in the infamous Carnegie Hall premiere of George Antheil's *Ballet Mécanique,* while Aaron Copland sat at an adjacent piano. And on December 30, 1928, and February 9, 1930, he performed in two Copland-Sessions concerts—another of the period's venues for presenting contemporary compositions. McPhee's interpretation of a sonatina by the Russian emigre Nicolai Lopatnikoff in 1928 gained good notices, such as the following: "[The work was] played with both intelligence and skill (two things that are not so often found together as might be supposed)."[15] But a review of his other Copland-Sessions performance—of the *North Country Suite for Piano,* by Jeffrey Mark—said little.[16]

During the late twenties McPhee also spent some time touring, both as soloist and accompanist. According to an advance notice in an Allentown, Pennsylvania, newspaper of late 1927, he was then in the midst of "his first all-American tour."[17] Although he must have visited other towns, no itinerary remains.

In January 1928 McPhee embarked on a month-long junket with a fellow Canadian, the soprano Eva Gauthier, who by then was renowned for her 1917 New York premiere of Stravinsky's *Three Japanese Lyrics* and for her 1923 recital with George Gershwin of popular songs. Gauthier and McPhee traveled as far as California, where they performed in Santa Barbara and Los Angeles and, farther north, in Piedmont. Late in the month they stopped off in Harrisburg, Pennsylvania, and presumably gave other concerts en route.[18] Each time, Gauthier sang five "new American songs," including "The Poet's Vision," Henry Eichheim's setting of a Chinese poem (Gauthier had premiered Eichheim's "Korean Sketch" from *Oriental Impressions* at Aeolian Hall in 1921), two Langston Hughes settings by John Alden Carpenter, "Berceuse Amoureuse," by Theodore Stearns, and " A Soliloquy," by James H. Rogers. Carpenter's music—especially his ballets *Krazy Kat* and *Skyscrapers*—was fairly well known in the twenties, and Henry Eichheim, while less widely celebrated, had his Asian-inspired orchestral works conducted by Leopold Stokowski and Frederick Stock. Stearns and Rogers were minor composers of the day who have since faded entirely from view. On these programs McPhee also played a small group of Debussy piano solos, and in Los Angeles he added his own *Sarabande* and his arrangement of *The Man I Love*.[19] He also accompanied the Viennese soprano Rena Pfiffer at least once: in her 1927 New York debut at Aeolian Hall. The program ranged from Mozart to Hugo Wolf.[20]

During this period McPhee was growing increasingly fascinated with African-American culture, and on April 15, 1928, he accompanied the black soprano and actress Abbie Mitchell at Engineering Auditorium in New York. Mitchell had earlier been married to Will Marion Cook, the important composer of works for the black musical theater, such as *In*

Dahomey and *In Abyssinia.* Although another pianist accompanied Mitchell for most of her 1928 recital, McPhee took over for a group of his own songs—*Petit chaperone rouge, Theris, Cradle Song,* and *C'est la bergère Nanette*—which were favorably characterized in the *Musical Courier:*

> The Pièce de Resistance was a group of songs by Colin McPhee,
> who proved to be an ultra modern but knows how to write
> effectively for the voice; the composer played the accompaniments to his songs, thus adding greatly to their effectiveness.
> Miss Mitchell sang them with intensity of feeling, overcoming all
> the difficulties with a charming ease that must have pleased the
> composer. They gave an encore to this group, also from the pen
> of Mr. McPhee.[21]

These scores, too, are lost.

Sometime in the late 1920s, most likely by mid-1928, McPhee found a steady job as full-time accompanist for the Schola Cantorum, a New York chorus conducted by Hugh Ross. The group included two hundred singers and gave several subscription concerts each year at Carnegie Hall, in addition to lecture-musicales in private homes and a series of concerts with the New York Philharmonic.[22] Ross had taken over the chorus in 1927 and met McPhee the next year. He was immediately impressed with the young man's exceptional gifts at the keyboard.[23] Again, as with Gauthier, there was a Canadian connection. Ross had become conductor of the Winnipeg Male Voice Choir in 1921 and two years later had taken the group on tour in Chicago, Detroit, New York, and Toronto—right at the peak of McPhee's Toronto period.[24] Also in 1922, when the Schola was conducted by Ross's predecessor Kurt Schindler, it had engaged J. Campbell-McInness as a guest soloist; McPhee was then Campbell-McInness's accompanist.[25]

According to Ross, McPhee was an extraordinary pianist. "Immediately when I found someone of Colin's capacity, he became our official accompanist. . . . I was interested in what music he was writing and in the fact that he could play anything at sight." The job was a time-consuming one, with two to three rehearsals a week and frequent performances. Ross has recalled that McPhee earned approximately $2,500 a year. For McPhee there were at least two outstanding moments in his tenure with the Schola: the premiere of his *Sea Shanty Suite* (1929) and his appearance as soloist in *The Rio Grande* (1931), by the British composer Constant Lambert.[26]

COMPOSITIONS OF THE 1920s

These few remaining vignettes of McPhee's life in New York during the late 1920s give a sense of varied activities and alliances, especially involvement with Cowell, Copland, Varèse, and others in the musical avant-garde and with Gauthier and Mitchell, who had strong connections to popular song and African-American idioms. Yet given the scarcity of documentation from this period, the most important part of McPhee's story lies within his extant scores. McPhee continued to be a productive composer during his early years in the United States, and his music gained the attention and respect of critics and fellow musicians. This is the first period from which any works survive following the Toronto publications of 1916 and 1917. Yet some compositions are still missing: the *Pastorale and Rondino,* the arrangement of *The Man I Love,* the songs performed by Abbie Mitchell, and *H₂O* and *Mechanical Principles,* scores to two Ralph Steiner films. In addition, there are pieces for which no evidence exists beyond a passing mention. In her *American Composers of Today* (1930), Claire Reis listed two such orchestral compositions by McPhee, both of which supposedly were in manuscript: *Sarabande,* a seven-minute piece dated 1927 (perhaps an orchestration of his earlier piano piece with the same title), and Symphony in One Movement, a twenty-minute work dated 1930.[27] Elsewhere, a string quartet, a work for chorus and orchestra, and a ballet are tantalizingly cited.[28] None has ever surfaced.

Despite these losses, publication has preserved several important McPhee works from the late 1920s: Invention and *Kinesis* for piano, the Concerto for Piano with Wind Octette, and the *Sea Shanty Suite.* They remain among his best. In them we see a gifted composer finding his personal approach to neoclassicism. We also see a composer fully in control of his craft.

Invention

McPhee's first surviving work after more than ten years of schooling in Toronto, Baltimore, and Paris is an Invention for piano, published by Henry Cowell's *New Music* in 1930. Although the Invention is signed "New York/Aug. 12, 1926," aesthetically it reflects McPhee's Parisian experiences.[29] A typical work to have emerged from that city in the mid-twenties, the Invention springs from the historical preoccupations of neoclassicism—here, more precisely, the inspiration is neobaroque. Lean and angular, with relentless forward motion, the Invention is tightly constructed in two-voice counterpoint and has a subject reminiscent of the G major Fugue in Book I of the *Well-Tempered Clavier*. Indeed, Bach and Stravinsky, the latter a powerful presence in Paris during the 1920s, are obvious models.

In writing of the *Pastorale and Rondino,* performed just a few months after completing the Invention, McPhee had described "definite tonalities in many places. . . . I consider both pieces [i.e., the *Pastorale* and the *Rondino*] as atonal music having used harmonic combinations for their sonorous value only." So too the Invention. Its harmonic language was typical of neoclassical writers in Paris during the twenties, where "atonality" had a special meaning—not the complete renouncement of traditional tonal resources but a realignment of their uses. The materials of tonality remained ever present, but their functions were often flouted. In the opening section of the Invention, for example, all the pitches come from a diatonic scale (in this case, D major), and snippets of the scale recur (ex. 2). But any conventional sense of a tonal center is confounded. The opening turn (measure 1) gives a sense of G major, not D, and strongly resonating dissonances—seconds, sevenths, ninths, tritones—occur on the downbeat of more than half of the first ten bars.

Rhythmically, the work is free-wheeling and asymmetric. While the opening subject draws upon eighteenth-century contrapuntal techniques, its approach to meter is wholly of McPhee's own era, with constant shifts that disrupt any sense of a regular downbeat. By combining these shifts with rhythmic cross-accents in individual lines, McPhee builds multiple

EXAMPLE 2   Invention, mm. 1−10.

EXAMPLE 3   Invention, m. 25. Brackets indicate pitch and rhythmic groupings.

levels of activity out of a two-voice texture. Measure 25 provides a compact example. There each voice has its own harmonic and rhythmic counterpoint, and when the two sound together the complexity increases. The pitches of the right-hand melodic pattern include four groups of three notes, but because they are beamed and more importantly accented as three groups of four, an internal cross-rhythm results (ex. 3). At the same time, the left hand has two six-pitch groups beamed as three groups of four. And for a final twist, a semitone pattern of C–D♭ juts between the voices, interlocking them irregularly (ex. 4).

McPhee's Invention, written at age twenty-six, shows strong connections to contemporary models, most noticeably the works of Stravinsky. In 1924, just two years before McPhee wrote this piece, Stravinsky had completed his Piano Sonata, and it must have been in McPhee's ear as he composed. Both works are suffused with two-part counterpoint, both play with widely spaced unison writing (compare example 5 with example 6), and both herald their closing statements with a sudden break in the

EXAMPLE 4   Invention, m. 25. Interlocking pitch pattern.

EXAMPLE 5   Invention, mm. 55–56.

EXAMPLE 6   Igor Stravinsky, Piano Sonata, first movement, mm. 149–50.

EXAMPLE 7   Stravinsky, Piano Sonata, first movement, mm. 156–60.

forward motion (compare example 5 with example 7). Other similarities include frequent meter changes and suspension of traditional diatonic relationships.

Stravinsky's was not the only brand of neoclassicism practiced in Paris during the mid-1920s. McPhee's composition teacher Paul Le Flem was himself a student of Albert Roussel, one of the stalwarts in the neoclassical movement. In 1924 Roussel had written to Nadia Boulanger of a "return to clearer lines, more emphatic accents, more precise rhythm, a style more horizontal than vertical," with a "sympathetic glance toward the robust frankness of Bach or Handel." [30] Other composers of that time and place showed similar tendencies, among them Virgil Thomson in his Five Inventions (1926), Francis Poulenc in his Suite in C (1920), and Heitor Villa Lobos in his *Cirandinhas* (1925). All strove for linear clarity, often expressed in stark two-voice writing.

Concerto for Piano with Wind Octette

With McPhee's next extant work, the Concerto for Piano with Wind Octette of 1928, the same crisp concision is apparent. In fact, the work has many traits found in the Invention: historical formal schemes, nontraditional uses of diatonic scale collections, supple meter shifts, and areas of intense, multilayered rhythmic activity. In the concerto these characteristics are heightened because of expanded instrumental forces and a richer harmonic vocabulary. Indeed, the large-scale, multimovement form seems to have kindled McPhee's imagination. Like the Invention, the concerto bears comparison with other neoclassical pieces of the day—in this case, ones for chamber ensemble, such as Stravinsky's Octet (1923), Roy Harris's Concerto for Piano, Clarinet, and String Quartet (1926), and Virgil Thomson's Sonata da Chiesa (1926)—especially in their acerbic wind timbres, brittle part-writing, and motoric propulsion.

McPhee's concerto was written between June and October of 1928, while he was staying in Woodstock, New York, and was published in *New Music* in January 1931. Like Prokofiev, Bartók, Stravinsky, and even his contemporary Copland, McPhee wrote concertos for himself to play. His two largest works prior to this had both been concertos, and he had been the soloist in their premieres. He was also at the keyboard for the first performance of the Concerto for Piano with Wind Octette, given in Rochester on February 22, 1929, under the direction of Howard Hanson, and he played it at least three more times before leaving for Bali in 1931.[31]

The concerto has three movements—Allegretto, Chorale, and Coda—and is scored for two flutes, oboe, clarinet, bassoon, horn, trumpet, and trombone.[32] Its tight structure, like that of the Invention, is a model of neoclassicism, with carefully crafted part-writing, translucent textures, and perpetual forward motion. Yet amid these cool, classical qualities are some warm touches: an opening modal melody, labeled "pastoral" by McPhee,[33] that rolls out in a lyrical $\frac{6}{8}$ meter, and a middle movement of spacious breadth and hymnlike simplicity.

The work's economy is apparent from the opening measures, where McPhee introduces most of the materials upon which the first movement is built. Rhythmically the underlying triplet in the left-hand piano part forms a cell basic to the structure (ex. 8), while tonally the opening also establishes a framework for the entire piece. It is tonic-centered, yet, as in the Invention, the tonic is often blurred and its role ambiguous. Here, McPhee immediately presents a modal duality. Although in typescript program notes he described the piece simply as opening in "E minor," in fact it is bimodal from the outset, with the right-hand piano part in E phrygian, the left hand in E minor (with an implication of its relative major, G), the clarinet and second flute together defining E minor, and the first flute ambiguously restating the third, fourth, and fifth degrees common to

EXAMPLE 8   Concerto for Piano with Wind Octette, first movement, mm. 1–11.

both modes. This bimodality allows McPhee to play with the tension between F♯ and F♮, the major and minor second in E.

Another harmonic device applied consistently throughout this work is the construction of chords from different parts of an eleventh or thirteenth. By doing so McPhee extracts two roots from a shared pitch collection, a twist on juxtaposing two modes with a shared tonic. A good example is found in measure 18 (ex. 9). Two triads—A major and G♯ minor—are derived from the same thirteenth chord (on F).

Ostinatos are central to the concerto's construction. Despite the use of traditional, organic forms—what McPhee called a "modified" sonata-allegro in the first movement and tripartite in the second and third—the subsections are modular, even self-contained, largely because they are built of ostinatos that spin within concisely circumscribed areas and then suddenly leap forward via modulation or sequence. In the first movement, ostinatos sound at different levels, not just in the overlayering established at the beginning (see brackets in ex. 8) but also in the very essence of the two principal theme groups. The opening piano part has an ostinato pattern in its accompaniment, and the second theme is itself an irregular ostinato. Although initially presented melodically, after two measures the latter becomes the accompaniment for a trumpet solo (ex. 10).

The tug of two against three, presaged in the piano as early as measure 11, is basic to this second theme. At first the rhythmic tension is

EXAMPLE 9 Concerto for Piano with Wind Octette, first movement, m. 18.

EXAMPLE 10   Concerto for Piano with Wind Octette, first movement, mm. 37–40.

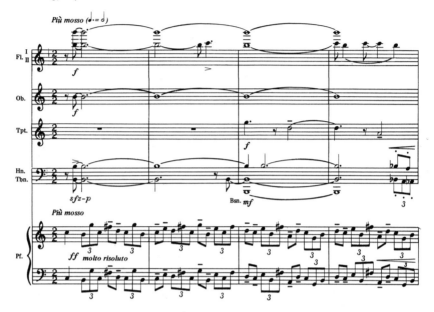

horizontal (ex. 10), but by measure 45 it becomes vertical within the piano part (ex. 11). And by measure 49 the piano and winds present the second theme one beat apart, so that two pull against three persistently (ex. 12).

Rhythmically, the concerto is disjunct and hard-hitting. In addition to the play of two against three just mentioned, meter changes unexpectedly jar the downbeat, and in the piano part of the third movement, McPhee introduces a pattern that in the years ahead will become one of his favorites—an asymmetrical subdivision of a measure into three plus three plus two (ex. 13).

Throughout the concerto, McPhee assigns the piano varying roles. In the first movement its solos, usually pared down to two voices, introduce both of the themes and inaugurate the development and recapitulation. When the piano becomes a supporting member of the ensemble, its role is often percussive, hammering out ostinatos against the winds (ex. 13). The

EXAMPLE 13   Concerto for Piano with Wind Octette, third movement, m. 35.

piano assumes a different guise in the second movement, becoming less soloistic and more consistently integrated into the ensemble. After an organlike statement of the opening theme by the winds, the piano offers a contrapuntal reinterpretation of the same material. With the third movement, the piano becomes persistently percussive, taking off with gusto at the start. It sounds constantly, pausing only occasionally for dialogue with the winds.

A prominent trait of this concerto—one that was to surface in many of McPhee's later works—is the use of thematic interconnections between movements. The first hint of such integration comes when the chorale's chordal texture is foretold by the winds in the first movement (m. 53). And when the second movement begins, it relates to the first by sounding E major in all the parts (a complement to the first movement's E phrygian-minor). In addition, its first melodic gesture (B reaching up to E) inverts that of the first movement (E moving to B).

In several respects, the third movement is the culmination of all that has come before. Although ostinatos had been prominent in the first movement, here they completely take over for a flashy, fast-paced conclusion. Tonally, the opening of the third movement nearly saturates the chromatic spectrum yet keeps a clear focus on a tonic C. Unison Cs are uttered irregularly in the winds, and they also form the focus of the piano's sixteenth-note pattern (ex. 14). The work ends in octave triplets leaping triumphantly up the length of the keyboard.

EXAMPLE 14   Concerto for Piano with Wind Octette, third movement, mm. 1–3.

Sea Shanty Suite

McPhee's next piece was a set of sea shanties, arranged for baritone solo, male chorus, two pianos, and two sets of timpani. It was composed for the Schola Cantorum and first performed in Carnegie Hall under Hugh Ross's direction on March 13, 1929. There were seven shanties in all: "Lowlands Away," "Billy Boy," "Stormalong," "What Shall We Do With a Drunken Sailor?" "Tom's Gone to Hilo," "Fire Down Below," and "Highland Laddie." All except "Fire Down Below" were published by Edwin F. Kalmus in 1930 as the *Sea Shanty Suite;* they bore the dedication "To Hugh Ross in friendship." [34]

In the sea shanties McPhee drew upon folk materials for the first time. Reworking preexistent music was not unusual for him, but taking folksongs and adapting them for concert performance signaled an important new direction. How he chose this particular genre is unknown. Perhaps the Schola Cantorum's tradition of performing folk music inspired him. Certainly he must have been attracted to the musical style of the shanty tunes, with their modal ambiguities and metric fluctuations.

For his first foray into ethnology McPhee made no excursion to the West Indies or the Scottish coast but chose tunes from an anthology that was considered reliable in its day—Sir Richard Runcian Terry's *The Shanty Book,* published in 1921.[35] According to a more recent shanty scholar, "Terry's . . . collection was accepted by schools and by baritone singers of the 1920s, the result being that his version of a certain shanty is the one generally found in circulation today." [36] McPhee used melodies and texts from Terry's collection in four of the six published shanties: "Lowlands Away," "Billy Boy," "What Shall We Do With a Drunken Sailor?" and "Tom's Gone to Hilo." The melody for "Stormalong" may have been taken from a shanty collection by Captain W. B. Whall; the two are similar although not identical.[37] In the introduction to his collection Terry set forth principles for folksong arranging and collecting. He felt that the accompaniments should preserve the purity of the melodies, and while he acknowledged that there were many variants of each tune, he published only one reading, which was a composite of the versions he had heard.

McPhee did not change a note in Terry's clean, simple melodies, and his arrangements for baritone soloist and male chorus present the shanties in the straightforward solo-chorus (i.e., shantyman–work gang) format basic to the genre. The accompaniments are understated and combine elements of McPhee's own style with a sympathy for each song. "Lowlands Away" is a good example. McPhee sets three full strains of the tune (each having four phrases) and presents them with an introduction and coda. Perhaps most striking is the way he highlights the rhythmic elasticity of the melody by stretching it over the accompaniment and emphasizing its rhythmic peregrinations. The simple rhythmic figure of ♩ ♩ (drawn from the opening two notes of the melody) generates much of this tension (ex. 15). Sometimes the pattern sounds on the beat, compatibly supporting the melody (see left hand in Piano II, measures 16–17 and right hand in Piano I, measure 17). Elsewhere it heightens the suppleness of the melody by vying with a duple vocal line (i.e., measures 18–20, not shown in examples here).

The phrases of the "Lowlands Away" melody are circular—one leads to another, and none solidly signals a finish. McPhee enhances this quality by alternating the accompaniment between major and minor and sometimes combining the two. In this way, he not only indulges his own compositional inclinations but also pays respect to a fundamental aspect of the performance style of shanties. According to Terry, "[There is a] tendency on the part of the modern sailor to turn his minor key into a major one." In the opening stanza of "Lowlands Away," the E♮ in both the melody (measures 5, 14, and 16) and the accompaniment (measure 10) tugs with the sustained E♭ pedal in the piano bass (measures 1–8), creating a C major-minor ambiguity. Later on this gentle major-minor contrast becomes more forceful, as in measure 52, where the Piano I bass sounds C major and the shifting ostinato under it defines C minor (ex. 16).

In all his shanty settings McPhee evokes the drone techniques of both bagpipe and fiddle players in British folk traditions. Open fifths and fourths abound, either sustained or regularly repeated. Often two fifths (sometimes even three) are stacked on top of each other. In "Lowlands" the suggestion of a drone combines naturally with the falling fourth of the

EXAMPLE 15   "Lowlands Away," from *Sea Shanty Suite,* mm. 1–17.

melody's first two notes. Another of the settings, "Drunken Sailor," is based almost entirely on quartal and quintal harmonies. The chorus first enters over a shifting drone, on the beat, with a scalar sixteenth-note figuration (ex. 17). At the chorus's next entrance, in measure 29, the drone challenges the regular scales with repeated thrusts of a new rhythmic pattern of 3 + 3 + 2.

What McPhee has done in the *Sea Shanty Suite,* then, is to derive the main elements of his accompaniment from the tunes themselves and from

EXAMPLE 16   "Lowlands Away," from *Sea Shanty Suite,* mm. 51–55.

EXAMPLE 17   "Drunken Sailor," from *Sea Shanty Suite,* mm. 13–16.

instrumental music of the British folk tradition, achieving a compatible synthesis with his own style of the period. Twelve years later, in reviewing a recording of early American ballads collected and arranged by John Jacob Niles, McPhee set forth his theory about writing accompaniments to folksongs. His attitude then reflected his practice earlier:

> The accompaniment is all that could be desired, for it never destroys the modal character of the melody by introducing inappropriate harmonies. It remains a discreet, purely sonorous background, serving to *scan* the stanzas more than anything else. This is not only the way it should be, but highly commendable; so many composers, including Brahms, have gone astray on that point, and have been tempted to sentimentalize modal melody with romantic or impressionistic harmonization.[38]

The sea shanties were well received at their premiere. In fact, the Schola's audience "seemed to enjoy them all immensely," so much so that "Billy Boy" had to be repeated.[39] All the reviews were complimentary, with perhaps the biggest boost coming from Samuel Chotzinoff, who called McPhee "one of the more talented members of New York's little group of serious composers."[40] The shanties were picked up by a number of college glee clubs during the late twenties and early thirties. Since then, the works have seldom been performed.[41]

Kinesis

In the summer of 1929, after the premieres of his Concerto for Piano with Wind Octette and *Sea Shanty Suite,* McPhee sailed for France, where he spent several weeks on the Riviera and in Paris before going on to Berlin and Munich. He was buoyed up by his recent accomplishments and wrote confidently to a friend in New York: "Though the critics did not like my concerto, *I* did. I do it in New York next season and I think it is to be played here [in Paris] also."[42] By fall he was back in New York, and during that winter he wrote only one piece, *Kinesis* for solo piano. The work is dated May 9, 1930, and was published in *New Music* in July 1930, together with his Invention of 1926. Despite the warm reception of his previous pieces, McPhee's confidence began to falter as the 1930s dawned. He told Wallingford Riegger, "My output has been small for the past few years, as I have found difficulty in finding myself and have mistrusted my natural facility."[43] *Kinesis* is a product of this transitional phase.

Although composed four years after the Invention, *Kinesis* seems to have been conceived as a prelude to the earlier work's fugue. It is toccata-like and free in form, balancing the Invention's tight, imitative counterpoint. The opening themes are related, and both use two-voice writing, exploit registral extremes, and incorporate irregular rhythmic shifts (ex. 18; compare with ex. 2).

True to its name, *Kinesis* is about motion, here of a rapid-fire sort. The tempo marking is "Allegro—138–160," and the lightning-fast writing is akin to that in the last movement of McPhee's Concerto for Piano with Wind Octette. The piece is a fantasia with some contrapuntal fragmentation and development, and throughout there is a strict stratification between the two parts. The right hand's stream of unbroken sixteenth notes speeds forward to the concluding chord, while the left hand moves independently in eighth notes that are interrupted by occasional rests and, in the penultimate section, by the addition of octaves.

But McPhee was moving in a new direction with *Kinesis*—toward

EXAMPLE 18   *Kinesis,* mm. 1–5.

uncompromising dissonance. Perhaps his summer in Berlin had affected his musical thinking, for with *Kinesis* he stretched tonality further than he ever would again. The piece's right-hand pitches are drawn from a series of tetrachords (ex. 19). Before the first two measures are repeated, at measure 3 of the right hand, McPhee uses eleven pitches of the chromatic scale. The twelfth is introduced in measure 5 (ex. 18), in the midst of scalar propulsion to a new pitch area.

Meanwhile, the left hand sounds economically constructed ostinatos, with F and G♭ revolving around B♭ (their internal cross-accents are bracketed in example 18). Similar ostinatos, resembling ones in McPhee's other works from the late twenties, turn up elsewhere in *Kinesis,* most notably near the close (ex. 20).

Besides its perpetual motion and harsh dissonance, another striking feature of *Kinesis* is its exploitation of register. The voices always keep a distance of two or three octaves from one another, and as the piece progresses they take turns pushing outward. In doing so they delineate separate sections. First the right hand reaches up to G³ (measures 10–22); then the left touches the lowest A on the keyboard (measures 23–36); later the right moves to A³ (measures 37–47). Finally, at the conclusion (mea-

EXAMPLE 19   *Kinesis,* outline of right-hand pitches, mm. 1–2.

EXAMPLE 20   *Kinesis,* mm. 55–56.

sure 48 on), both stretch in opposite directions, gripping the outer reaches of the piano.

McPhee's style in *Kinesis* was a brief side trip on the long road to redefining his musical language. It signaled the beginning of a period of indecision and insecurity as a composer. Neoclassicism had become barren and constricting to him, and like many young American composers in the early thirties, he was beginning to examine his responsibility to a broad audience, or one broader than attended new music concerts. In 1931 he clearly articulated his frustration, but no solution was yet in sight:

> Music of today has become terribly erudite and more than ever
> difficult for the average ear to derive pleasure from. The
> Schonbergian [*sic*] school delights in inverting, reversing, and
> augmenting its themes. Stravinsky now denies himself the luxury
> of sensuous sound or rhythmic excitement. Wherever we look
> we find composers imposing upon themselves restrictions inter-
> esting to musicians but completely unintelligible to the layman.[44]

H_2O and Mechanical Principles

McPhee composed his next two works—H_2O and *Mechanical Principles* of 1931—as a way of addressing these issues. The scores accompanied films by Ralph Steiner (later one of the photographers for *The Plow That Broke the Plains,* for which Virgil Thomson composed the score). With them McPhee hoped "to give the music I have written a more direct and widespread appeal."[45] He clarified his newly evolving philosophy in a statement quoted in *American Composers on American Music:*

> The "Concerto" represents the time when I was chiefly inter-
> ested in economy of means and formalism. "Mechanical Prin-
> ciples" shows my change to more elaborate material, form,
> rhythm, the use of polytonality, etc. From that work on I have
> been trying to express through music an emotion resulting from
> contact with daily life—its noise, rhythm, energy, and mechani-
> cal daring. Do not think I mean program music. I have no more
> definite, concrete idea in mind than the construction of logical

51

music whose rhythms derive from mechanics, whose tonal
structure, while orderly and complete, is as complex as the
structure of a large bridge.[46]

With its emphasis on "noise" and "mechanics," McPhee's language reflected the then-current union of science and art, especially as found in
New York's famous "Machine-Age Exposition," which had opened in May
1927 in Steinway Hall. He also revealed a lingering connection to the ideas
of Varèse and to his own *Pastorale and Rondino* of 1926.

The film scores were McPhee's last compositions before leaving for
Bali. They were performed only once, at the final concert of the Copland-
Sessions series on March 15, 1931, conducted by Hugh Ross, which
included another Steiner film, *Surf and Seaweed,* with music by Marc
Blitzstein, as well as two films with scores by Darius Milhaud (*Actualités* and
La P'tite Lilie), Copland's *Music for the Theatre,* and Roger Sessions's *Suite from
the Black Maskers.* The program was billed as "the first attempt by serious
American composers and serious artists of the films to coordinate their
efforts."[47] McPhee wrote his pieces for an orchestra of 30 players;[48]
unfortunately, the scores are now lost.

McPhee and Steiner sought independence between the film and its
score. As McPhee put it, "They are parallel creations in two different
media."[49] The subjects were mundane. *Mechanical Principles,* filmed in the
Chicago Museum of Science and Industry, captured the workaday spirit
and rhythmic vitality of machines, "showing plungers and cogs and strange
mechanisms . . . in action."[50] And H_2O was a celebration of water in its
many incarnations, juxtaposing individual shots to create a collage. Olin
Downes, in his review of the concert, wrote: "The pictures of Ralph
Steiner, which are abstract designs, are themselves symphonic in the
development of the ideas, the rhythms of line and mass and light, and the
sense of cumulative development. . . . [They are] essentially music, thrilling, intoxicating as tone itself to eye."[51]

One year later McPhee told his friend Carl Van Vechten that "the
music with cinema" had made a "good impression."[52] Downes's review
confirmed this, calling the Steiner-McPhee works "the climax of the
evening. . . . To [*Mechanical Principles*] . . . Mr. McPhee has written very

carefully considered music, which often conveyed the sense of stark and irresistible power." But Downes was troubled that the films and music were not well synchronized. Other critics focused on the chaos that resulted when the film of *Mechanical Principles* broke repeatedly, making coordination with live orchestra impossible. Steiner later recalled, "When one film happened to end with the end of the music a loud cheer of relief went up from the audience." [53]

Despite McPhee's positive experience with *Mechanical Principles* and *H_2O*, he seems to have hit an impasse soon after they were written. Like other young composers of his day, he had become impatient with the abstract, esoteric music of the late 1920s and had tired of writing for small audiences. As he and his contemporaries moved into the 1930s, they attempted various solutions. For Copland, Harris, and Thomson, among others, American folk music would become a guiding inspiration. McPhee, however, was to set his sights much further afield.

3

ASIA BECKONS

 **1928–31**

At some point in the late 1920s, amid work as a performer and composer, Colin McPhee heard newly released recordings of the Balinese gamelan. It was a decisive event, exposing him for the first time to the delicately clangorous music of this distant people, and it had a powerful effect:

> The clear, metallic sounds . . . were like the stirring of a thousand bells, delicate, confused, with a sensuous charm, a mystery that was quite overpowering. I begged to keep the records for a few days, and as I played them over and over I became more and more enchanted with the sound. Who were the musicians? I wondered. How had this music come about? Above all, how was it possible, in this late day, for such a music to have been able to survive?
>
> I returned the records, but I could not forget them. At the time I knew little about the music of the East. I still believed that an artist must keep his mind on his own immediate world. But the effect of the music was deeper than I suspected, for after I had read in the early books of Crawfurd and Raffles the quite

fabulous accounts of these ancient and ceremonial orchestras, my imagination took fire, and the day came when I determined to make a trip to the East to see them for myself.[1]

McPhee claimed to have heard these recordings "quite by accident." But looking back over his life during this period, the event begins to seem almost inevitable. New York in the late 1920s was a place of prosperity and experimentation where "the *new*—the thing of the latest moment— became almost violently desirable and important," as one chronicler of the period has put it.[2] Among these "new" ideas was an interest in the exotic, whether found in nearby Harlem nightclubs or far-off South Sea islands. Through a widening circle of friends, McPhee came in touch with several key figures, including especially the anthropologist Jane Belo, the writer Carl Van Vechten, and the artist Miguel Covarrubias, all of whom were involved in exotic explorations. By 1931 he found himself at the edge of an exciting musical frontier.

Developments in McPhee's personal life were crucial in pointing him toward Bali. Central among them was his relationship with Jane Belo. The two met in Paris—McPhee's friend Minna Lederman, the editor of *Modern Music,* has recalled that he first saw Jane as she passed on the street while he sat at a cafe table[3]—and they were married in 1930. Since Belo had long been interested in other cultures, she helped stimulate McPhee's growing curiosity. When the two eventually traveled to Bali, they did so because Belo could finance the trip.

Belo was the child of wealthy Texans.[4] A student first at Bryn Mawr, later at Barnard (1923–24) and the Sorbonne (ca. 1925), she focused primarily on psychology. At Barnard she became interested in anthropology through her work with Franz Boas and Ruth Benedict, and her captivation with non-Western cultures was further stimulated by travel to the Middle East.[5] In 1925 she married the painter George Biddle, son of the Philadelphia Biddle family, whose past would greatly affect her own future. Biddle had lived in Tahiti from 1920 to 1922, and aspects of his stay there bore striking parallels to the trip that McPhee and Belo would make to Bali ten years later. Biddle built a house in Tahiti; he adopted a native boy (named Moerai); and he even wrote a book about the house, the child, and the entire island experience.[6]

Biddle also traveled with Jane Belo after their marriage, especially in the Caribbean. Unlike most wealthy pleasure-seekers of the day, they approached these journeys not simply as vacations but as opportunities to study other cultures. After one such trip they jointly published an article in *Scribner's* entitled "Foot-Hills of Cuba: A Cross-Section of Spanish-American Civilization" (1926), with illustrations by Biddle.[7] The article recorded observations about the village's class distinctions and racial inter-mingling, closing with a comparison of blacks in Cuba with those in Harlem. It was a genuinely serious, if amateur, anthropological study.

Colin reentered Jane's life in New York at some point in the late twenties, and by late spring and early summer of 1928 their relationship began to intensify. Early that summer, Jane was staying at the home she and Biddle owned in Croton-on-Hudson, New York, while Biddle was off painting in Mexico. Colin and Jane's mother were house guests during much of May, and Jane wrote her husband about meeting Carlos Chávez, "Colin's Mexican composer friend."[8] Colin was around to "play [piano] accompaniment to packing" before Jane closed the house in late May and left for Rhode Island.[9] In June he followed her there for a short vacation and then in early July set off on his own for Woodstock, where he completed his Concerto for Piano with Wind Octette, which was dedicated to Jane. For her this was a period of self-exploration; as she told her husband, "I'm just drifting—having a beautiful time, and never think more than a week ahead. That's the essence of this scheme of mine for liberation."[10]

Jane achieved that freedom in the fall of 1928, when she separated from Biddle. She never joined him that summer in Taxco, Mexico, as originally planned, and in a letter postmarked December 1928 she revealed to him that she and Colin had been having an affair. From the beginning she knew Colin was homosexual, yet she saw their relationship as a necessary phase in her own sexual development. Her lengthy self-analysis bore the marks of her studies in psychology:

My present stage of being in love with a feminine man has aspects of masculine protest and narcissm [sic] on my part. . . .
[Colin and I are] two people of unlike sex and like temperament.
The relationship between unlike or opposite temperament plus
opposite sex is the mature one, theoretically. . . . Heaven knows
what stages of change I still have to go through, and how long it
will take before I can be the mature female.[11]

Colin and Jane were married on May 6, 1930.[12] They took a honeymoon
trip to Italy, traveling from Naples to Venice. From there they went to the
south of France and rented "a charming little house" in Cassis-sur-Mer,
between Toulon and Marseilles, on the Mediterranean coast.[13] Colin wrote
ebulliently to a friend in New York, "With my usual luck I happened upon
[the house], and we were installed with a piano and Citroën only eight
hours after seeing the place."[14]

The two shared many interests. Both wrote poetry—Colin had
published at least one poem in Canada, and Jane had done so in American
literary magazines—and in the summer of 1928 they spent much time
drawing.[15] Colin had been making sketches since adolescence; a group of
his caricatures had been printed in the *Peabody Bulletin* in 1921, and he had
done some printmaking.[16] Ultimately, however, their most important link
was a fascination with the exotic, something they shared with many friends
at the time.

Chief among their contacts was the music critic and novelist Carl
Van Vechten, a man well known for giving parties that drew together some
of the most challenging minds and eccentric personalities in New York.
Almost any night of the week one could find a distinguished group of
celebrities at Van Vechten's West Fifty-fifth Street apartment—people
such as George Gershwin, Theodore Dreiser, Langston Hughes, James
Weldon Johnson, Somerset Maugham, Paul Robeson, Helena Rubinstein,
Bessie Smith, and Ethel Waters. Van Vechten had been a music critic for
the *New York Times* between 1906 and 1913, and by 1920 was writing occasionally for popular magazines such as *Vanity Fair*. His *Vanity Fair* articles
were of two types: either they gave important early notice to contempo-

rary European composers, such as Satie (whom Van Vechten profiled as early as 1918), or they focused on aspects of American music that had not yet been fully accepted in traditional circles. Van Vechten wrote about composers of popular songs, at one point counting Irving Berlin among "the true grandfathers of the Great American Composer of the year 2001," and was especially interested in African-American spirituals and the blues.[17] He spent much time in Harlem, particularly in its famed nightclubs, and he cultivated friendships with black intellectuals and musicians. His most controversial novel, *Nigger Heaven* (1926), told the story of a violent love affair between two Harlem blacks.[18]

Langston Hughes, in his memoir *The Big Sea,* recalled seeing McPhee and Belo at Van Vechten's parties.[19] And several letters show that Van Vechten was interested in McPhee's music. He attended at least two performances: Abbie Mitchell's recital in 1928, with its group of McPhee songs, and the New York performance by Georges Barrère's Little Symphony in 1930 of McPhee's Concerto for Piano with Wind Octette, with McPhee at the piano.[20]

The Van Vechten circle included two other figures—the black writer Zora Neale Hurston and the Mexican artist Miguel Covarrubias—who were crucial to McPhee and Belo's anthropological interests. Hurston had been friends with Jane since Barnard, when both were students of Boas and Benedict, and in her autobiography, *Dust Tracks on a Road,* she recalled a dinner party given for her by Van Vechten in the late twenties. Among the guests were Blanche Knopf, Sinclair Lewis, Ethel Waters, and "my old friend Jane Belo."[21] Hurston and Belo stayed in contact at least through the early 1940s, when they traveled together to South Carolina on a recording expedition financed by Belo.[22]

Miguel Covarrubias brought Colin and Jane in touch with even more remote possibilities. After arriving in New York in 1923, supported by a scholarship from the Mexican government, he had been championed immediately by Van Vechten. His caricatures appeared regularly in the *New Yorker* and *Vanity Fair,* and his work during the twenties showed a growing involvement with black Americans. Covarrubias designed the sets for Josephine Baker's 1925 Paris debut; he was the illustrator for W. C. Handy's *Blues: An Anthology* (1926); and a selection of his sketches was issued by Van Vechten's publisher Alfred A. Knopf under the title *Negro Drawings* (1927). In his introduction to the latter volume, *Vanity Fair* editor Frank Crowninshield credited Covarrubias with being "the first important artist in America . . . to bestow upon our Negro anything like reverent attention." [23]

Covarrubias responded not only to African-American culture. He too went to Bali, one year before Colin and Jane, and he too wrote a book about the experience. His *Island of Bali* is essentially a travel narrative, yet it is filled with detailed observations about daily life and social patterns. In his introduction to the book, Covarrubias claimed, "When I sailed with [my wife] Rose [Rolanda] for the remote island, no one seemed even to have heard of the place; we had to point it out on the map, a tiny dot in the swarm of islands east of Java." [24] The Covarrubiases stayed just six months, returning in 1931 via Paris, where Balinese dancers and musicians were "the sensation" of the International Colonial Exposition. There they happened upon their old New York friends, Colin McPhee and Jane Belo, who were about to embark on their first Balinese journey. As Jane later remembered, "By great good luck we ran into Rose and Miguel Covarrubias on the Rue de la Paix—and they had just returned from their first six-months' stay in Bali and were bursting with enthusiasm." [25]

Marriage to Jane Belo and friendships with Covarrubias, Van Vechten, and others reaching outside of European traditions certainly influenced McPhee's decision to go to Bali. At the same time, he joined other creative artists of the day in seeking an antidote to the anxieties of urban life. It was a period of paradoxes. Americans revered their skyscrapers and fast-paced machines, memorializing them in art and profiting from them on the stock market, yet they also sought means of offsetting their dehumanizing potential.

In later years McPhee called his trip to Bali "an escape from the vulgarity of America . . . the sordid materialism, the competition, and all the modern virtues." [26] He was not alone in these sentiments, for writings by his contemporaries showed the same dissatisfaction—a nostalgia for simpler days and a yen to escape the confusions of postwar, industrial society. In *Exile's Return: A Literary Odyssey of the 1920s* (1934), one of the most widely acclaimed windows on this period, Malcolm Cowley called the decade "The Age of Islands." He saw these islands as both real and metaphorical. *Escape* was the reigning byword:

> [It was] an age when Americans by thousands and tens of
> thousands were scheming to take the next boat for the South
> Seas or the West Indies. . . . Or without leaving home they
> could build themselves private islands of art or philosophy; . . .
> they could create social islands in the shadows of the skyscrapers,
> groups of close friends among whom they could live as uncon-
> strainedly as in a Polynesian valley, live without moral scruples
> or modern conveniences, live in the pure moment, live gaily on
> gin and love and two lamb chops broiled over a coal fire in the
> grate.[27]

Years later McPhee used strikingly similar language in describing his ideal existence. He spoke of the world "outside of the United States" as "a beautiful place, filled with mystery and unexpected loveliness." He went on: "I once said all I asked of life was . . . the sociability of the village, a hut, and some savory haunch broiling over the coals."[28]

Escape as a remedy for underlying dissatisfaction was a recurring theme of the 1920s and early 1930s. Morley Callaghan, the Toronto novelist and contemporary of McPhee, recalled his motivation for traveling to Paris in the twenties:

> Could the dream I had had for years of being in Paris [have] been
> only a necessary fantasy? A place to fly to, a place that could give
> me some satisfactory view of myself? . . . And indeed it was my
> conviction now that for most men there had to be some kind of
> another more satisfactory world. . . . The saints, tormented by
> the anguish of the flesh, wanted to reject the human condition,
> the world they lived in. But whether saints or café friends there
> in Paris, weren't they all involved in a flight from the pain of
> life—a pain they would feel more acutely at home?[29]

Waldo Frank, in his *Re-Discovery of America* (1929), one of the most im-portant assessments of contemporaneous American culture, also found faraway lands more appealing than home: "There is more famine in the Sahara, but more comfort. There is more misery in Poland, in Egypt, and more comfort. All western Europe, despite primitive farms, decadent towns, and the growing gnaw of dynastic discord, is vastly superior in common comfort to our comfort-worshipping Republic."[30]

▓ Musically, the forces of escape were also at work, as the centuries-old European concert tradition came under attack. "Modernism" donned many hats. McPhee responded to this broadening of musical options, and in his own compositions began moving toward Bali. In 1928, when he wrote accompaniments to sea shanties, he turned to a folk genre—a significant new direction. Another strong element was his close friendship with Henry Cowell, whose fascination with non-Western musics stretched back to childhood. Cowell claimed to have heard Japanese *shaku hachi* music before he knew Brahms, and beginning in the late 1920s taught a course at the New School for Social Research entitled "Music of the World's Peoples." Both he and McPhee were active in the Pan American Association, and Cowell's *New Music* had published McPhee's *Kinesis,* Invention, and Concerto for Piano with Wind Octette.

McPhee had other contacts with non-Western musics. In 1930 or 1931 he became involved in a rather elusive organization called the New York Polyhymnia, which had an exotic purpose: "to foster international exchange of unknown musical cultures and of unknown works, old and new."[31] The Polyhymnia presented concerts in Berlin, Vienna, and Milan before it gave its first—and perhaps only—New York program in April 1931. McPhee belonged to its "Technical and Advisory Board"; Ruth St. Denis, the dancer so steeped in Asian traditions, choreographed the New York concert; and Lazare Saminsky served as "Founder and Executive Director."[32] Saminsky was one of the period's proselytizers for a union of the musics of East and West. In his book *Music of Our Day* (1932), he predicted "an all-embracing synthesis, aesthetic and racial" that would yield a "new tonal language." His rhetoric was extravagant:

> Marvelous are those flare-ups of a renaissance appearing from an
> Eastern racial direction just in this era of marasmus and death, in

an age of visible petrification in Western European music! . . .
This new and triumphant cortège of the musical East, augurates
a real return to our common racial spring, heralds a reunion
of the musical creeds, a tonal merging of the Orient and the
Occident.[33]

In the midst of these involvements, McPhee heard the gamelan recordings that were to have such a profound impact on his career. The records were produced in 1928 when Odéon and Beka, German sister companies, sent technicians to Bali and recorded ninety-eight sides with the aid of Walter Spies, a German then living on the island. Five sides were made commercially available in the West in 1931, when Erich von Hornbostel issued them as part of an Odéon set called *Musik des Orients*.[34] However, the entire group of Balinese discs was pressed in 1928 for an Indonesian market. McPhee was lucky enough to hear some of the pre-Hornbostel releases because two of his friends, Claire Holt and Gela Archipenko, brought them to New York when they returned from a trip to Indonesia, probably in 1929.[35]

McPhee's musical sensibility was perfectly attuned to the gamelan. He loved intricately layered textures, irregular ostinatos, and shifting rhythmic patterns—characteristics that form the very essence of Balinese music. Years later he looked back on his musical progress and recalled his search, from childhood on, for a special kind of sound.[36] At age twelve he had written a piece for children's percussion band with a few strings and other instruments. In it two plates were dropped and smashed. He had been unhappy with the result but said he was thinking of "frail china splintered on marble." Ten years later, when he had composed a concerto for the Toronto Symphony, he again sought this elusive timbre. In the Scherzo he directed one percussionist to shake Chinese glass wind-chimes, the kind one hangs on the verandah in the summer, but the conductor would not allow it. McPhee continued his pursuit, however: "I had in mind some idea of crystal sound, something aerial and purely sensuous. It is strange that another ten years should find me in Java and Bali where music sounded exactly like that."

4

THE FIRST TRIPS TO BALI

 1931-34

In the late spring or early summer of 1931 Colin and Jane sailed for Bali via Paris, where they ran into Rose and Miguel Covarrubias, who gave them a firsthand account of life on the island as well as letters of introduction to two Europeans living there: Walter Spies, a German painter and musician, and Bobby Bruyns, a Dutch travel agent. Most likely Colin heard the Balinese gamelan that was performing in the Dutch pavilion at the International Colonial Exposition—the first appearance in the West by a Balinese group. At least two of McPhee's future Balinese musical friends played in the ensemble: I Madé Lebah and Anak Agung Gedé Mandera, both from the village of Peliatan.[1]

Colin and Jane continued their journey through Marseilles on one of the Dutch Rotterdam Lloyd Royal mail liners. From Marseilles it was a twenty-day trip to the East Indies, with the departure time usually set for Fridays around 1:00 P.M. The ship went along the western coast of Italy, through the Straits of Messina, and then across to Crete. It sailed through the Suez Canal, across the Red Sea, and on to the Indian Ocean for "four or five real 'sea days' [with] nothing to be seen save the silent beauty of the sea and, at night, the beautiful tropical sky with the bright stars." After stopping in Ceylon and Sumatra, the ship continued to Batavia, Java (now

Jakarta), billed by the company as "the starting point of your trip through an earthly Paradise."[2]

Colin and Jane spent at least part of the trip learning Malay, then the *lingua franca* of the East Indies, while enjoying the comforts of the ship.[3] Margaret Mead, writing home to friends during her own voyage to Bali five years later, gave some sense of the accommodations:

> It is a trim, quiet little ship with a sort of furry, warm precision about it which is Dutch. There is discipline, but it is not too intense; there are very good meals and a French menu and a white steward who, himself as thin as a maypole, hovers solicitously in the background and tries to make the officers fat.[4]

The final leg of the journey was between Surabaya, Java, and Buleleng, the north port of Bali. The ship left Surabaya in late afternoon and arrived in Bali the next morning. Both Colin and Jane remembered those early morning approaches to the island as breathtaking: "We never found anything as lovely as our beautiful Bali, and, as we returned, we always stood on the deck at sunrise, just as the ship which bore us was coming in to port, and saw the mountains looming in the early mist behind the stretches of beach and waving palms."[5]

Bali was at a turning point in its history when Colin and Jane arrived there in 1931. A small island of some 2,900 square miles, it was densely populated, with six hundred people per square mile and a total population of approximately 1 million. It had been independent and largely isolated until 1906, when the Dutch moved in. From then on, increasingly large numbers of Western tourists had arrived, and Bali, like Tahiti, had become a metaphor for paradise—a luscious, tropical retreat. Under the Dutch, the Balinese royalty was deposed, and a process of cultural jostling began. When McPhee arrived in 1931, vestiges of the old civilization remained.

> Bali was a medieval, agricultural society that had changed little in spite of closer contacts with the outer world. Houses were still built from surrounding trees and grass, land cultivated and law administered in ways that had long since proven sound and

practical. The Dutch had made roads, schools and hospitals, ruled firmly but discreetly, with a regard and even admiration for native law. A Balinese version of Hindu religion was still the force that held the people together and dominated every activity.[6]

As soon as Colin and Jane reached Bali, they headed for the city of Denpasar, located on the south coast of the island, directly opposite the port of Buleleng. Although they stayed at the Bali Hotel, the usual haunt for Westerners, they kept a distance from tourists. The hotel offered daily itineraries for guests who wanted to cram visits to the sites of Bali into a few days. But Colin avoided such common junkets: "I preferred to drive at random through the island, getting lost in the network of back roads that ran up into the hills where, as you looked down towards the sea, the flooded ricefields lay shining in the sunlight like a broken mirror."[7] He was mesmerized by "the sound of music . . . forever in the air." As the days passed, the seductive appeal of the music increased, and Colin gradually realized he could not leave. He and Jane broke out of the hotel's stuffy European environment and rented a small house in the village of Kedaton, just north of Denpasar. The house was immediately outfitted with servants, and the couple settled into a peaceful tropical existence.

This first house was "small and square, with a roof of corrugated tin and walls covered inside and out with damp white plaster."[8] It had four rooms and a cement floor, and in traditional Balinese style the kitchen and bath were in a separate building. Light came from coconut oil lamps, and servants brought water up from the springs.[9] "The doors creaked; the rooms were musty; the place had been shut a year. But from the deep veranda in front you looked out through the palms over gleaming ricefields and caught a glimpse of the sea beyond."[10]

Suddenly, in January 1932, Colin and Jane sailed back to Paris.[11] Their six-month visitors' permit had expired, and, as Colin described it, they had completely lost track of time. To stay they would have had to take up resident status, and they were not yet ready to make such a commitment.

In Paris they rented "a small apartment" at 35, rue de Fleurus. The transition back to Western life was hard. McPhee felt a tension in the air around him, partly due to the political uncertainty after Hitler's recent election but also to the contrast of European existence with his idyllic Bali sojourn. That spring he wrote Carl Van Vechten in New York: "Life seems cold, sad and dreary after the charms of Bali. We had a marvelous time there, and are thinking seriously of returning in June to stay indefinitely. The world is a horrible place at present, and I feel quite out of it." [12]

During these months McPhee grew disenchanted with Western music. He found himself "restless" at concerts and claimed that "the programs of new music that I once delighted in now seemed suddenly dull and intellectual." He longed for the magic of the "sunny music" of Bali. [13] For McPhee, Balinese music, with its vibrant rhythms and bright timbres, had an overwhelming attraction: "Such music appealed strongly to my imagination, rich as it was in implications of a time when the world was young, and men had simple needs." [14]

DAILY LIFE IN BALI

To uncover the secrets of this musical culture, Colin and Jane returned to Bali in May 1932. On board the Rotterdam Lloyd headed for Bali from Marseilles, he calmly announced his future plans to Carl Van Vechten: "Well, we are on the way back to Bali. . . . We shall build a house there, in the Balinese style, and live quietly and happily." [15]

Immediately after arriving, Colin and Jane began looking for property. The Anak Agung of Saba, a friend who lived in a village on the southeast coast of the island, tried to convince them to live near him. Nyoman Kalér, a fellow musician, hoped they would settle once again in Kedaton. But Colin had other ideas. He searched for a spot high in the hills, where it was cooler, quieter, and more conducive to work. The site he found was all that and more. It lay on the outskirts of Sayan, a small village perched on a mountain ridge not far from Ubud. The property overlooked a deep ravine, at the bottom of which rushed a broad stream. Terraced rice fields lined the other side, and the mountains of Tabanan were visible in the distance. The view was stunning.

"The forest was flooded with a soft golden light that glanced off the surface of huge thick leaves, turned others transparent, and penetrated caves that lay between tense, clutching roots" (*A House in Bali*). Photograph by Colin McPhee.

In choosing a village such as Sayan, Colin and Jane reconciled themselves to a life that would hew to Balinese customs. Sayan was small and a bit off the beaten track; it was quiet and conservative, "a peasant village, not very old, but running according to old Balinese law."[16] There were no shops, only "a small market every two days."[17] Few there spoke Malay, so the McPhees had to start learning the Balinese language, a complex one with three variants—high, middle, and low. Margaret Mead later described the "intricacies" of Balinese:

> [There were] endless small conventions that governed the speech
> of people of different rank and caste in Balinese. We had to learn
> to deal with seventeen levels of vocabulary. . . . And words were

extraordinarily specific. If you showed a Balinese a loaf of bread and asked him to slice it, but used another verb instead of the one that meant to cut in even slices the thickness of which was less than their length and breadth, he would look at you with an absolutely blank expression.[18]

Mead intimately knew the subtleties of the language because when she arrived with her husband Gregory Bateson in 1936, they decided to live in a village even more remote than Sayan—the mountain town of Bayung Gedé. Mead found the people there "sulky and frightened" and the culture "simple and inarticulate."[19] Yet she realized that the simplicity of the mountain people forced her and Bateson to acquire a better knowledge of Balinese and that the cool mountain climate brought "health instead of languor."

The McPhees' house in Sayan was built, in Balinese style, of bamboo with a thatched roof. According to an undated inventory of the property, they constructed at least four buildings: a "large house" with a verandah, dining alcove, studio, and balcony; a "bedroom house" with two verandahs and two bedrooms; a bath house; and a "kitchen house."[20] There was also a separate garage. Teak, durian, nutmeg, coconut, and "several other untranslatable woods" went into the structure.[21] All the materials came from Bali, except the floors, which were of polished Borneo cement. The McPhees' chauffeur and musical informant, I Madé Lebah, has remembered the main building as simple, with no sculpture or paintings. It had exceptionally high ceilings, beautifully carved rafters, and many Balinese textiles. Its design accommodated Colin's work:

> It had been built in the style of a theater pavilion, and the long veranda was large enough to hold both gamelan and dancers. A wide lower step ran around the entire pavilion where an audience might sit and look on. . . . At one end of the pavilion, where the curtains that concealed the actors might have hung, I had closed off a room for my piano and books. Above was a little balcony which overlooked the veranda. Here I wrote. The pavilion stood at the very edge of the cliff, and as I looked out from

the balcony through the break in the sloping roof, out and down over the ravine and curving river, it was like looking out from a plane.[22]

Colin was a talented cook and had two kitchens built on the property. One was fully outfitted for preparing an array of international cuisines. The other was "purely Balinese":

> It was a simple thatched pavilion with neat mud walls on three sides, wide open on the fourth. The stove was built of hardened clay, in which only the dried ribs and fronds of the coconut palms around the house were burned. I insisted that all utensils be Balinese; an array of earthen pots stood in a line for stewing, steaming rice, etc. The strainers and sieves were of bamboo; the coconut grater of prickly ratan. Ladles and spoons were made from coconut shell; there was a low bamboo bench for a table, on which the cook sat while she prepared her spice. A couple of thick cross sections of giant tree trunk served as chopping blocks. There was a stone mortar and pestle, a thick earthen plate for grinding spice, and several large shallow Chinese pans for frying. With this simple equipment, like a show case in a natural history museum, she turned out elaborate, and delicious Balinese food—hashes, steamed things, forcemeats and dumplings, grills, curries and meats fried crisp in fresh coconut oil.[23]

Sketches for some of these buildings exist in the McPhee Collection at UCLA. All are in the hand of Walter Spies, a German living in Ubud. According to Spies, he, Colin, and Jane drew up the plans together.[24] In *A House in Bali,* McPhee described walking around the property with his friend to "discuss the best position for the house." Like McPhee, Spies was a refugee from the West, having come to Java from Germany in August 1923. He had first worked as a pianist in a Chinese movie theater in Bandung and then began giving piano lessons to Russians living in Java. From there he went to Jogjakarta, where he became master of the sultan's music. In 1927, after a few brief excursions to Bali, he decided to move

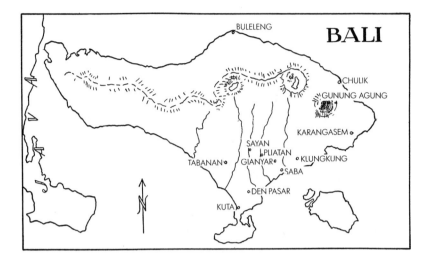

Map from McPhee's *A House in Bali*. Ubud is near P[e]liatan; Bayung Gedé, where Mead and Bateson stayed, is in the mountains directly north of Sayan; and Gilimanuk, where McPhee took the trip described in chapter 6, sits on the far western tip of the island.

there and settled in Ubud. By early 1928 he began building a house at Campuan, on the outskirts of Ubud, northeast of Denpasar. Spies's house, like McPhee's, was in native style. It still stands today.

Colin and Jane rented Spies's house while their own was being built, and Spies stayed in another building on the property. Writing to his mother in October 1932, Spies described his carefree days with the McPhees: "The McPhees and I live together very quietly and happily. He has bought a Steinway grand piano, and so we play much two-piano music. Perhaps, although it's very unlikely, we will make a small concert tour through Java! We have a lot of fun at home." [25] Spies went on to call McPhee an "exceptionally good cook."

Despite its Balinese style, the McPhee house stood out in a simple village such as Sayan. Not only did the buildings have exceptional details, but their inhabitants were Westerners. Colin was aware that their presence could be disruptive, and difficulties did occur. While they were still planning the house, a problem arose in negotiating a lease to the land, a

Panorama of the Sayan house. Photograph by Colin McPhee.

matter that eventually was resolved.[26] Later, demons were thought to have appeared, partly because there was a graveyard next door.[27] Perhaps the most disturbing event occurred when a neighbor arrived one day to survey the house and pronounced it a "palace."[28] Colin, who wanted to slip unobtrusively into the community, was hurt by this remark. Yet he took some comfort in knowing that the Balinese princes living in real palaces were not haughty at all but undertook menial tasks side by side with the villagers.

Certain aspects of the McPhees' life might have made it seem a privileged one to the Balinese. Like other Westerners there during the 1930s, they had a large retinue of servants. In 1933 Colin wrote to Van Vechten, proudly describing his tropical establishment: "How I wish you could see [the house] . . . Twelve servants—all beautiful and naked to the waist."[29] Ni Murni, an Ubud woman whose mother worked for McPhee, has recalled six servants in the McPhee kitchen alone: several to carry water up from the river (a big job with such a large household), one to wash clothes, others to cook.[30] Colin names several servants in *A House in*

Interior of the Sayan house. Photograph by Colin McPhee.

Bali. Rantun was special among the cooks, and there was a stream of houseboys and chauffeurs: Kesyur, Durus, Pugig, and I Madé Lebah, the most important of them all. Lebah was not only McPhee's chauffeur but his principal musical informant. He has recalled being treated well by McPhee; they had good times together. The pay was generous, and McPhee had compassion toward him: "If I was sick, he would cry and go look for a doctor for me."

Jane was accustomed to this grand life. Coming from an affluent family, she accepted servants as a usual part of daily existence. Yet she was not considered arrogant or ostentatious by friends. Zora Neale Hurston, writing to Jane in 1939, gently chided her for being so sheepish about her money, and Rhoda Métraux, an associate of Mead who also worked with Jane, called her "modest" and "generous." [31]

Despite the McPhees' large household establishment, life in Bali was rugged in a number of ways. There was no plumbing or electricity and few shops or cars; travel to the West involved a twenty-day trip by ship; and access to the materials needed for research was difficult—books and paper were at a premium, and even newspapers arrived two months late. Mail was delivered not to their door but to the Bali Hotel in Denpasar. In

Katharane Mershon (left) and Jane Belo (right) in Bali. Photograph by Colin McPhee.

addition there was the isolation of working in a foreign culture for six years, with only a few breaks.

Other Westerners in Bali lived similarly. When Margaret Mead and Gregory Bateson arrived in 1936, they also hired help for research and household tasks. "When we came home at midnight, dinner would be waiting, hot and delicious." [32] Both had years of fieldwork behind them— Mead in Samoa and New Guinea and Bateson in New Guinea. Mead saw Bali as a "paradise" for the anthropologist. Ceremonies, both in their village and in others nearby, were easily accessible for daily observation, and "informants, scribes, secretaries were ready to be trained for the asking." But in a letter written from Bali in 1937, Mead revealed how taxing fieldwork could be, even in circumstances as optimal as those in Bali: "One realizes what a strain conscientious anthropological research in a native village of 500 people is—people whose every word, grunt, scratch, stomach-ache, change of wearing apparel, snatch of song sung on the road or jest flung over someone else's wall is *relevant*." [33]

McPhee seems to have combined a pleasant existence with a determination to document the musical culture around him. Although he had no formal training in fieldwork or any aspect of scholarship, he fell into anthropological research with natural ease. The secure comforts of a gentleman scholar gave a firm foundation to his efforts. In the 1933 letter to Carl Van Vechten already cited, he described life in Bali as "lazy and unproductive. I leisurely collect Balinese music and make notes for a book, and the rest of the time plant trees and flowers, or ride the horse." [34] Yet the quantity of his transcriptions and the quality of his writing on Balinese music show that the pace, if "leisurely," was nonetheless dogged. In later years Mead told the folk music collector Sidney Cowell that "Colin worked hard in Bali." And I Madé Lebah, who was by McPhee's side for so much of the Bali stay, has described a rigorous schedule in the Sayan house. [35] Most days Colin practiced the piano for several hours in the morning; then he and Lebah settled down to a long session of transcription. McPhee's tone in describing his daily life to Van Vechten was much like the one he would later use in *A House in Bali*—that of fantasy. Unlike Mead, he did not succinctly describe his work in practical terms.

During their years in Bali, the McPhees not only observed the culture but also became active community members who adhered closely to local customs. Lebah has affirmed that they were liked by the people of Sayan. They took part in temple ceremonies and were accepted as part of the community. Hugo Bernatzik, a Viennese ethnologist and explorer who stopped in Bali on the way back from a field trip in the Solomon Islands and New Guinea, gave a Westerner's perspective on Colin and Jane's sympathy for the Balinese:

> Among all the whites whom I met on my travels they were the only ones who, amid the beautiful tropical scenery, did not live in barracks and had not, though their means would have permitted, built themselves houses in the loud colonial style. They had real artistic natures, whose whole endeavour was to encourage and maintain the good characteristics and disposition which the Bali people so richly possess. . . . My hosts were tireless.[36]

A COMMUNITY OF RESEARCHERS

Colin and Jane lived in Bali during an active period of anthropological research there. Years later Jane gathered together essays by Westerners who had worked on the island during the 1930s and published them under the title *Traditional Balinese Culture*.[37] The volume opened with an introduction in which she discussed the work of this community.

Walter Spies was the group's acknowledged leader. The first to settle in Bali, he painted local scenes in a naive, Rousseau-like style, and he also published with Beryl de Zoete a book entitled *Dance and Drama in Bali* (1938). Any Westerner arriving on the island sought out Spies immediately, for he was renowned for his generosity in helping others get settled. As Margaret Mead said, "Walter . . . has welcomed and entertained all the interesting people who have come here."[38] And there were a lot of "interesting people": Charlie Chaplin, Noël Coward, the Duke and Duchess of Sutherland, and Leopold Stokowski, as well as many scholars and writers.

Margaret Mead in Balinese festival dress with local children, Bayung Gedé, Bali. Library of Congress; courtesy of the Institute for Intercultural Studies, Inc., New York.

Westerners working in Bali during the thirties generated a long bibliography of writings. Jane remembered Gregory Krause's *Bali* (1926), a photo album, as inducing many Westerners to set sail for the island.[39] Krause captured the tropical density of Bali in photos remarkable for their formal concision and effective play of light. That same year Hickman Powell, an American newspaperman, produced a Bali adventure story, *The Last Paradise* (1930), with photographs by André Roosevelt. Besides the previously cited *Island of Bali* (1937), by Miguel Covarrubias and his wife Rose, the novelist Vicki Baum, celebrated author of *Grand Hotel,* arrived in 1935 to learn about Balinese life and two years later published *A Tale from Bali.* It was a historical novel about the 1906 battle between the Dutch and the Balinese Raja of Bandung, in which many Balinese committed suicide rather than submit to outside rule.

Others took decades to complete their books. Belo's *Bali: Rangda and Barong* appeared in 1949, her *Bali: Temple Festival* in 1953, and her *Trance in Bali* in 1960. Katharane Mershon, who built a house at Sanur Beach with her husband Jack, published *Seven Plus Seven: Mysterious Life-Rituals in Bali* in 1971, thirty years after leaving the island. Claire Holt, a student of dance and sculpture who worked both in Java and Bali, wrote a number of studies about the area, the most important of which was *Art in Indonesia: Continuities and Change* (1967). And McPhee's *Music in Bali* did not reach print until 1966.

The most famous Western scholars on the island during the thirties were Mead and Bateson, whose principal publication from the period was *Balinese Character: A Photographic Analysis* (1942). When they arrived in 1936 they joined Belo and Mershon in studying the arts of Bali, as well as aspects of family life and temperament. Jane later said of her relationship to her colleagues: "We were not exactly a team, yet we communicated and were aware of the ongoing studies being made by each of us. There was cross-stimulation, and cooperation when it was needed." [40]

Photography played a major role in their research. A complex method was devised for rapidly shooting photographic stills of a given occasion at the same time as a moving-film record was made. Notes were taken simultaneously by several observers, both Western and Balinese. Mead and Bateson shot some 25,000 stills during their Bali years. They purchased a rapid winder and bought a developing tank to handle ten rolls of film at a time. Mead saw this research method as revolutionary: "In 1971, when the American Anthropological Association held a symposium of the newest methods of using and analyzing film and tape, Gregory's films of Balinese and Iatmul parents and children still were shown as models of what can be done with photography." [41]

Mead, Bateson, Mershon, and Belo worked together with their Balinese secretaries, yet all was not peaceful within the group; artistic natures clashed with scientific method. According to Mead, "This brought us into some conflict with our artist-hosts, a conflict that intensified when Jane Belo . . . rebelled against what she called 'cold and analytical' procedures." [42] In her preface to Belo's *Trance in Bali,* Mead described the research roles assumed by each member of the group:

> [Jane] participated actively and eagerly in our experiments with
> new methods of recording, even though the rigor of time

observations, matter-of-fact cataloguing, and firmly schooled translations seemed at first to be a way of dissecting and denaturing the beauty of the whole. But she was as convinced a scientist as she had been an artist. . . . Initially, we worked along parallel lines, [Jane] in the village of Sajan, Gregory Bateson and I in the village of Bajoeng Gedé, and our two secretaries, Madé Kalér and Goesti Madé Soemeng worked in parallel as we developed the complex methods of recording necessary to cope with such a complicated culture. It soon became apparent that an appropriate division of labor would be for Jane Belo to take over the study of trance. . . . Katharane Mershon, who had lived and observed and participated in the life of the village of Sanoer, District of Intaran, out of her previous experience as a dancer, was also drawn into the project. Ketoet Moerda, the youngest of the three Balinese secretaries [Mershon's adopted child], learned to touch type and record in Balinese. . . . Occasionally we all met, to record some particularly complicated trance drama, and messengers went back and forth across Bali, carrying our notes to one another.[43]

Colin and Jane also took many photographs for their own research, even before Mead and Bateson arrived. "We had invested in our first movie camera and, using a Rolleiflex and a Leica, were learning to capture the moment in the sequences of behavior."[44] Colin alone shot hundreds— perhaps thousands—of photographs in Bali. A few were included in his various publications, but most have yet to reach print.[45] In 1941, applying for funds for yet another fieldwork project (this one in South America), McPhee described his use of photography in Bali. His method was similar to that of Mead and Bateson:

I began my work by taking motion-pictures of the different orchestra-types (together with performances), and attending as many ceremonies as possible. In these pictures stress was laid on technic of playing the different instruments, which were photographed at great length. Stills were made at the same time, which were later converted into slides, thus supplementing in detail the motion pictures.[46]

According to Jane, she and Colin learned much from other photographers living in Bali, especially Jack Mershon and Hugo Bernatzik.[47]

FROM COMPOSER TO ETHNOMUSICOLOGIST

During these first years in Bali and indeed throughout his stay there, Colin kept involved with Western music by playing the piano and listening to the phonograph. Within his first six months on the island, while living in the rented house in Kedaton, Colin found a piano, "a shrill upright," which he got from another resident on the island. He was eager to have a piano around, both because his fingers were feeling stiff and because he wanted to play some of the gamelan music he had been transcribing. The Steinway grand that Spies has described Colin purchasing in 1932 was supposed to be resistant to tropical weather but emerged a bit waterlogged from its first rainy season. Colin played frequently, both at home and on board ships anchored in the Bali port, where, according to Lebah, he would entertain visiting Westerners. Lebah has remembered him mostly playing jazz.

Yet despite a continued connection to Western music, composition moved to the background for McPhee during these years. While in Paris in the spring of 1932, he admitted to Carl Van Vechten:

> I've written no music since I left N.Y. So I imagine the good
> impression created by the music with cinema [i.e., H_2O and
> *Mechanical Principles*] has quite evaporated by now. Slonimsky
> wanted to play [the Concerto for Piano with Wind Octette] in
> one of the Paris Concerts, but I said no (for several reasons) and I
> am getting the reputation as the composer who doesn't care.[48]

In *A House in Bali* McPhee described himself as arriving in Paris with one goal: to compose. But the muse stubbornly eluded him. "The weeks passed and the pages on the piano were filled with no more than scraps of themes."[49] The restlessness he had felt in New York, before coming to Bali, did not diminish.

Lebah has claimed that McPhee did little composing after he returned to Bali from Paris and built the house. Most likely, the excitement

Jane Belo in the garden of the
Sayan house. Photograph by
Colin McPhee.

of encountering the music of a new culture eclipsed the urge to compose,
especially when the music was as intoxicating as that of Bali. Mantle Hood,
a composer who also turned to ethnomusicology, believes his own experience in some ways parallels McPhee's:

> I went to Java as a composer, not an ethnomusicologist. I took a
> stack of score paper three-feet high and all my black pencils. I
> came back after two years with the same blank score paper. I
> couldn't write a note. And I didn't write again for ten years.[50]

McPhee's description of himself around 1934, after several years of inten-
sive study of the gamelan, reminds one of Hood's:

> I was now entirely absorbed in work. Everything seemed of
> greatest interest, from the detail of the 'flower parts' in a far-off
> village by the sea, to the bare and simple melodies of the
> mountain gamelans. As the days passed, I found myself thinking
> less and less of composing. I began a work for orchestra, but I
> knew I should not finish it. I wrote a few short pieces and forgot
> about them a week later. The urge to write music had left, it
> seemed.[51]

Yet in this same passage McPhee acknowledged there was more to his waning interest in composition than simply the desire to explore Balinese music. Composing had become an "oppressive responsibility." As the drive to write music left, he felt "free and happy, liberated from [something] in which I no longer believed." [52]

More and more McPhee's attention turned to study of the gamelan. Yet even though he stopped composing for a time, he never fully saw himself as a scholar but as a composer working within a brotherhood of fellow musicians, inquiring how persons like himself functioned in another culture. In *Music in Bali,* the most scholarly outgrowth of his fieldwork, McPhee began the introduction with a flat declaration of his status: "The present book is a composer's account of music in Bali." [53]

The pace of McPhee's discoveries about Balinese music is difficult to chart since most of his field notes and transcriptions are undated. He must have begun his research soon after arriving there in 1931, because when he describes his sudden realization in 1932 that his visa is about to expire, forcing him to return to Paris for a while, he calls his last two weeks on the island ones of "feverish activity." He photographed musicians and instruments and took "endless moving pictures." He worked steadily with musicians making transcriptions. "When I at last gathered my pages together and locked them in my trunk I had the feeling of storing a folio of pressed flowers." [54]

McPhee learned about Balinese music by working closely with musicians on the island, several of whom played prominent roles in his life there. Nyoman Kalér was the first. The two met soon after McPhee rented the house in Kedaton in 1931. Kalér was a teacher of *légong* dance, a style performed by young girls, and was the leader of all three gamelans in McPhee's *banjar.* [55] "He was a slight man, perhaps thirty, with intelligent eyes and a smiling, well-shaped mouth that was both sensual and vaguely sarcastic." [56] Kalér filled McPhee's ears with tales of court gamelans from bygone days. He gave him tips on special performances to attend and introduced him to artists in the area, such as Ida Bagus Anom, a scholar and *dalang* (puppeteer in the shadow play). Through Kalér, McPhee first began to understand the music's intricacies. Several times a week McPhee attended rehearsals of Kalér's *légong* club, across the road from his house:

> At first, as I listened from the house, the music was simply a
> delicious confusion, a strangely sensuous and quite unfathomable
> art, mysteriously aerial, aeolian, filled with joy and radiance.
> Each night as the music started up I experienced the same
> sensation of freedom and indescribable freshness. . . . [It was]
> sound broken up into beautiful patterns. . . . Already I began to
> have a feeling of form and elaborate architecture.[57]

Kalér began teaching the gamelan instruments to McPhee. He brought over a *gendér* from an *angklung* ensemble, later a drum, then a *gangsa*. "Soon the house was filled with gongs, drums, cymbals and flutes, looking like a museum in disorder."[58] Together they began the painstaking process of transcribing. Kalér would play a melody on the *gendér*. McPhee would write it down in Western notation and play it back on the piano. Kalér would suggest corrections. "Nyoman had all the patience in the world. We would work for an hour or so each morning or late afternoon, to relax afterwards by driving down to the sea with Kesyur and Chetig or Tantra [house boys] for a swim."[59] McPhee described Kalér's character on several occasions. In field notes McPhee called Kalér "pedantic" or, as he put it in *A House in Bali,* "the soul of the academic."[60] He also drew the portrait of a jealous man. Once McPhee innocently asked about the gamelan in a neighboring *banjar,* which turned out to be a rival to Kalér's own group. As Kalér answered McPhee's question, "his voice was suddenly thin. . . . He sat for awhile, preoccupied and no longer communicative, and soon he rose and took a ceremonious departure."[61]

Kalér withdrew similarly when McPhee enthusiastically asked to meet I Lotring, a composer from Kuta, a village on the southwest coast of the island. Lotring was a man McPhee had wanted to know for some time. He had first heard Lotring's music in the 1920s, as played by his *légong gamelan* on the Odéon recordings. Lotring's gamelan had been famous then, but in 1929 internal tensions forced it to disband and store the instruments, leaving Lotring without an ensemble. McPhee finally met

Lotring through Kesyur, one of the house boys. At the time Lotring was making a modest living as a goldsmith. He also trained dancers for other clubs, and his wives wove mats. In field notes McPhee gave an impression of Lotring:

> Short, slight, about 30, a mild, guileless smile, hair very thin (this is rare) 'from so much thinking'; a goldsmith; a famous cook; lives by the sea in a very poor house; several wives; unreliable and a little tricky; dreams of pieces at night; . . . studied together with Kalér; same style but Kalér a pedant and Lotring imaginative.[62]

Lotring and McPhee spent a little time together before McPhee went to Paris in 1932. But it was after his return that "our acquaintance developed into a friendship that was to last as long as I remained in Bali."[63]

As McPhee learned more about the Balinese gamelan, he yearned for concentrated periods of work with individual groups so that he could better understand their playing technique and repertory. What he sought was a laboratory-like environment, where musicians could be observed closely over extended periods of time. Suddenly, when presented with Lotring, a composer from whom he could learn much yet one who lacked a gamelan, McPhee had an idea; he and Lotring would revive the Kuta group. That way Lotring would have the stimulus to compose, and McPhee would be able to observe and learn. McPhee later remembered, "As I listened to the records [of Lotring's gamelan] I felt I would not rest until I had succeeded in bringing the gamelan back to life."[64] At the time McPhee was obsessed by the desire to grasp one of Lotring's pieces— *Gonten (Djawa),* included on the Odéon recording. It was one that only the Kuta gamelan could play. "At one time Lotring had tried to teach it to me. But I never got past the melody. The rest was impossible to grasp except through a performance."[65]

Negotiations began with the men of Kuta, and soon a plan took shape for forming a new group. Some old members refused to return, but their investment in instruments was reimbursed (or, as McPhee says, they were "bought off"). A budget of 240 *rupiah* ($144) was drawn up, which included costs for repairing the gold leaf on the instruments (which had long been in storage), bringing in a tuner, buying back the big gong from the local pawn shop, purchasing cloth and goldleaf for costumes, and paying the old members. McPhee volunteered to shoulder 150 *rupiah* of the expenses. In return, he asked the men of the gamelan to build him a hut on the beach.

The hut was soon completed, and McPhee immediately settled there for three straight months of work in Kuta, returning only occasionally to Sayan. The hut provided a welcome retreat:

> It stood at the edge of the beach, beneath the palms, and through
> the open door you looked straight out on the sea. It was long and
> narrow, and the palm-thatch came down like a tent, touching
> the ground. The pillars were thick columns of coconut that had
> been planed smooth, and rested on heavy round blocks of coral.
> The floor was the white sand.[66]

The Kuta gamelan revived quickly and soon was playing even better than before. Lotring composed steadily, and the club gained fame.

Lotring enthralled McPhee, not only because he was one of the few composers McPhee worked with in Bali but also because he gave a close-up view of how the Balinese imaginatively reworked existing material. As McPhee observed, "These transferences always seemed surprisingly natural, and gave continually new aspects to the original melodies and ornamental figuration."[67] The rhythmic complexity of Lotring's music appealed to McPhee as well. In *Music in Bali* he returns repeatedly to this aspect of Lotring's style, and in one example of the composer's cross-accentuation focuses on a passage using rhythmic devices much like those in McPhee's own Concerto for Piano with Wind Octette of 1928, with its shifting pitch patterns and accents (exs. 21 and 22).

McPhee gave euphoric accounts of working with Lotring and the Kuta gamelan. Here was the situation he had longed for—not a library with records of dead traditions but a living art, growing in front of his eyes:

EXAMPLE 21   Concerto for Piano with Wind Octette, third movement, piano, mm. 113–15.

EXAMPLE 22   I Lotring, *Angkatan*. Transcription by McPhee from *Music in Bali* (ex. 218, mm. 1–2).

> Often, as I sat on the floor of the clubhouse, listening to the men rehearse, I would ask a g'nder player to move aside while I took his place for a while. . . . This was enough . . . for me to experience the sensation of being, at least for the moment, completely united, in close and absolute sympathy with the players, lost with them in the rhythm of the music. I knew the melodies by heart, and as I played I felt both peace and exhilaration in this nameless, tacit accord. Here there was no conductor's stick to beat time, no overeloquent hands to urge or subdue. The drumming of Lotring was at times barely audible; you felt it rather than heard it, and the music seemed to rush ahead on its own impetus. You were swept along the stream, no longer knew what you were doing. It was something free and purely physical, like swimming or running.[68]

Two other Balinese played a central role in McPhee's musical activities before he returned to New York in 1935: I Sampih and I Madé Lebah.

Sampih was a child of about eight when McPhee first met him in 1932, while the house was being built. As McPhee tells the story, one day he walked down to the river below his house and was suddenly caught in a flash flood. Sampih saw him struggling, leaped in, and led him to safety. The two struck up a tentative friendship, and soon Sampih was stopping frequently at the McPhee house. Eventually he came there to live. McPhee probably never adopted Sampih officially. In *A House in Bali* he does not use the term "adoption," although he talks of custody negotiations with the child's parents.[69] Katharane Mershon also took in a Balinese boy; hers was named Murda. She has claimed she paid Murda's family about a dollar a month so she could keep the child; she also educated him. In return, Murda taught her Balinese and became her secretary.[70]

One day, quite by accident, McPhee discovered that Sampih had talent as a dancer:

> I came home unexpectedly one evening to find the phonograph on the floor, playing the loudest and most syncopated gamelan record, and Sampih seated beside it improvising a wild kebyar dance. . . . Although he stopped the moment he saw me it was not before I had a glimpse of melodramatic gestures, coquettish eyes and flashing hands that caught with surprising precision the violent and abrupt accents of the music.[71]

Sampih was a lively, precocious child, with a personality as wild as the *kebyar* dance he improvised. On the first day Colin met him he noticed that Sampih was "one of the more boisterous, . . . the leading spirit" of the group of children he was playing with.[72] Another time, when McPhee had a group of twenty-five boys at his house, all waiting to work with a *génggong* (jew's harp) teacher, he again described Sampih's energy: "He could not be suppressed, but always took the lead, laughing and dancing with his shoulders."[73] But there was a rough, moody side to the child, too. His parents were peasants, and while living with them he had been exposed to a violent life. Before meeting McPhee, Sampih had stolen money from his father and run away from home after watching his father beat his mother. Another time McPhee and Sampih found Sampih's

Sampih dancing *kebyar.* Photograph by Colin McPhee.

mother lying in a field, her head split open by a blow from her husband. She recovered quickly, but Sampih did not. McPhee watched a sinister transformation occur in the child as he planned retribution: "'I will surely *kill* [my father] when I am older,' he said [to McPhee] in a low voice that was tense with ferocity." McPhee went on to observe that Sampih's face had become "dark, . . . it suddenly resembled his father's." [74]

McPhee was devoted to giving Sampih every opportunity to grow as a dancer. That devotion is apparent throughout *A House in Bali* and is remembered by those around McPhee, such as Lebah, who has recalled how intensely McPhee loved the boy. McPhee brought the best dancing teachers in Bali to Sayan. Sampih's first teacher was Nyoman Kalér. But Kalér had little sympathy for Sampih's temperament. What to others might have seemed dynamic was crude and wild to Kalér. He thought it "vain to spend time on this mountain child." [75] But McPhee persisted. He then brought Champlung, a young woman *légong* dancer from Bedulu, to Sayan a few days a week to teach Sampih. Immediately the child began to grow artistically.

> [Champlung's] style had sweep, imagination, a fluidity that made Nyoman's teaching seem dry and superficial. . . . she put all her youthful energy into these lessons, difficult, moreover, for her to give, for she had a willful and far from supple boy to deal with. . . . Sampih adored her. Their bright peasant natures understood each other.[76]

Two musicians came with Champlung—a *génder* player and a drummer. The latter was I Madé Lebah, already mentioned as McPhee's chauffeur.[77] Lebah lived in Peliatan, a village not far from Sayan, and was a member of its gamelan, one of the most famous on the island. He had gone to Paris in 1931 to perform in the Colonial Exposition, and his background made him the ideal musical informant and comrade for McPhee.

> He was a high-strung, rather fragile youth, perhaps twenty, filled with some mysterious nervous energy, for even when he was not rehearsing, his long slender fingers were forever drumming lightly against some vibrant surface, and when he laughed his voice was high and excited. He had the most agreeable nature in the world.[78]

According to McPhee's field notes, Lebah "never went to school" but was "always learning music" and was "always in demand. . . . he is an instinctive rather than a technical musician. . . . His culture is restricted. . . . Loves to teach."[79]

In the mid-1980s Lebah still fit McPhee's description.[80] A man with a wiry frame, his words tumble out in a high-pitched torrent. He is shy, yet beneath the shyness is complete self-assurance. The passing of the years has raised Lebah's status to that of *guru*. When McPhee discovered him, he was young and unknown. Since then, he has become a major musical figure in Bali.

Lebah's presence brought calm to McPhee's work. Once he joined the household, the two began a stint of uninterrupted work. When McPhee had worked with Kalér and Lotring, both lived outside Sayan and could stay only for short periods. With Lebah in residence, however, it was possible to get into the rhythm of a regular routine.

Transcription was the learning tool they used. McPhee recalled their daily schedule:

> In the afternoon Lebah would sit down near the piano, to play
> phrase by phrase some g'nder melody while I wrote. Or he
> would pick up a drum to show the rhythm in a certain part of
> the music. Seriously, leisurely, we worked together till sundown.
> At last we would decide to stop. We would walk down the
> hillside to bathe in the spring halfway down, or else in the pool
> far below, where through the ferns the water fell from
> overhead.[81]

Lebah's memory of the transcription process concurs with McPhee's. "I played, he listened, and then he wrote. He'd play back on the piano and that's how we checked for accuracy. He couldn't play actual gamelan instruments. He knew the music but he couldn't play the instruments."[82]

The work with Lebah was interrupted for a time when McPhee returned to the United States in 1935, but it would resume when he came back two years later.

5

A WESTERN INTERLUDE

 **1935–36**

En route to New York in the spring of 1935,
McPhee heralded his arrival in a letter to Henry Cowell: "After those years
of silence, and geographical remoteness, I announce my return to the land
of the living." [1] His letter overflowed with plans. He was "in the middle of"
a book on Balinese music and expected "to have a couple of orchestral
work[s] finished by fall—a prelude and tocatta [*sic*], and a 'fantasia' for
piano and orchestra on Balinese melodies and rhythms—authentic stuff
and not dished-up impressionism à la Eichheim." (Henry Eichheim's
orchestral works, *Java* and *Bali,* had been written in 1929 and 1933,
respectively.)

Colin and Jane left Bali in late December of 1934, just as the rainy
season descended. [2] They did so for several reasons. One month earlier
Colin had written Carl Van Vechten grumbling about the growing numbers of tourists and missionaries in Bali, and he was perturbed by the high
taxes levied against Westerners. [3] In *A House in Bali* he mentioned having
"business to attend to" in the United States: "I also felt I needed to
get away." [4]

Soon after reaching New York, the McPhees headed for Toronto to
see Colin's parents, the first visit he seems to have made there since
leaving for Paris in 1924. It was one of two occasions on which his family

93

met Jane.[5] Augustus Bridle, the critic who had so faithfully followed McPhee's career, wrote in the *Toronto Daily Star* that Colin and Jane had arrived via Canadian Pacific Railroad and stayed only a day or two.[6] According to Colin's sister-in-law, Janet McPhee, he and Jane went to Campbellville to visit his family and then stopped overnight in Montreal, where Janet and Colin's brother, Douglas, were living. Jane's worldliness enchanted her sister-in-law: "She was beautiful, very elegant, every hair in place, and perfectly dressed. I was very naive and thinking how Dougie and I were living out on a lakeshore then, lugging big stones to build our driveway." Jane seemed especially glamorous as she described her life in New York that coming winter, with gallery openings and concerts as daily fare. But Janet and the rest of Colin's family found her friendly.

This was probably the last time Colin went home. Yet the trip had a purpose beyond simply visiting family: since he was not yet an American citizen, Colin had to return to Canada in order to stay in the United States for an extended period.

Back in New York in the summer of 1935, Colin and Jane found that conditions were different from when they had left four years earlier. The Depression had worsened. Franklin Roosevelt was in the third year of his first term as president. The Works Progress Administration had been established in May of that year; soon after came the Federal Music Project and its offshoot, the Composers' Forum-Laboratory. McPhee was luckier than many composers in having an independent income, and he remained untouched by the radical political movements that galvanized others.[7]

As in 1926, McPhee hit New York's new music turf with a determined stride. Although only in the city for the 1935–36 concert season and the fall of 1936, he managed to pack the time with activities, and his status among New York's community of composers remained strong. Soon after arriving, he was offered a commission by the League of Composers that included a guarantee of performance. The other League commissions that year went to Joseph Achron (for a string quartet), Aaron Copland (for *Statements*), Leo Ornstein (for *Dance of the Fates*), Quincy Porter (for a string quartet), and William Grant Still (for *Kaintuck*).[8]

While at work on a piece for the League, McPhee began preaching about Bali with a missionary's zeal, especially in "The Absolute Music of Bali," which appeared in the May-June 1935 issue of *Modern Music*. It was the first article about his island experience, and it was clearly directed to other composers. As McPhee related how Balinese music fit snugly into society as a functional craft rather than a rarefied art, he mused about whether the same could ever be true in the West, whether the music produced by contemporary composers might be integrated into the flow of daily life.[9] McPhee admired most the rhythmic vitality of Balinese music, and he opened and closed with an invitation to explore the repertories of this small island. In between he cited specific aspects of the music that might appeal to Western composers, especially the uses of ostinatos, polyrhythms, and syncopation.

McPhee brought the sounds of Bali to New York's Cosmopolitan Club on November 6, 1935.[10] The program featured three of McPhee's films of Balinese musicians accompanied by appropriate segments from the Odéon gamelan recordings and three groups of McPhee's own gamelan transcriptions for two pianos. It even included a Balinese dinner. Each of the two-piano segments was curiously subtitled "Music recorded for two pianos" (*recorded* must have meant *transcribed*). Marc Blitzstein, who had been a friend of McPhee at least since the days of the Copland-Sessions Concerts, played the second piano.

In January 1936 McPhee began a series of radio programs entitled "Modern American Music" that were broadcast on Sunday evenings at 8:30 P.M. on WEVD (New York), the same station that three years earlier had aired a series sponsored by the Pan American Association of Composers.[11] McPhee chose the programs and provided commentary. Included were works by Ernst Bacon, Evelyn Berckman, Marc Blitzstein, Paul Bowles, Carlos Chávez, Aaron Copland, David Diamond, Harrison Kerr, Charles Ives, Otto Luening, Walter Piston, and Elie Siegmeister.[12] The final broadcast, entitled "The Influence of Jazz on Europe," featured the music of Darius Milhaud and Arthur Honegger. Soon after the series started, McPhee wrote Cowell about having to cancel a performance of Cowell's "new quartet" (which must have been the "Mosaic" of 1935). In the same letter McPhee had something to say about women writing music:

"Berkman's [i.e., Evelyn Berckman's] Hebrides vocalises went very well [on the show]; I liked them in spite of my disfavor of female composers, and I was not grudging in my enthusiasm when I spoke to her afterwards."[13] Then in early February McPhee went up to Hartford to judge a composition festival held by the Friends and Enemies of Modern Music, the group that had given the premiere of Virgil Thomson's *Four Saints* in 1934. The other two judges were Harold Berkeley and Aaron Copland. Ross Lee Finney took first prize for three songs.[14]

In the midst of this musical activity Colin and Jane led a busy social life. They stayed at her mother's apartment in Gramercy Park and occasionally entertained there, giving at least one memorable dinner party attended by Minna Lederman and her husband Mell Daniel. Two dozen guests, including Carl Van Vechten and his wife, sat around a table in an apartment that was "a very pleasant place with a few Balinese and other Indonesian objects around."[15] Colin prepared an elaborate *rijstafel,* which took two or three days to cook and involved the services of Mrs. Belo's staff. Lederman has recalled the event vividly: "The feast was overwhelming. I stopped eating halfway through, but my husband, who was fond of rice, ate to the end. It was apparently the thing to do. It was an absolutely gorgeous evening, and the first indication to us that Colin was a master chef."

On March 27, 1936, McPhee reentered New York as a composer with the premiere of *From the Revelation of St. John the Divine,* the work commissioned by the League of Composers. It was performed in the Grand Ballroom of the Waldorf-Astoria by the Princeton University Glee Club, conducted by James A. Giddings.[16] After having declared composition an "oppressive burden" several years earlier, McPhee chose a curious way to return to it. For one thing, there is little hint of why he selected texts from Revelations. Israel Citkowitz, who reviewed the work for *Modern Music,* thought it was because of the book's "terrifying visions of war, famine, and destruction [that have] a distinct bearing on the catastrophic events of the present."[17] Three years earlier McPhee had acknowledged that he found the growing world political turmoil to be "horrible."[18] At the same time, though, McPhee was brimming with the sounds of Bali and was at work on the orchestral piece that would become *Tabuh-Tabuhan*. Perhaps *From the Revelation of St. John the Divine* provided a break from Indonesian music, a means of reconnecting with the West.

Three days before the premiere, McPhee wrote his new friend David Diamond, a younger composer whom he had met the year before, giving the fullest extant account of his feelings about the piece:

> I wonder if you will like the work. It is so different from your
> own musical tastes. . . . As you know, it is my first work after
> four years, and I had to bestir myself to write it, and I am curious
> to find what impression it makes on my different friends. It
> seems to have developed into a 'dramatic' work, much to my
> surprise, and become almost pictorial at times under Giddings
> direction. But the form au fond is very simple, and I think the
> music moves forward in the most direct manner from beginning
> to end. I don't know why I should try to present the work to
> you in these rather flattering terms, but I felt I had to tell you
> something about it.[19]

Another letter, this one written to a different friend in the 1940s, reveals that *From the Revelation of St. John the Divine* was scored for men's chorus, two pianos, three trumpets, and two sets of timpani—a combination reminiscent of the *Sea Shanty Suite* of 1929.[20] It lasted twenty minutes.[21]

In his *Modern Music* review Citkowitz, a composer of limited productivity known especially as a songwriter, was none too flattering. He felt that the texts of Revelations presented "almost insuperable difficulties in setting" because their "sheer allegory" made it "impossible to seize hold of that kernel of poetic thought and concentrated expression which permits a choral form to develop in all musical freedom." Citkowitz criticized McPhee's work for suffering "from the excess of verbal detail and image which the music is called upon to digest." The words were largely declaimed in recitative, a technique that lost its grip "after a highly effective opening." David Diamond, on the other hand, has recalled being "overwhelmed" by the piece: "I said, 'Colin you have to orchestrate it, for a big orchestra.'"[22]

Not only did McPhee fail to take up Diamond's suggestion; he withdrew the piece after its premiere. In the early 1940s, a New York University choral group asked for the score, but McPhee turned down the request. He thought the work had "sounded well" in its original version but said he had "always wanted to change it and alas, have not done so." The music must have been in storage then because McPhee claimed, "I can't get at the score to work on it, and it would need all new parts." [23] At about the same time, the conductor William Strickland tried to get the music from McPhee for a performance but was unsuccessful. "He wouldn't let me have it, and everybody talked about it as such an interesting work." [24] Today the score is lost. [25]

In the spring of 1936 McPhee published in *Modern Music* four reviews of New York concerts, reestablishing himself as a music journalist. His association with the magazine had begun in 1931, when he wrote a similar group of concert reviews. It continued briefly in the spring and fall of 1936 (with his final review published in January 1937, after he had sailed back to Bali), and then accelerated after his final return to New York from Bali early in 1939. Although he had published some writing before, *Modern Music* was the first—and only—journal to which he contributed regularly. His pieces from the spring of 1936 show him to have been an avid concert-goer with wide-ranging tastes and strongly formed opinions. They also reveal a gifted writer. Among his contemporaries he admired Marc Blitzstein, Paul Bowles, Carlos Chávez, Aaron Copland, David Diamond, Frederick Jacobi, Walter Piston, Wallingford Riegger, and Lazare Saminsky—an eclectic mix suggesting that his tastes were broad.

McPhee freely aired his aesthetic preferences. In the January-February issue of the magazine, he praised Copland's ballet *Hear Ye, Hear Ye!* for its "vitality, exhilaration and pungent orchestration, particularly in the jazz parts." He went on, "Not the least of Copland's many gifts is the ability to write the most exciting jazz I know." [26] In the same issue he compared Berg and Hindemith and spoke as a graduate of the neoclassical school:

> The texture of Berg's music is always of too rich and complicated
> a weave for my own ultimate enjoyment; there is too much to

admire, too much to be asked to digest. I find the atmosphere rather suffocating. The clean-cut lines of the Hindemith work [Viola Concerto] seem to me far more eloquent.[27]

On occasion McPhee could be caustic. Reviewing *Joseph and His Brethren,* a "ballet-pantomime" by Werner Josten, he voiced opinions about how non-Western materials should be used:

> The music wavers between angular pedanticisms (neoclassic?)
> and the sort of Oriental melodies formerly heard at the circus in
> the vicinity of the snake charmers. From the standpoint of phras-
> ing and rhythm, I do not see how it could possibly stimulate the
> body to expressive motion. The music is pricked with dissonance
> like a pincushion stuck with pins.[28]

But McPhee aimed his sharpest barbs at the music of Roy Harris: he had no sympathy whatsoever for the man's work. Reviewing a Philadelphia performance of *Farewell to Pioneers,* he wrote:

> In *Farewell to Pioneers* the orchestra labored along far more wearily
> than did any of the most fatigued pioneers. The sonority was
> weak and lacking in resonance. . . . Why the music had been
> published before performance is a mystery to me, for much will
> have to be done to it before it can sound.[29]

A MEXICAN SUMMER

During the winter of 1935–36 McPhee renewed his friendship with Carlos Chávez, an alliance that was to affect his career greatly, especially in the birth of *Tabuh-Tabuhan.* The two had known each other since at least November 1926, when both had works performed on a concert by the International Composers' Guild, and they traveled in common circles. Both were friendly with Copland, Cowell, and Varèse. Both were involved with the Pan American Association. And both came to New York from neighboring countries. Chávez had lived in New York from 1926 to 1928 and settled there again during the winter of McPhee's return from Bali.

McPhee was a strong admirer of Chávez's music, especially *Sinfonia de Antigona* (Symphony No. 1) of 1933 and *Sinfonia India* (No. 2) of 1935–36. In January 1936 *Sinfonia India* received its premiere over CBS radio. Soon after the performance McPhee wrote Cowell: "Chávez did some new works over the air, all Mexican . . . and very good, and including an Indian symphony of his own (very short) which was simply ripping. I wish you could see your way to publishing it. I don't know when I've enjoyed a new work more." [30] That spring McPhee reviewed the same piece in *Modern Music* with more detailed enthusiasm. He responded most to Chávez's use of ethnic materials (in this case Mexican Indian), which he found true to their source: "One feels on hearing this music first of all a primitive energy that has nothing of the exotic but is a clear and forceful expression of racial vitality both youthful and healthy." McPhee was relieved to hear "none of the Europeanisms or French impressionism still lingering in the works of so many Latin-American composers." Chávez's workmanship appealed to him, with its orchestration "in primary colors," its "hard and penetrating" sonorities, and its "resilient percussive base." [31]

Since at the time McPhee was at work on *Tabuh-Tabuhan,* his favorable response to a composer using ethnic materials comes as no surprise. Throughout the spring of 1935 and the fall and winter of 1935–36, references to a work based on Balinese materials began to appear. On the boat to New York McPhee had written Cowell of plans for two orchestral works on Balinese themes: a "prelude and toccata" and a "fantasia for piano and orchestra." [32] In the May-June 1935 issue of *Modern Music* he was identified as being at work on "a *Rhapsody* on Balinese themes." [33] By the May-June issue of the following year the piece had a title—*Tabuh-Tabuhan.* McPhee was said to be "completing a symphonic work . . . which is Balinese in motif and in musical construction. Mr. McPhee is now on his way to Mexico." [34] Around that time he wrote Cowell that he was composing "a concerto for piano and large orchestra using Bali-jazz-and-McPhee elements. [35] As McPhee recalled many years later, the genesis of *Tabuh-Tabuhan* was simple and Chávez's role significant:

It was in the mid-30's, back in New York for a year, that I
suddenly had the idea, partly suggested by Carlos Chavez, of
writing an orchestral work utilizing material I had collected in
Bali. "Come to Mexico City," he said, "write it, and I will play
it with the orchestra." [36]

McPhee did just that. He and Jane arrived in Mexico City by early June
1936. They spent a week visiting the ruins of Yucatan and then settled in a
small house in Taxco, just south of Mexico City, while Colin finished his
work. [37] They rented a piano immediately, and Colin began arranging for
Chávez to see the score. On June 4 McPhee told Chávez about his progress
on *Tabuh-Tabuhan;* he was composing with ease—no doubts, no blocks.
"The score is going so very well. I hope you will like the nocturne—the
slow movement. It's quite short. I hope to have the whole work finished
inside of two weeks." [38] The summer was spent putting finishing touches
on *Tabuh-Tabuhan* and rehearsing it, with a short breather in Acapulco.

Chávez had founded the Orquesta Sinfónica de México in 1928. In
the summer of 1936 it performed eight subscription concerts, beginning
July 17, at the Palacio de bellas artes, in a concert hall so magnificent that it
boasted a "million-dollar Tiffany glass curtain." [39] In addition, it gave a
concurrent series of popular concerts for workers, for which tickets were
distributed through labor unions. The orchestra presented a balanced fare
of standard European orchestral literature and contemporary Mexican,
American, and Spanish works. [40] That summer it performed Bach's second
and third Brandenburg Concertos, Beethoven's Seventh and Ninth symphonies, Tchaikovsky's "Pathétique" Symphony, and works by Mozart,
Haydn, Scarlatti, and Monteverdi. Gustavo Pittaluga and Ernesto Halffter
were the Spanish composers represented; the Mexicans included Candelario Huízar and Chávez himself. The only two North Americans were
Copland and McPhee. McPhee wrote to his friend Eva Gauthier in early
September about the group's summer program:

Chávez . . . has done excellent work with the orchestra here. I
think he is a fine musician, particularly in modern things. He is

very eager to be a good 'classical' conductor at present, and is
doing Beethoven, Vivaldi, Mozart, etc. It is hard to tell just how
sure he is of himself yet in these, as such works show up the
orchestra here very much. . . . They are excellent in modern
works, but still lack finish for classics.[41]

That summer Copland also visited Mexico to work on *The Second Hurricane*.
But it was his Concerto for Piano and Orchestra of 1926 that Chávez
performed in July.

As early as June 27 McPhee and Chávez were arranging rehearsals for
the premiere of *Tabuh-Tabuhan,* to take place on September 4 (it had
originally been scheduled for August 21).[42] They began by working with
the two pianists, Francisco Agea and Eduardo Hernandez Moncada, and
then moved to full orchestra early in August. That same month, as
rehearsals of *Tabuh-Tabuhan* became more frequent, Colin and Jane settled
"in town" at the San Angel Inn, "just outside of Mexico City."

It was formerly an old monastery, and has a beautiful quasi
tropical park all about it. From the verandah you can see the
snow-capped volcanoes, glistening in the sun like plates of ice
cream. . . . A lot of New York friends have turned up during
the summer, for Mexico seems very popular, in spite of strikes,
bandits, and assassinations. Safer than Europe, however.[43]

The McPhees saw Rose and Miguel Covarrubias almost every day.

In late August McPhee gave a lecture-concert on Balinese music at
the Palace of Fine Arts in Mexico City, the same program he had presented
in November 1935 with Marc Blitzstein at New York's Cosmopolitan Club.
This time Moncada played second piano.[44] McPhee's presentation was
received enthusiastically by "a large and delighted audience."[45]

McPhee's letters of that summer resonate with hope. He was forging
an individual style based on his experiences among the musicians of Bali,
and he seemed confident of the product. Most important, an orchestra was
waiting to perform his new work.

TABUH-TABUHAN

From beginning to end, *Tabuh-Tabuhan* is a celebration of the Balinese gamelan. Its title is "a Balinese collective noun, meaning different drum rhythms, metric forms, gong punctuations, gamelans and music essentially percussive." Its instrumentation pits a "nuclear gamelan" of two pianos, celesta, xylophone, marimba, and glockenspiel—all Western instruments except for two Balinese gongs—against a standard symphony orchestra.[46] And its themes, rhythms, and textures are drawn from McPhee's own gamelan transcriptions. In many ways *Tabuh-Tabuhan* was conceived with the same missionary spirit that energized the pages of "The Absolute Music in Bali" and was behind McPhee's concerts of transcriptions in New York and Mexico City. He was eager to share his recent musical discoveries with others.

As McPhee acknowledged in a letter that summer to Eva Gauthier, *Tabuh-Tabuhan* was the most ambitious piece he had ever written. Its subtitle, "Toccata for Orchestra and 2 Pianos," is warranted by the flash and flare of much of the instrumental writing, yet "Concerto" would have been equally appropriate. McPhee's large works before *Tabuh-Tabuhan* had all been concertos, and here again the concerto principle predominates; McPhee even called it once a "concerto grosso," for indeed the "nuclear gamelan" often functions as a solo group, the full orchestra reserved for tutti passages.[47]

McPhee was attempting to resolve the crisis he had reached before leaving for Bali. He had gone through several approaches to composition during his last few years in the United States—neoclassical, folk-inspired, dissonance-saturated—and had ended up, in *Mechanical Principles* and *H_2O,* seeking a less elite art. He spoke of these works as having a connection "with daily life—its noise, rhythm, energy, and mechanical daring."[48] His trip to Bali had brought him in contact with an aesthetic close to his own. There, as McPhee stressed in the opening sentence of "The Absolute Music of Bali," music "play[ed] a most important part in the life of the people."

Tabuh-Tabuhan, then, marks the union of McPhee the composer and

McPhee the ethnomusicologist. The work draws on many of McPhee's transcriptions from Bali and also emulates the very process by which Balinese music is composed. McPhee described that process in "The Absolute Music of Bali":

> Retaining its traditional melodies and phrase formulae [the music] receives new treatment by successive generations of *gurus* (teachers) who take the place of the composer. The present tendency . . . is to break up the old compositions and weld fragments or episodes from these into new works. . . . *In Bali music is not composed but rearranged* [emphasis added].[49]

Tabuh-Tabuhan draws on this principle but modifies it somewhat, for in the piece McPhee combined composition with rearrangement.

Throughout the work McPhee's Western training stands alongside Balinese methods and materials. In terms of form, there are three well-balanced movements, perhaps in keeping with a concerto-like conception: the first and last are spirited, and the middle is slow. Each presents a parade of transcriptions, creating what Richard Mueller, in an exegesis of McPhee's Balinese borrowings, has termed "a montage-like structure."[50] The first movement is sectional, with each theme group drawing upon a separate transcription. After all the themes are stated, there is a reprise. The second movement uses three transcriptions and closes with a return to the opening material. The third, however, moves continually forward with no final reprise. It has four principal sections and quotes from several gamelan compositions. Yet despite its continual forward push, this movement recalls motives from the first.

The harmonic materials of *Tabuh-Tabuhan* are Balinese in some ways, Western in others. Chords are generated from four- and five-note scales, drawn from various forms of the Balinese *pelog* and *slendro*. Several pitch groups often sound simultaneously, yet on the whole they remain the same throughout a single transcription (i.e., each section of a movement), adhering to Balinese models of pitch constancy within a single composition. Where the Westerner enters is in the transitions between those sections, most of which move to a new set of pitch groups. In the opening of the first movement, for example, McPhee uses two four-note patterns, one based on E (in the flute, clarinet, marimba, and Piano II), the other a transposition of the first on A (in Piano I; see ex. 23). Beneath both sounds an ostinato on C and G—significantly, the two missing axis pitches from the four-note groups. The patterns interlock in different ways (ex. 24). The

EXAMPLE 23   *Tabuh-Tabuhan,* first movement, mm. 1−6. (All instruments not shown here are tacet.)

(*continued*)

EXAMPLE 23 (*continued*)

shift to new pitch material begins in measure 25, where a D♯ is introduced in the flute, slightly modifying one of the original patterns. Juxtaposed in Piano I, however, is the original D♮—a familiar McPhee technique from the late 1920s. One pitch area overlays another in this transitional passage until new patterns are reached at measure 49. Similar procedures are found throughout the work.

The first page of the score reveals much about McPhee's compositional procedures in the piece. From the outset he finds common ground

EXAMPLE 24   *Tabuh-Tabuhan,* pitch collections used at the opening of the first movement.

between his own compositional preferences and Balinese techniques. This fusion is apparent in the irregular ostinatos, stratified registral placement, and, on many levels, a layering of materials. The first movement is entitled "Ostinatos," a reference to its fundamental building blocks. At the opening, five separate ostinatos sound. Each has internally shifting pitches and accents. All interrelate (ex. 25). Ostinato B is an augmented version of A; C is built of pitches transposed from A; D uses the two missing pivotal pitches of A, B, and C; and E reinforces the 3 + 3 + 2 rhythmic accentuation of C and similar pitch grouping of D. Each ostinato falls into broader patterns of repetition; those patterns, in turn, overlap irregularly (see brackets showing ostinato length in ex. 25). McPhee carefully distributes the registers of these ostinatos. Most stay within a closely circumscribed area; ostinato B is doubled at the octave. By doing so, he achieves a transparent layering in which each individual line is delicately delineated.

McPhee's use of transcriptions in *Tabuh-Tabuhan* varies from literal to free. The second movement, "Nocturne," provides a concise summary of his various approaches. The movement has four sections, the last of which recalls the first. Each of the first three features a separate transcription. McPhee later identified the sources: "The first [section] is my arrangement of a Balinese flute melody. The second is the quiet passage from the modern gamelan piece, *Kebiar Ding*. The third is the . . . *gamelan angklung*. This last represents the style rather than the actual music, which I composed myself." [51]

The opening of the "Nocturne" is modeled on *Lagu ardja,* a flute-piano piece by McPhee that is itself an amalgam of transcription (the flute line) and arrangement (the piano accompaniment). McPhee later commented on his method in *Lagu ardja:* "I tried composing light, percussive accompaniments for the piano, choosing tones that would suggest gongs

EXAMPLE 25   *Tabuh-Tabuhan,* first movement, five ostinatos from the opening. (All instruments not shown here are tacet.)

and other Balinese instruments. . . . Here, you might say, the composer emerges somewhat, although remaining discreetly in the background."[52]

In the "Nocturne" McPhee transfers the first two-thirds of his arrangement of *Lagu ardja* nearly literally to the orchestra. The melody is transposed down a step, and a few ornamental details differ. In the orchestrated version phrasing is added to clarify the shape of the flute part, and the tempo is slower. Yet the melody notes are mostly preserved, and the accompaniment is much the same. McPhee retains the spareness of the piano accompaniment by whittling the instrumentation down to clarinets, marimba, two pianos, cellos, and basses. Here again registral independence is prominent. The F♮ pedal in the low strings and Piano I bass sounds against an F♯ high above in the flute (ex. 26). McPhee adheres less closely to the flute-piano transcription once its second section is reached ("Nocturne," measure 33), adding a string counterpoint to the flute part and moving to a new pitch area at the end of the section.

The part of the second movement that stays closest to its transcribed source—*Kebyar ding*—comes next. *Kebyar ding* appears on the Odéon recordings from the late 1920s in much the same form as in *Tabuh-Tabuhan*

EXAMPLE 26   *Tabuh-Tabuhan,* second movement, mm. 1–11.

(*continued*)

EXAMPLE 26 (*continued*)

EXAMPLE 27   *Tabuh-Tabuhan,* second movement, mm. 49–56.

(*continued*)

EXAMPLE 26 (*continued*)

EXAMPLE 27 (*continued*)

(*continued*)

EXAMPLE 27 (*continued*)

EXAMPLE 28 *Kebyar Ding.* Transcription by McPhee from *Music in Bali* (ex. 328).

(and later transcribed in *Music in Bali*) (compare ex. 27 with ex. 28). *Kebyar,* during McPhee's day, was a relatively new style of gamelan music, described by McPhee as having "freedom of form," "lavish and varied

orchestral effects," and "bold syncopations and intricate passage-work." [53]
In the "Nocturne" *Kebyar ding* is transposed (as was *Lagu ardja*), this time
up a half step from the transcription. (The starting pitch of the music on
the Odéon recording lies between C♯ and D.) The scoring of this section,
like the opening of the "Nocturne," is pared down and percussive. The
first part (measures 49–72) uses piano and celesta and assigns the drum
part to pizzicato strings.

Next comes the section based on *angklung*. As at the opening of the
first movement, here McPhee captures the essence of the style in both
pitch and rhythm yet without direct quotation, conveying what he describes as the core of the *angklung* idea: "The constant interlocking of . . .
parts, and the sudden rhythmic breaks that occur from time to time,
maintain a steady tension throughout the music." [54] One of McPhee's
transcriptions from *Music in Bali* illustrates the style he was imitating
(compare ex. 29 with ex. 30). *Lagu ardja* returns at the close.

In "The Absolute Music of Bali" McPhee writes that the Balinese
gamelan's "chief strength is its rhythm." Accordingly *Tabuh-Tabuhan* can
be seen as an essay in rhythmic intricacy. Again McPhee expanded on a
prominent aspect of his previous works. As early as 1926, in his statement
about the *Pastorale and Rondino,* he focused on "vigorous" rhythmic
changes. The Invention from the same year had polyrhythmic areas. And
the Concerto for Piano with Wind Octette of 1928 thrived on the layering
of rhythmic groups and on shifting ostinatos.

EXAMPLE 29   *Tabuh-Tabuhan,* second movement, pianos, mm. 77–78.

EXAMPLE 30   *Pengechét Bérong,.* from the *gamelan angklung* repertory. Transcription by McPhee from *Music in Bali* (ex. 244).

In *A House in Bali* McPhee gave further evidence of his fascination with the complex rhythms of Balinese music:

> I sat watching the concentration of the players. . . . The music
> was rapid, the rhythms intricate. Yet without effort, with eyes
> closed, or staring out into the night, as though each player were
> in an isolated world of his own, the men performed their isolated
> parts with mysterious unity, fell upon the syncopated accents
> with hair's-breadth precision. . . . This, I thought, is the way
> music was meant to be, blithe, transparent, rejoicing the soul
> with its eager rhythm and lovely sound.[55]

McPhee's writings are filled with observations about Balinese rhythm, as, for example, when he recognizes its role in creating tension: "The oriental relies on rhythm to create dissonance; he is unconscious of it melodically (or harmonically). Polyrhythm means dissonance."[56]

A glance at any page of *Tabuh-Tabuhan* reveals a stratification of rhythmic patterns that are usually presented as separate ostinatos. These multileveled patterns form part of a greater scheme in which the layering of individual lines—either through the simultaneous use of distinct registers, pitch patterns, or ostinatos—is a central concept behind the work. McPhee's rhythmic levels in *Tabuh-Tabuhan* are sometimes compatible, articulating different subdivisions of a regularly sounding beat; often, however, they are not. The piece starts off with a bold cross-accent and proceeds to incorporate a variety of cross-rhythms. Two examples from the first movement follow.

While some cross-accents are simple, such as in measure 5 (ex. 23), occasionally a rhythmic counterpoint appears (ex. 31). Most frequently,

EXAMPLE 31   *Tabuh-Tabuhan,* first movement. Rhythmic patterns used in m. 181.

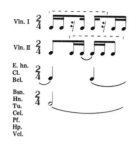

EXAMPLE 32   *Tabuh-Tabuhan,* first movement. Rhythmic patterns used in m. 56.

the patterns derive from some version of the grouping of eighth notes within $\frac{4}{4}$ (or sixteenths within $\frac{2}{4}$) as $3 + 3 + 2$—a division of the bar that McPhee later called "complex and of apparently inexhaustible vitality." It appears often in Balinese music, as McPhee illustrated in "Eight to the Bar," a *Modern Music* article of 1943, and it figures prominently in *Tabuh-Tabuhan.* The pattern occurs as early as measure 5 of the first movement; it returns briefly in measure 44; by measure 49 it is in full evidence; and in measure 56 it sounds against $4 + 4$ (ex. 32). Many other examples of rhythmic complexity could be given.

In writing *Tabuh-Tabuhan,* McPhee was well aware of the pitfalls of using exotic material. In his first known reference to the piece, he reas-

115

sured Henry Cowell that he was writing "authentic stuff," [57] and in "The Absolute Music of Bali" he addressed the issue squarely:

> Just how much, and in what manner a so-called primitive music can be utilized by the occidental composer is a question for each individual conscience. The difference between a pastiche and a creative work in which foreign material has been so absorbed by the artist as to become part of his equipment is something which has never been completely recognized. [58]

Tabuh-Tabuhan, as a work thoroughly imbued with the sounds and techniques of the Balinese gamelan, invites evaluation on this very level.

In notes to the published score of *Tabuh-Tabuhan,* McPhee acknowledged the inspiration of Balinese materials but firmly asserted his own role: "I consider it a personal creation." Indeed *Tabuh-Tabuhan* was his own, especially in the ways that it reflected McPhee's style before he went to Bali. The cross-rhythms, irregular ostinatos, sectional structures, and layered textures of *Tabuh-Tabuhan* all appeared in McPhee's work from the late 1920s. In subsequently incorporating materials and techniques from Bali, he did not simply tack on exotic effects but found in the music of the gamelan traits common to his own personal voice. At the same time, however, he drew directly upon gamelan transcriptions and applied the Balinese method of composing through rearranging. The marriage of his musical aesthetic to that of Bali retained respect both for himself and for the tradition he was honoring.

Tabuh-Tabuhan was written in a decade when many American composers were turning outside the Western concert hall for inspiration. Some, such as Virgil Thomson in *The Plow That Broke the Plains* or Roy Harris in his *Folksong Symphony,* used American folk melodies. Others drew upon a variety of folk and non-Western musics: Henry Cowell in *Ostinato Pianissimo* and *Pulse,* Aaron Copland in *El salón México,* even Carlos Chávez in *Sinfonía India. Tabuh-Tabuhan* occupies a singular—even a leading—position within these works of ethnic inspiration as well as the whole of twentieth-century American music. It is one of the earliest attempts by a Western composer to meet the East on its own terms.

A BRIEF RETURN TO NEW YORK

The premiere of *Tabuh-Tabuhan* on September 4, 1936, was a huge success. Colin and Jane left Mexico City soon afterwards, sailing to New York on the S. S. *Orizaba,* of the New York and Cuba Steamship Line. Colin felt pleased with his achievement, and Bali lay once again in the future. Jane realized how important this event had been to Colin's life as a composer, and she wrote Chávez from the ship, acknowledging his role:

> I wanted to thank you for our Mexican summer, because you
> were responsible for our coming, and for making it a great
> success. It was marvellous for Colin. If he hadn't had you behind
> him he probably would never have finished the work, and to
> have the performance right away was a great stimulus to him.
> I am so glad, because when he was in Bali I really thought he
> might never write anything again.[59]

Even before the premiere McPhee began dreaming of a glorious future for the piece. He had plans for a recording, "which I hope will succeed, and am sure will succeed."[60] He went on to say that Stokowski had written asking about the piece, "but as St. is always a bit vague as to near dates, I prefer to have Chávez." By early September McPhee's sights were set even higher: "Carlos wants to do [*Tabuh-Tabuhan*] next season, but wants to broadcast it, as he says it would sound very well over the air. However, I prefer Carnegie Hall, and hope to induce him that way."[61]

During the fall of 1936 Copland and Chávez, the two composers who had heard McPhee's new work, tried to help him arrange a New York performance. Copland wrote McPhee a warm letter of introduction to Serge Koussevitzky in Boston, inviting the conductor to listen to *Tabuh-Tabuhan:* "I think you will find it full of exotic charm and new sonorities."[62] And Chávez promoted *Tabuh-Tabuhan* in letters to five conductors— Stokowski, Koussevitzky, Artur Rodzinsky, José Iturbi, and F. Charles Adler:

> In my series just past in this City I gave the premiere of McPhee's
> Tabu Tabuhan [*sic*]. This is, I think, a superb work, and I believe

you will have real interest in looking at the score. I am suggesting
[to] McPhee to see about the possibility of having a copy available for you.[63]

In the same mail he sent McPhee carbons of the letters, advising that Colin
contact the conductors himself.[64] By mid-December Adler, Iturbi, and
Rodzinski had all responded positively and asked that McPhee bring them
the score.[65] But it appears that McPhee visited only Koussevitzky and
Stokowski and then gave up.

That fall Jane went back to Bali ahead of Colin, leaving sometime in
mid-October.[66] Colin sailed in late December and wrote Chávez from the
boat—apparently the first letter he had sent him in some months. He
thanked Chávez for his efforts on behalf of *Tabuh-Tabuhan* but described
them as futile: "I played [*Tabuh-Tabuhan*] to Koussevitzky early in October—nothing. I also gave a score to Stokowski, who professed so much
interest in Balinese music—nothing."[67] A sense of failure, even self-pity,
weighs down the letter. McPhee seemed to ignore the fact that his
situation was not unique. Many American composers struggled for performances, especially of orchestral works. When in 1928 Virgil Thomson
played Koussevitzky the last movement of his *Symphony on a Hymn Tune,* a
work that would wait until 1945 for its premiere, he was turned down
"cold." But Thomson resiliently retorted, "I knew it was pretty good but
hadn't really imagined it that good."[68] McPhee, however, retreated in the
face of rejection. More than ever, Bali became an escape, as he wrote
Chávez: "I don't really care [about Stokowski and Koussevitzky's reac-
tions], as my heart is in the East, and this time I feel I am going out for
good. Nothing matters to me except to shut out the hideous nightmare
which is called civilisation."

McPhee was easily defeated: "Although I feel injustice, too, I have
not the energy to demand that things should be different." He went on to
say that his true musical calling might not be as a composer: "I feel that if I
must function in life, it is as a recorder, a preserver of musical ideas which
we call primitive, but which will prove to be of great value to future
musicians." And in closing, he made a plea for sustaining their friendship:
"I feel you are one of the few people who can see my point of view. . . .

And you are the only one in my life to have shown real enthusiasm for anything I have written."

Although McPhee realized that with *Tabuh-Tabuhan* he had taken a major step toward fusing the musics of East and West, he was impatient for immediate recognition. While *Tabuh-Tabuhan* would wait some time for an American performance, its value was assessed by Henry Cowell ten years after the Mexican premiere when Cowell reviewed a radio broadcast of the piece: "It seems to me certain that future progress in creative music for composers of the Western world must inevitably go towards the exploration and integration of elements drawn from more than one of the world's cultures. I think *Tabuh-Tabuhan* will prove to be an important landmark." [69]

6

THE LAST YEARS IN BALI

 **1937–38**

Sometime in late January 1937 Colin arrived back at his island home. Jane had preceded him by a few months. That March Colin wrote his Peabody classmate Ann Hull a letter full of enthusiasm for his work in Bali. It contrasted sharply with the defeated attitude he had shown toward composing just months before.[1] The people of Sayan staged an elaborate welcoming celebration for the McPhees: "The whole village turned out. . . . [There was] dancing and music and feasting, and offerings made for our safe return." And Colin's response to Bali remained strong: "Place looks as beautiful as ever; eight different kinds of orchids in bloom at the moment; a mother monkey with two babies brought as a gift; the babies just learning to jump from the piano into the ink."

During their New York interlude, Colin and Jane had received news of Bali from Walter Spies, who wrote mostly of Western visitors he was entertaining.[2] Spies's letters show how Bali was fast becoming a chic tourist spot, an island retreat for wealthy pleasure seekers. Others returning to the West from Bali observed the same trend. In her introduction to *A Tale from Bali* (1937), Vicki Baum claimed, "Bali has become the fashion. . . . [There is] an invasion of Bali bars and Bali bathing suits and Bali songs."[3] Perhaps the most popular of those songs was *On the Beach at Bali-Bali,* which was recorded by at least eight American bands in 1936.[4]

Colin McPhee on an outing in
Sumatra.

Colin also noticed this change in Bali after his return. By the next
spring he was complaining, "Many people from god-knows-where are
building houses. . . . Every one wants to be Robinson Crusoe, and takes
other footprints in the sand as personal insults."[5] But one aspect of life
remained untouched: "The music . . . is still marvelous." There were
other, more serious visitors to Bali, especially Margaret Mead and Gregory
Bateson, who had arrived in the spring of 1936 and worked in the mountain village of Bayung Gedé. Their presence gave added incentive to both
Colin and Jane's work.

Immediately upon his return to Bali, Colin laid composition aside
and settled down to study the music with renewed purpose. Although at
times old doubts and insecurities surfaced, he seemed to have a steady
sense of the importance of his research. By building on contacts made
during his first years on the island, McPhee was able to intensify his pace.

Scattered among Colin's field notes are various thoughts about his
role in the musical life of Bali. He described a process of piecing together

"scraps of knowledge [that] lay scattered within the isolated minds of musicians all over the island."[6] In some ways he was overwhelmed by the task at hand. Increased study revealed greater complexity: "The inner meaning of the music seemed to recede the more I knew it." Yet he felt a strong conviction about his fieldwork, a conviction that resonated from a number of letters to friends. Early in 1938 he wrote Copland:

> I am really glad I came back, for there has been loads of new
> material to absorb; all that I really studied before and knew well
> was the outer surface, the beautiful shell. The metrical forms
> and construction of the different kinds of music I never really
> analyzed till now. I feel sure that this work is going to have great
> value for western musicians, if they survive.[7]

McPhee expressed similar confidence in letters to Chávez and Van Vechten. To the latter he wrote: "Perhaps 50 years from now if life still persists in any organized form, there will be musicians who will get ideas from the neat patterns and fascinating technic."[8]

When McPhee arrived in early 1937 the island was bustling with plans for a three-day all-Bali festival, scheduled for late June. Its purpose was to celebrate the restoration of self-government. Lebah met McPhee at the boat, preoccupied with preparations for the festival. The Peliatan *gamelan kebyar,* of which Lebah was a member, was to take part in a competition with ensembles from across the island. For this occasion they had commissioned a dazzling new piece by Gedé Manik, a drummer and composer who lived on the north side of Bali. Manik's drumming was so spectacular that McPhee once described him as playing "with the energy of the devil."[9] In *A House in Bali* McPhee gave a detailed account of the intrigue that preceded the festival, an example of just how seriously the Balinese took such contests. The Peliatan gamelan had to ward off spies from the village of Blahbatu, who were trying to steal its new piece. Ultimately the Peliatan men won, after catching the spies, and Lebah could return to Sayan to work with McPhee.

In October of that same year McPhee and Spies presented a program of gamelan transcriptions for two pianos as part of a congress staged in Bali by the Java Institute of Jakarta. Programs for three concerts of two-piano transcriptions by McPhee and Spies exist at UCLA; none is dated. In a letter to his mother, Spies described their performance at the Bali Congress:

> In October we are having a congress sponsored by the Java
> Institute. Three-hundred people will come from all over the
> world. . . . With McPhee I will give a two-piano concert of
> Balinese music in transcription as proof that it can be played on
> and transcribed for pianos—and overall because it is beautiful,
> even without gamelan.[10]

In *A House in Bali* McPhee told of a later performance with Spies that was given at the Harmony Club in Denpasar. It was a repeat of their Bali Congress program.

> This time I invited the Regents and a few musicians to come and
> hear what their music sounded like when arranged in this way.
> They were quite delighted. . . . When it was over the Regent of
> Tabanan made a quite charming little speech of compliments, in
> which he lamented only that the tuning of the piano did not
> always match.[11]

Spies had been transcribing Balinese and Javanese music since the mid-1920s, when he worked as music director for the sultan of Jogyakarta. While there, he learned to play gamelan instruments and began making arrangements of the repertory for two pianos, which he performed with a German woman living in Java. Jaap Kunst, who did fieldwork in Java during the 1920s, was a great admirer of Spies and, in a letter written to Erich von Hornbostel in 1926, described scores for six Balinese gamelan works that Spies had transcribed and performed for him. Kunst wrote of the problems in transferring Balinese tunings to the piano and then exclaimed about Spies's transcription: "Wie schön war es!"[12]

Just how many transcriptions Spies made and how much they influenced McPhee is not known. McPhee's decision to score so many transcriptions for two pianos was probably not a coincidence. He had previously shown some interest in that instrumental combination with his *Sea Shanty Suite* of 1929, where two pianos formed the basis of the accompaniment. But once he reached Bali that scoring became a mainstay in his translation of Balinese music into Western terms. Lebah remembers that McPhee and Spies made music together frequently. They played two-piano works for a time but mostly gave solo performances for each other.[13]

GAMELAN REVIVALS

During the summer of 1938, after the excitement of the Bali festival was over and Lebah had returned to work in Sayan, he and McPhee began discussing plans to start a gamelan in Sayan, one devoted to the music of *semar pegulingan*. This was a special ensemble dedicated to Semar, the god of love ("God of the Pillowed Bed"), that had been performed in the palace courtyards, mostly in the afternoons and evenings.[14] After the courts had been disbanded under Dutch rule, the *gamelan semar pegulingan* had all but disappeared. McPhee found this music ravishing. The instruments were decorated with carvings of flowers and dragons in red lacquer and gold leaf, and their sound was "elegant, sweetly poignant."[15] But for McPhee the strongest appeal was that of a mysterious, nearly lost genre, vital in bygone days when Bali was still untouched by the West.

This was not the first gamelan McPhee had organized in Sayan. After Sampih joined the household, McPhee had formed a *gandrung* club to accompany the boy's dancing. (*Gandrung*, or *jogéd*, was a popular dance form using an orchestra of bamboo xylophones.[16]) Working with this club took the edge off the long Sayan evenings, which McPhee found too quiet. There was no other gamelan active in Sayan at the time; a previous one had disbanded some years before. Besides, it took a while to build up rapport with the villagers, to establish the kind of trust that would allow them to accept an outsider's participation in their music making. The *gandrung* club was short-lived; McPhee claimed he had only moderate success with the group.

McPhee's luck with the *gamelan semar pegulingan* was quite different.

The *gamelan semar pegulingan* founded by McPhee in the late 1930s. Photograph by Colin McPhee.

By the 1930s the style had become mostly a historical one. Few sets of instruments remained, and even fewer clubs performed upon them. McPhee first heard about the music through Nyoman Kalér during his early days on the island. But not until the summer of 1932, when the Sayan house was being built, did McPhee confront the music itself. With two houseboys he traveled to remote villages, east of the base of Gunung Agung, the most sacred of Balinese mountains. In one of those villages he found an incomplete *gamelan semar pegulingan*—just enough to whet his appetite. He was able to hear a complete ensemble on only a few occasions in the old palace in the region of Gianyar. In *Music in Bali* McPhee based his discussion of *gamelan semar pegulingan* upon an ensemble in Badung. So, with musical activity nearly nonexistent in Sayan and Lebah at hand to help out, McPhee decided to found an ensemble of his own:

> I had no idea of bringing about a belated renaissance in Sayan, for
> I did not expect much enthusiasm over my plan among the young
> men of the village. But for me there would be both pleasure and

profit, for I was tired of going about the island with a notebook, asking questions like a government official. By forming a club not only would I have music near the house once more, but I could learn the forgotten court style of playing in the most natural way possible, by hearing it pass from teacher to pupils.[17]

The instruments were borrowed from Anak Agung Gedé Mandera of Peliatan, whose family had won them in battle from the palace in Negara, south of Peliatan.[18] After the instruments were acquired, McPhee called together the men and boys of Sayan and formed a club in the Balinese style. Each member made a small deposit upon joining, and fines were assessed for missed rehearsals. Lebah was elected the leader.[19]

The next step was to find a teacher, someone acquainted well enough with this old repertory to pass it on to the musicians of Sayan. McPhee was fortunate in locating I Lunyuh, who thirty years earlier had been a leading musician in the palace of Payangan, approximately ten miles from Sayan, which in its heyday had boasted a beautiful *semar pegulingan* ensemble. After some coaxing, Lunyuh accepted the invitation. McPhee described Lunyuh as

> about 60, slightly deaf, naive, phlegmatic, pock-marked, hasn't bathed for years [in *A House in Bali* McPhee writes, "he smelled rather like a dried fish"], thick-set, clothed in the old-style, has a marvelous memory, and plays trompong and drum in excellent style.[20]

It was Lunyuh's *trompong* playing (a principal element in *gamelan semar pegulingan*) that especially appealed to McPhee. McPhee recorded "surprise at the grace and agility of his style, his free syncopations." He went on to observe, "The rest of the gamelan was a background. He was like a star pianist at a concerto." [21] In describing Lunyuh McPhee also attempted to convey the paradox of Balinese music, which is so animated while the physical bearing of the musicians is impassive:

> The guru [Lunyuh] had begun very simply, but soon his playing began to take on life. . . . The music had become almost a dance,

a dance that was light, agile, filled with sensuous grace. Yet he
sat there, a stolid figure of apathy to the outside world, never
moving, except to reach out for the farthest gongs.[22]

With Lunyuh, as with Lebah, Lotring, and Kalér, McPhee feverishly wrote
out transcriptions, taking down the old tunes as they poured forth from
the man's memory. McPhee claimed that Lunyuh knew much more music
than he could ever teach the club during the three days he spent working
with them each week.[23]

According to Mandera, who followed the group's progress, all the
musicians in McPhee's *gamelan semar pegulingan* were from the area surrounding Sayan, except Lebah. Sometime after McPhee's days there, the
instruments were moved back to Peliatan, which is also Lebah's home
village. They lay unused until 1968, when Lebah revived the ensemble;
recordings of them have been made since, including *Gamelan of the Love God*

McPhee's *gamelan semar pegulingan* performing in Peliatan, Bali, in 1984. The
musicians are seated under a banyan tree. I Madé Lebah is the drummer on the
left. Photograph by author.

I Madé Lebah (right) in performance, 1930s. Photograph by Colin McPhee.

(Nonesuch H-72046, 1972). Today the group performs much of the traditional repertory, including works by Lebah, Lunyuh, and Lotring. Lebah, although now retired as leader of the group, still plays with it occasionally.[24]

McPhee also started another ensemble in Sayan to perform an older repertory—that of *gamelan angklung*. This time the group was made up of village children between the ages of six and eleven. According to McPhee it was unique on the island for that reason. McPhee wrote a good deal about the founding of this ensemble. Its story fills a chapter in *A House in Bali;* he published an article about it for *Djåwå* (1938), a journal of Indonesian studies issued by the Java Institute; and in 1948 he turned the tale into the charming children's book *A Club of Small Men.*

As with *semar pegulingan,* McPhee had been enchanted with *gamelan angklung* since his early days in Bali. It was a musical style at the opposite end of the social scale from that of *semar pegulingan:* it had no court connection at all but rather was music of the village people, a "folk

The *gamelan angklung* of Sayan, founded for village children by Colin McPhee in the late 1930s. Photograph by Colin McPhee.

orchestra," as McPhee called it in *Music in Bali*. Although *angklung* ensembles, made up mostly of four-keyed metallophones, were not uncommon in Bali during McPhee's time, the incorporation of the actual instrument called *angklung* was. McPhee described the instrument as having "three bamboo tubes of different lengths which are hung within a light wooden frame and tuned to sound a single tone in three octaves when the frame is shaken." [25]

The founding of the children's gamelan seems to have grown naturally out of other research being conducted in Sayan. Because of Sampih, there were many children in the McPhee house, and they were entranced by the *semar pegulingan* when it first began. McPhee described them hanging around at rehearsals and then sneaking off to try out the instruments while they were not being used. During this period both Jane Belo and Margaret Mead were working closely with children on the island, probably contributing to his interest in them.[26] But equally compelling was the *angklung* music itself; McPhee wanted an ensemble of his own close at hand to study and enjoy.

Once again, McPhee had to find a teacher for the ensemble—this time, someone who knew the musical style and could also work with children. McPhee chose I Nengah, from the village of Selat, whom he described as being "perhaps forty, shy, gentle, a man of few words."[27] Nengah came to live in McPhee's house and was a great favorite with the children. Through Nengah's work with the *angklung* ensemble, McPhee had a chance not only to study its repertory but also to observe Balinese pedagogical methods. McPhee found Nengah's method of teaching a new work "strange" yet typical on the island.

> He says nothing, does not even look at the children. Dreamily he
> plays through the first movement. He plays it again. He then

Kayun, leader of the children's *gamelan angklung,* playing the *gendér.* Photograph by Colin McPhee.

131

The *gamelan angklung* of Sayan, performing in 1984 in a local temple. The *angklung* in the foreground (racks of bamboo tubes with streamers at the top) were given to the group by McPhee in the 1930s. Photograph by author.

plays the first phrase alone, with more emphasis. He now indicates that the children are to commence. . . . Bit by bit the
children who are learning the melody go from phrase to phrase,
forgetting, remembering, gaining assurance.[28]

The Sayan *gamelan angklung,* like the *gamelan semar pegulingan,* still plays
together today. The small men have become big. Although some of the
original members have died, approximately half of the ensemble of thirty-
six is from the founding group; some are sons of original members.
Although they have purchased a new set of instruments since the 1930s, at
least one of their *angklung* was a gift from McPhee. They remember him
and smile proudly when discussing their connection with his work.[29]

In his field notes McPhee mused over what benefit, if any, these
revivals brought to the people of Bali. In one entry he stated, "A revived art
is always futile (necromantic)." [30] Elsewhere he compared the work of
Lotring, Lebah, and Lunyuh and then considered his own role:

As for me—I had succeeded in helping prolong the past. To
delay it even for a day, change which brought inevitable decline,
was my one wish. . . . Who had benefitted? None. But at the
same time, none were harmed by this look toward the past, and
from it much pleasure had been derived, many evenings of diversion had been the result.[31]

To McPhee it seemed as if these gamelan revivals mostly aided his own
study. Even in his introduction to *Music in Bali,* he talked of them as
preserving a "record" of Balinese music, especially of older styles. But
McPhee underestimated the lasting effects of his work. I Madé Bandem, a
Balinese dancer, musician, and scholar who is director of the Arts Academy
of Indonesian Dance in Denpasar, Bali, has studied in the West and hence
has an outside perspective on his people's music. He claims that two of
McPhee's great contributions to the music of his island were to revive
these old styles and to expose musicians to works from other villages.

McPhee had a great reputation for bringing new repertoire to
certain clubs by bringing teachers from one village to another.

Members of the Sayan *gamelan angklung* in 1984 looking at pictures of Sampih in McPhee's *A House in Bali*. Photograph by author.

He exchanged repertoire between north and south Bali. In 1938, north Bali had a great repertory called *kebyar légong.* They were fanatic about it in north Bali, and Gedé Manik taught one of their pieces in Beluluan, Denpasar. As an exchange, a club from South Bali—I Madé Regog was the leader—brought their own *kebyar* style to the group in north Bali. All of these ideas came from McPhee. I was told by my teacher Nyoman Kalér about that.[32]

Through his gamelan revivals McPhee not only preserved a record of dying repertories but also brought the music back to life.

TRAVELS AND ATTEMPTED RECORDINGS

McPhee's other principal means of studying Balinese music was to travel across the island searching out as many varieties of gamelan playing as could be found. While crisscrossing Bali, he kept detailed notes, many of which are preserved in the McPhee Collection at UCLA. In them a process of systematic exploration and inquiry is revealed.

Lebah accompanied McPhee on many of those trips. He drove McPhee's 1931 Chevrolet and served as a go-between with the villagers, reassuring them about the purpose of this white man's visit and coaxing them to share their music. Lebah remembers long stays in Kuta (to work with Lotring), in Karangasem, and in Desa Culik and also recalls the care McPhee took in taking notes. According to Lebah, McPhee kept a notebook for each principal Balinese musical style; this is confirmed by the organization of the books of transcriptions at UCLA.

Excerpts from these field notes reveal something of life on the road and the musical characteristics that particularly interested McPhee. From the village of Tenganan he wrote:

> I lie in the hard iron cot, half suffocated by the thick mosquito netting and the lack of air in the stuffy little room. . . . Through the air floats the music of the selunding, sweet, mechanical, like the leisurely chiming of a giant music-box. . . . As I listen I think of the enigmatic indifference, the weary reverence with which the men turn out this music. It is strange music, in its aura of legend, secrecy and taboo, in its lovely chiming tones, its organisation, its endless repetition without the slightest change of nuance. . . . All is timeless, ageless, colorless, neither slow nor fast, a resonant, metallic chorale in honor of the gods who long ago gave this gamelan and its melodies to the village.[33]

In his notes, McPhee repeatedly compared the music of south Bali, where he lived, to that of the north. He found not only the music but also the people to be different. At one point he asked, "Where is the real Bali? In the exuberant North, or in the more mysterious, more reserved South?"[34] He went on to note the contrast of the north with Sayan: "Once more back in Sayan, the whole North Bali excursion seems like the exploration of another land, where people are brusque, energetic, cordial, careless, and emancipated. A land of sunshine and loud music, bold gestures, handsome people, uninhibited sex impulses."

Suling players from the court of Tabanan in the 1930s. McPhee included *suling* melodies in his arrangements of *Lagu ardja* and *Kambing slem*. Photograph by Colin McPhee.

McPhee was by no means so enamored of Bali and its music that he suspended critical perspective. In writing of the *angklung* in the village of Sibetan, for example, he spared few words: "Disagreeable and rude people, noisy and always on the defensive. Bad playing. . . . Gamelan only interesting for its five notes and example of decadence." [35] Another *angklung,* in the village of Prasi, west of Karangasem, was, "a strange sekaha of men who seem half wild, half crazy, and very fantastic. Willing, however. Gamelan set out in complete disorder. Gending and sonority most interesting."

Some trips were purely for pleasure. One page in the field notes is titled simply "Holiday" and describes an excursion to Gilimanuk, on the western tip of Bali, with Lebah and Walter Spies. McPhee says the car was loaded down with provisions "piled around us like sandbags." Included were necessities such as food, including a pot of curried anteater, as well as luxuries: "rum, Dutch gin, cigarettes, a portable tent, the portable phonograph, folding chairs, dominos, cameras, a batch of Ellingtons, frying pans." [36]

McPhee often took time in these notes not only to jot down observations in some short, efficient form but also to shape stories. He wrote frequently and seemed to be thinking always about the books that lay in the future. Words were inspired by every level of experience, from visiting the local market to observing musicians, and a narrative sense is ever present. He recounted another trip to Gilimanuk, this one in August 1937:

> Spent a week at Gilimanoek with Walter, Jane, and the boys. We put up two tents. Spent the days sailing in praus across the straits of Java. Frigate birds high in the air in the late afternoon. Each evening at dusk the flying-foxes come out by the hundreds from the mangrove swamps and flap slowly over our heads across the water to Java, where the mango trees are plentiful and ripe. We shoot through the wings of several; they are close enough for us to see the hole left. A weird, Doré-like sight. We spend the afternoons—the tide is out at this time—walking over the coral reefs, and peering down into crystal depths. Small fish of incredible brilliance, gold, scarlet, crimson, ultramarine and silver; enormous starfish; the coral life a window in the Museum of Natural History. Gaping below are the huge Bear Paws or giant clams—the same whose shells are used in Cathedrals of France for l'eau benit (Tridacna maculatus?) We thrust a bamboo pole in one; it closes at once and no human strength can remove it. Alas for the pearl diver whose foot entered here. As we return we find two of these giant clams near the surface. With the help of the boys we pry them loose of the coral and bring them out of the water. One measures a foot and a half, the other is slightly smaller. They seem to weigh a ton. [37]

McPhee also traveled a good deal outside of Bali. Originally he had envisioned his stay on the island as the first leg in a journey throughout Southeast Asia, including Burma, Thailand, Cambodia, and Laos. [38] But the

"I preferred to drive at random through the island, getting lost in the network of back
roads that ran up into the hills
where, as you looked down towards the sea, the flooded
ricefields lay shining in the
sunlight like a broken mirror"
(*A House in Bali*). Photograph
by Colin McPhee.

appeal of Bali held him there for most of his time in Asia. McPhee's travels
outside Bali are sketchily documented. In *A House in Bali* he mentioned
several trips to Java, and in letters to Van Vechten he described his route
back to the United States in 1934 through Southeast Asia, as well as a trip
to Java.[39] There are also twenty-one typewritten pages of notes from trips
to Colombo, Sumatra (two separate sets of notes), Java, and Peking.[40] All,
except for the second set on Sumatra, are couched as though planned for a
guidebook of some sort, a plan that never materialized. The notes include
nothing about music but describe especially appealing sights, good restau-
rants, and comfortable sleeping accommodations. The second set of
Sumatra notes (with a beginning date of January 20, no year) is a daily
digest of a trip McPhee took from Padang north across the equator.

Toward the end of McPhee's days in Bali, one bitter disappointment
cast a shadow upon work that had otherwise been consistently gratifying.
Through Columbia University he had received a grant of one thousand
dollars to support his fieldwork; part of the money was to go toward
recording Balinese music, a project he desperately wanted to complete.[41]
The Odéon recordings of 1928 were the only ones that had been made of
Balinese music, and the unsold stock had been destroyed by a salesman in

Denpasar during the 1930s. McPhee's hope was to record many of the gamelans he had worked with—to have aural documents that would complement his written transcriptions. In a detailed letter to Ruth Benedict at Columbia University, he described the failure of his effort, "which breaks my heart."[42]

He worked with a thirty-two-year-old Austrian musicologist, one Dr. Halusa, who was in charge of musical instruments at the museum in Batavia, Java. Halusa was said to have made recordings in Sumatra and was recommended to McPhee by Willem Stutterheim, an anthropologist, director of the Batavia museum, and author of *Indian Influences in Old-Javanese Art.*[43] McPhee advanced Halusa the money to order five hundred records, as well as needles, from Sweden. But, as McPhee told Ruth Benedict, when Halusa arrived in Bali in August 1938 the equipment refused to function properly: "From the standpoint of recording sonority the machine was good; it would not, however, record without an alteration of pitch once, twice or more during the record." Various remedies were tried. Extra batteries were purchased; an expensive transformer was brought in. A mechanic was also consulted: "Gamelans were scheduled to come to the house; they did so, sitting there all day while we wasted record after record. This went on two and a half weeks; we had used 60 sides without getting satisfactory results."

The failure of this project not only dashed McPhee's hopes for aural documentation of Balinese music but also was a direct blow to his pride. He felt that he had been duped by Halusa. After Halusa's failure in Bali, McPhee found out that the Sumatra recordings had not yet been heard by anyone. McPhee told Benedict that the museum people in Batavia were "furious" with Halusa and that the local papers had published articles exposing his incompetence. That September Walter Spies wrote to Jane, who was then in New York, of Colin's failure with the project. He seemed to think Colin might have been able to make a success of it with a little perseverance:

> Of course you heard of all the misfortunes that poor Colin had
> with his recording! It is too dreadful—and I think he is a fool

not to try to do it in some other way. Now that everything is prepared—and . . . o god—it is so difficult to speak to him about it.[44]

For McPhee a unique opportunity had been lost. Whether because of funding limitations or simple procrastination, he had waited until the very end of his stay in Bali to attempt the recordings. It was the only chance he would ever have to make them.

PERSONAL AND POLITICAL TURMOIL

As for McPhee's personal life in Bali, especially his relationship to Jane Belo, the picture is sketchy at best. The two had been married not long before traveling to the island in 1931, and they were divorced in July 1938, close to the end of their stay.[45] They had lived separately for some time in Bali, and Jane finally left in late March 1938 with Mead and Bateson. Her traveling companions went on to New Guinea, and she returned to the United States. Her relationship to Colin is a key element in understanding the whole Bali experience.

Although Colin and Jane both felt strongly devoted to Balinese culture, they were able to live there only because Jane had the money to do so. She paid for the house in Sayan, and from all indications she completely supported Colin financially during their marriage.

Nowhere in his writings about Bali does Colin acknowledge this financial support. In *A House in Bali* he not only never mentions Jane but also couches his tale, from beginning to end, in first-person singular. To readers of that book, it appears as if Colin went to Bali alone, built the house himself, and experienced every detail of life there as a single man.[46] Only when *Music in Bali* was published, posthumously in 1966, did Jane's name appear—in the acknowledgments, within a list of several people thanked "for further collaboration in the field."[47]

Lebah is perhaps the person who knows most about Colin and Jane during the Bali years because he lived in the Sayan house. But he has little to say about the relationship. Madé Peghi, a Balinese woman who was married for a time to Theo Maier, a Belgian painter living in Bali, has recalled that Jane spent a lot of time away from Sayan in "her mountain house."[48] What Peghi is probably referring to is Jane's many trips to Bayung Gedé, where Mead and Bateson were working.

In a letter to Margaret Mead, written from Sumatra on his final trip back to the United States, McPhee rued: "There is so much I would like to say to you . . . about Bali, Jane, and even Me. No one will know my sense of loss in regard to Jane, my regret that it did not last, my awareness of myself as a destructive factor."[49] Although McPhee's other writings from the 1930s reveal little about his life with Jane, in the next decade he reflected on the marriage in several letters to Sidney Cowell. In one, he responded to a proposal that he stay in Shady, New York, while both Sidney and Henry were there. Colin was sure such an arrangement would not work:

> I never expect to live with anyone again, and I have gradually realized that even the warmth of a romantic attachment cannot compensate for the loss of cool solitude. Groan as I may at coming home forever to an empty place, an empty life, I seem actually to prefer it so. . . . . If I were different, I'd probably still be happily married to Jane. As it was, we lived in separate houses in Bali, as far apart as possible on the grounds.[50]

In another letter he acknowledged that he could be difficult: "I realize that everyone of my few friends have reproached me, at one time or another, with either my harshness or withdrawal. That does not exclude either Margaret [Mead] or Minna [Lederman]. Or George Davis or a boy called Vinny. And most of all Jane. . . ."[51] In yet another he recognized his difficulty in accepting and nurturing love:

> It is my great and basic, unfortunate trait that the warmth and affection which you (and Henry) have given so wholeheartedly, to which I owe my life today, and which I have, in one form or another, seemed to depend upon all my life, I feel at times I must

deny and destroy. I managed that to perfection with Jane, to both our ruin. I don't want to destroy, by following the same pattern, our friendship.[52]

Around the same time he wrote David Diamond: "I certainly was in love with Jane. And yet I wanted that solitude, and was never satisfied until we broke up, most unhappily, and I went back to live alone."[53]

Even though Jane had known from the beginning that Colin had male lovers, she eventually found this intolerable. In his Bali field notes Colin occasionally alluded to affairs with Balinese men, but he was mostly discreet and extremely private. Several of his friends have suggested that one of the appeals of Bali was its openness to homosexuality.[54] Colin later bluntly described to Sidney Cowell at least one reason for the end of his relationship with Jane:

> My few emotional-sentimental relations have not penetrated too deeply. My alliance with Jane was broken off by me in a final fit of stubbornness, and on the whole I don't regret it, for she had turned into what for me was a prig, probably because she was tired of my untidy and carefree attitude towards life. Anyway, I was in love at the time with a Balinese, which she knew, and to have him continually around was too much for her vanity. So it all ended as I had foreseen at the beginning, and Jane was unbelievably loyal long after there was any reason for it. . . . Anyway, my one experience with marriage and the opposite sex was quite enough.[55]

Jane also gave a picture of their life together. Soon after divorcing Colin, she married Frank Tannenbaum, a scholar and author on Latin American topics, and she wrote Margaret Mead about her relief at living with someone who was not hypersensitive in his work habits: "Isn't it lovely that [Frank] can write with me in the room? He said to me a little while ago, between pages—'I'm not the sort of person who has a fit if someone sneezes'—I wonder if he realizes how welcome to me is that sort of ease in a creative person."[56]

Yet Jane seems to have been sympathetic to Colin's struggles with composition and to have encouraged him during the years they were together. Besides writing Carlos Chávez after the premiere of *Tabuh-Tabuhan* to thank him for bringing Colin back to composition, she conveyed similar concern to Willem Stutterheim in Java after she and Colin were divorced:

> I heard Colin reached New York, and had a splendid reception.
> I do so hope he will get started now and write a lot of lovely
> music. That's what he should have been doing, you know Stutt,
> all these years. Working on Balinese music is all right, very good,
> but he is a *composer*. [57]

Colin stayed alone in Bali for nearly a year after Jane left. He sailed from Batavia on December 26, 1938. A number of factors conspired to make him leave. The first was a lack of money. Although Jane seems to have supported him for a time after their divorce, she would not do so indefinitely. During this period he got his first outside grant—the one thousand dollars from Columbia University—but such funds were not plentiful. Political events also forced his departure. By late 1938 the impending war in Germany and Japan began to affect an island as small as Bali. In October 1938, shortly after the Munich crisis, a Japanese photographer suddenly visited McPhee's house. He claimed to be showing a friend sights on the island, but McPhee sensed that his house was being surveyed—"his friend seemed to be counting even the coconuts in the trees." [58] Around the same time the Dutch authorities in the East Indies mounted what Margaret Mead has called "a witch hunt against homosexuals." [59] Many Westerners in Bali were under suspicion, and several, including Walter Spies, were thrown in jail. Spies's arrest took place on December 31, 1938, only five days after McPhee had left Bali. Nowhere does McPhee record that he might have been the object of such suspicion, yet the timing of his departure suggests he was affected. Besides, he had not allowed Jane to tell anyone that they had been divorced the previous summer. [60]

A dispiriting tone pervades the closing pages of *A House in Bali,* as

McPhee describes his preparations for departure. He spent his final evening there driving with Lebah along his favorite roads, and Lebah took him to the boat the following morning. McPhee sailed via the Cape of Good Hope and Halifax to New York, where he arrived in mid-February of 1939.[61]

McPhee was at peace in Bali, enjoying an inner contentment that no environment would ever again provide. In 1942, as he followed from America the effect of the war upon his cherished island, he wrote:

> Everyone carries within him his own private paradise, some
> beloved territory whose assault is an assault on the heart. Some
> felt this when Paris was taken, others when Britain was bombed.
> For me it was Bali, for I had lived there a long time and had been
> very happy.[62]

Jane returned to Bali in January 1939, not long after Colin had left, and found it quite different. On one level it was hard "to pick up the life again without Colin to make things interestingly difficult."[63] On another, all Westerners on the island were being harassed by the Dutch authorities as part of a general crackdown against the growing movement for Indonesian independence. The purpose of Jane's trip was to finish her research on Balinese trance.[64] En route in Sydney, Australia, she met Mead and Bateson, who had just finished their fieldwork in New Guinea and were debating whether or not to return to the United States. The situation in Bali was unsettled enough that they decided Jane should not travel alone. So they accompanied her and spent six weeks following up on work they had done one year earlier.[65] Jane offered to pay the increased expenses of the trip, and Mead and Bateson accepted on the condition that the money be given through the Museum of Natural History. After a brief stay with Katharane Mershon in Sanur, the three moved to the house in Sayan.

As they did on Colin and Jane's return to Sayan in 1937, the villagers celebrated her return: "The people all seem delighted to have me back; they gave me a tremendous welcome party with the 2 orchestras that Colin had trained, the dancing girls who now number 34, . . . and dozens of beautiful offerings were brought by all my friends." [66] Walter Spies had taken over stewardship of the two Sayan gamelans immediately after Colin left Bali. But when he was thrown into jail in December 1938, the task became a bit complicated. [67] By late January Spies was writing to Jane expressing concern for the future of the groups; he asked that she let the children continue to practice at the Sayan house. [68] In March Jane reported to Willem Stutterheim that Spies continued to direct the groups while in jail. [69]

Westerners on Bali were not having an easy time of it. Accusations of homosexuality had been flung at many; even Jane was harassed:

> All of us who lived in a pleasant way in Bali have been investi-
> gated—police in and out of our houses, all our servants arrested
> and questioned. Of the 34 dancing girls in my village, all were
> questioned on my habits, down to the 3 year olds. Thank heaven
> I had a free conscience and could stand up in a haughty manner
> and demand an explanation for such bandying of my good name. [70]

Since Colin had kept their divorce a secret, she had difficulty convincing the authorities that she was "an individual, with a name, a passport, and a soul of my own." Finally, after several days of questioning, she was allowed to live in the Sayan house again. Jane was among the lucky ones, because "at least half of the people living in Bali have been asked to leave, or have left of their own accord, one dares not wonder why. . . . The Balinese think the whole white caste has gone mad."

Several letters written by Jane during her final months in Bali remain; all center around the problem of getting Walter Spies released. Jane was devoted to Spies, and together with Mead, Bateson, and Katharane Mershon, she found him a lawyer and worked on his behalf. In letters written during this period Jane was circumspect in describing the charges against Spies, primarily because the mail was being censored. Evidently Spies had been arrested on several counts, especially for turning his house in Ubud into "a rendezvous for homosexuals" and for having sexual relations with minors. [71] The handling of the case was confused enough that

Jane, who spoke out repeatedly in his defense, was unclear about what was happening:

> There is a good deal of feeling that the case against Walter is a
> little bit unjust, that he has simply been caught up in the tur-
> moil—semi-political, I gather—that started in Java, and that he
> is actually innocent of the charges which do apply to some of
> the other charming residents of our island—the point about
> minors.[72]

The Balinese were baffled. Homosexuality was not a crime to them, and Spies had been a good friend, with much sympathy for Balinese culture. One day a man from the village of Selat spoke with Jane about the situation. Jane's papers contain notes of the conversation:

> He made the statement that according to Balinese law the offence
> is not recognized. In Bali, he said, to be 'salah mekoerenan'
> (wrongly married) is to have relations with an animal, or for a
> man to take a girl not yet mature, or a woman of higher caste.
> *Mekoerenan* means male with female (*lanang-istri*), and male with
> male cannot be *mekoerenan*.[73]

The days of joy for Westerners in Bali were temporarily over. Although Spies was released on September 1, 1939, nine months later, when Hitler's troops invaded the Netherlands, he was put back in prison, and all Germans living in the Dutch East Indies were arrested. Spies died on January 18, 1942, while being transported with other prisoners by boat from Sumatra to Ceylon. The boat was downed by a Japanese plane.

Jane's stay in Bali lasted until June 26, 1939. She finished her field-work and then made plans to rent the house. Her hope was to hold onto it as a retreat:

> The house is altogether too nice to sacrifice, and it was too much
> trouble to build, not to keep it up for whenever I or any of our
> friends want to come to Bali for a few months. My idea is not to
> be a resident. As a tourist, one can come and go—which really

suits me better. One gets more work done if one stays a short time.[74]

That plan was partially successful, at least for a little while. Rudolf Bonnet wrote Jane in June 1940, reporting on the condition of the house and life on the island. He had just had dinner there the previous evening with Theo Maier, who was renting the place.[75] According to I Wayan Rima, who today lives next to the McPhee property, the Japanese eventually ransacked the house; they confiscated furniture and cut down the beautifully carved rafters.[76] The other parts of the buildings were eaten by white ants. Today only the foundation remains.

7

HARD TIMES IN NEW YORK

 **1939-52**

           On the way back to New York in January 1939, McPhee once again announced his return in a letter from the ship. This time his spirit was subdued, without the buoyant self-confidence of 1935. He told Carl Van Vechten that upon reaching the city he wanted to see him "at once."

> That may sound a little high-pitched, but I assure you it's true;
> I have been literally starved for friends, and since Jane left last
> March have spoken nothing but Malay. The Balinese are good
> comrades, but there is still a lot left to be desired in their
> friendship. [1]

As in 1935 McPhee immediately published an article about Bali in *Modern Music,* yet his mood was changed. In "The Absolute Music of Bali" he had touted the glories of the island's music, hopeful of its potential for Western composers. But "The Decline of the East" (1939), his first post-Bali publication, expressed despair. [2] He reviewed changes on the island since the Dutch take-over at the turn of the century and charted a steady cultural demise:

> The radjahs [Balinese nobility] have now given up all pretense
> of elaborate court-life; they are no longer interested even in
> encouraging Balinese arts. Nearly all their gamelans have been
> discarded; now they buy cars, motorcycles and European
> clothes, send their sons to school in Java or even Europe,
> discuss the price of sugar and Hitler. . . . The visible general
> effect of all this is sordid, deplorable.

It was a bitter article, full of anger at Western society for savaging the East. At its core lay a personal lament. Not only did traditional Balinese music stand in danger of being lost to the people of the island; in an immediate sense it had been lost to Colin McPhee.

Stripped of his house in the Sayan hills, with its servants and breathtaking view, and of the money that had provided these comforts, McPhee was adrift in New York, trying to find a solid mooring in seas that became rougher with each passing year. The life of a gentleman-scholar had suited him perfectly. He loved good food, good drink, the good life. Now, the man who had existed in Paris on the generosity of patrons, in New York on piano accompanying and solo jobs, and in Bali on the beneficence of his wife suddenly found himself with no financial support. His creative energy, which had flowed unpredictably even under the most comfortable circumstances, began to wheeze in tortured spurts. He acknowledged to Carlos Chávez that his luck had "turned" when he split with Jane, and in a letter to Sidney Cowell he stated just how closely money was related to that luck: "I'll never be happy or contented with a small amount of money, first of all because money that comes from work seems to me somehow tarnished, and secondly, the only things in life that I want are the things money can buy." [3]

The late 1930s would have been a hard time for any composer to reenter the United States, especially after an absence of nearly a decade. But as would become the sad pattern, McPhee failed to acknowledge that most American composers were facing difficulties in being accepted and supported. He was easily discouraged. In 1939 money remained tight, and attention was focused on the war abroad. In March, just a month after his return to New York, the Germans invaded Czechoslovakia and then Poland; the Russians invaded Finland. While the surrounding world was in crisis, McPhee's own saga became one of deepening despair.

At first things went modestly well. By March 1939 McPhee had found an apartment on East Tenth Street in New York and had begun trying to build a new life. However changed his mood, he remained determined to spread news of Bali. Soon after his article in *Modern Music* came a piece for the *New York Times,* "Report on Bali's Music" (March 5, 1939), which was essentially a reworking of "The Absolute Music of Bali" from 1935.[4] Other articles followed in *Musical America,* the *Peabody Bulletin, Modern Music,* and *Asia and the Americas.* As a result, many New York composers and others learned about Balinese music. Minna Lederman, *Modern Music*'s editor, recalls, "Colin's Bali was in the air; we all seemed to be familiar with Bali."[5]

McPhee was injecting Balinese music into a New York air increasingly receptive to Asian influences. Henry Cowell had been teaching a course entitled "Music of the World's Peoples" at the New School for Social Research, and his articles in *Modern Music* reflected a growing concern with the musical resources offered by the East. Cowell's "Music of the Hemispheres" (1929), for example, was merely a story of his encounter with a Chinese musician, but in "Towards Neo-Primitivism," written four years later, he exhorted his contemporaries to look outside their own culture:

> Now the time has come for a strong new countermovement, full-blooded and vital. . . . This tendency [i.e., of contemporary composers to explore non-Western musics] is obviously neo-primitive in its drive for vitality and simplicity. It is not an attempt to imitate primitive music, but rather to draw on those materials common to the music of all the peoples of the world, to build a new music particularly related to our own century.[6]

Similar *Modern Music* articles by other musicians followed. In 1934 Raymond Petit wrote "Exotic and Contemporary Music"; in 1943 Paul Nettl published "The West Faces East"; and in 1946 John Cage produced "The East in the West."[7]

Cowell and McPhee had shared an interest in Asian musics since at least the late 1920s, when they listened to the famous Balinese recordings together. Cowell later recalled:

> When good recordings of Balinese music were made with Odéon and Beka labels in the 1920's, McPhee and I heard them together and wondered enthusiastically over them. He went to Bali, stayed seven years, became intimately acquainted with this music. I stayed home, read McPhee's writings, and listened to more recordings.[8]

In the early 1940s McPhee gave some sense of the bond—and the conflicts—between them:

> I find [Henry] has a really sensitive ear, at least when it comes to discriminating listening to exotic records, and it is a pleasure to play Javanese and what-have-you records to him and discuss them. At the same time he is stubborn and pedantic, with the mind of a child, and I simply avoid any clash by keeping away from serious discussion. As a matter of fact, he has indicated quite a lot of folk music about which I knew nothing, and been very generous in lending me records which were both rare and interesting.[9]

After returning to New York McPhee cultivated friendships with others interested in non-Western musics, such as the ethnomusicologist George Herzog. The two recorded Javanese musicians at the 1939 New York World's Fair and shared an interest in American Indian repertories.[10] McPhee had other such colleagues: Carleton Sprague Smith, a scholar of Latin American music, and of course Carlos Chávez.

Again, as in 1935, McPhee brought the sounds of Bali to New York. In 1940 G. Schirmer published three of his two-piano transcriptions under the title *Balinese Ceremonial Music,* and the next year issued a recording entitled *The Music of Bali* (Schirmer 17), which included transcriptions for

I. a) Christian Bach : Sonata in G major
        Allegro — Menuetto

b) Domenico Zipoli : Suite in four parts (transcribed
        by Heinrich Simon)

c) Friedeman Bach : Sonata in F major
        Allegro moderato — Andante — Presto

II. Béla Bartók : Four pieces
        Serenata — Allegro diabolico —
            Scena della Puszta —
                — Per finire

Intermission

III. a) Colin Mc Phee : Balinese Ceremonial music
            (transcription)
            Pemoengkah — Gambangan —
                — Taboeh teloe

b) Béla Bartók : Six pieces from Mikrokosmos:
        Chord and Trill Study — Perpetuum
        mobile — New Hungarian Folk-Song
            — Short Canon and its Inversion
            — Ostinato

IV. Fr. Liszt : Concert pathétique

Program for Béla Bartók's performance of McPhee's *Balinese Ceremonial Music* at Amherst College, Amherst, Massachusetts, February 1942. It is in Bartók's hand. (See page 179.)

two pianos and for flute and piano. Both attracted attention in the *New York Times,* where the published works were hailed as "a unique contribution, opening up new vistas in the tonal realm."[11]

All three pieces in *Balinese Ceremonial Music* are dedicated to Margaret Mead (see Chapter 9 for a discussion of the music). The first two, *Pemoengkah* and *Gambangan,* date from 1934; they had been performed on McPhee's 1936 concerts of Balinese music in New York and Mexico City. McPhee must have submitted them to Schirmer while in New York during 1935–36, because after returning to Bali he wrote his Peabody chum Ann Hull:

> I would like to ask you a favour. Before I left I sent in to Schirmers the ms. of two Bali pieces for 2 pianos—the ones accepted last year. I also wrote to Engel about them. No word. Could you phone Miss Daniels and ask what is doing about them? I would also like to have word from them regarding the pieces, and also a contract.[12]

The third piece in the collection, *Taboeh Teloe,* was completed in 1938, after McPhee had returned to Bali.

The Schirmer recording of McPhee's transcriptions featured McPhee and Benjamin Britten at the pianos; Georges Barrère was flutist. The album included seven pieces—the three published ones, as well as *Rébong* and *Lagu délem* (both for two pianos) and *Lagu Ardja* and *Kambing Slem* (both for flute and piano). Three ten-inch records were released, and the set sold for $2.50.[13] McPhee wrote Copland after the records came out, "I must say they are not bad; . . . they are not flawless, from my point of view, but on the whole I'm pleased."[14] Listening to the original 78s today, the poor recording quality makes it difficult to perceive subtle performance nuances. Presumably Britten played second piano, because his score for *Balinese Ceremonial Music* has that part circled.[15] The two closely followed McPhee's performance suggestions in the published score. In *Pemoengkah,* for example, their touch is "light" and the texture "transparent," as McPhee asks in the introduction. And in McPhee's opening solo to *Gambangan,* his playing has a fluid rhythm and resonant, ringing timbre, in keeping with the "noble and robust" tone of the *gamelan gong* described in his preface. This is the only extant recording of McPhee at the piano.

Britten's biographers have traced his later involvement with Oriental musics back to this early collaboration with McPhee. It was 1956 before Britten actually traveled to Bali.

Benjamin Britten was one among a circle of friends who entered McPhee's life after his return to New York. Many would help sustain him in the years ahead. Carlos Chávez, Aaron Copland, and Henry Cowell hailed from the pre-Bali days. These three, together with Oliver Daniel, whom McPhee met in the mid-1940s, encouraged McPhee to compose and helped him find grants and commissions. Chávez visited New York occasionally and, when in Mexico, kept up a lively correspondence with McPhee. Carl Van Vechten, another friend from the twenties, seemed to fade out of McPhee's life.[16]

Through all this time there were four women in whom McPhee confided regularly: Sidney Cowell, Elizabeth Mayer, Minna Lederman, and Margaret Mead. A fifth, Marian ("Marne") Eames, came on the scene in the late forties. Because most of them saved his letters, we have a fairly full view of his life during this period.[17]

McPhee met Sidney Cowell in the summer of 1942 in Woodstock, New York. He was renting "a house with a shed with a screen porch added on," and Henry and Sidney, who were recently married, also rented while they looked for a house to buy.[18] While Colin had known Henry for some years, Sidney was new to him. They immediately became great friends (he later told her, "You I liked at once"[19]), and his letters to her are more revealing than any other group of documents. They include laments about his personal life and work problems, as well as charming anecdotes about shared loves: cats, food, books.

Elizabeth Mayer entered McPhee's life for a shorter time, yet she was a special confidante. Their friendship grew out of McPhee's connection with Britten, for it was Elizabeth Mayer and her husband, Dr. William Mayer, who housed Britten during the war. Between 1939 and 1943 McPhee also was a frequent guest at the Mayers' home in Amityville, Long Island. There McPhee mingled not only with Britten but also with his old friend Copland, as well as Peter Pears, W. H. Auden, and Chester Kallman.[20] Elizabeth Mayer was a pianist who had studied at the Royal Conservatory of Music in Stuttgart and, for a time, had dreamed of a professional career. In 1942 Colin gave her piano lessons; once he even signed the Mayers' guest book by adding the name of the famous writer of piano exercises to his own, "Colin (Pischna) McPhee." In July 1942 Mrs. Mayer wrote Britten, "Colin was down here for two days, giving me excellent lessons, writing some marvellous exercises for my fingers, and even promising to write some piano pieces for me."[21]

McPhee's acquaintance with Margaret Mead continued after they returned from Bali and was both personally and professionally sustaining. She encouraged him to finish *Music in Bali*—his letters to her are preoccupied with the topic—and also helped him obtain grants. McPhee found her optimism inspiring: "You have a remarkable gift for imparting courage and faith."[22] Yet her spirit was so unlike his own as to be exhausting. He once confided to Sidney Cowell, "I love Margaret M. . . . but at intervals, and at a distance. I'd hate to have that YWCA energy around me for more than a couple of hours."[23]

McPhee had known Minna Lederman since he started writing for *Modern Music* in 1931, and Marian Eames came into his life in 1948, when he wrote a piece for *Dance Index,* the journal she edited with Lincoln Kirstein. All these women were sympathetic to McPhee's struggles.

❚ 𝕸 ❚ During the 1940s McPhee lived in several different places, never settling anywhere for long. At first he found an apartment on St. Mark's Place in the East Village.[24] Then in June 1941 he was awarded a residency at Yaddo, in Saratoga Springs, New York, where he remained until December.[25] During those months he got a good start on both *Music in Bali* and *A House in Bali* and seemed content: "The country is simply magnificent just now, unbelievably, unbearably beautiful. I am staying here till I have enough text to show a publisher, which ought to be soon. . . . I love being here."[26]

From September 1943 until June 1947 he lived in a Brooklyn Heights brownstone at 7 Middagh Street, where he had the top floor—a "tranquil" place—to himself.[27] The house had been leased by George Davis, then fiction editor at *Harper's Bazaar,* and rooms were rented to an illustrious group of artists: W. H. Auden, Carson McCullers, Paul and Jane Bowles, Benjamin Britten, Peter Pears, Oliver Smith (the stage designer), and Gypsy Rose Lee. Truman Capote, a longtime Brooklyn Heights resident, later recalled, "Each of the tenants in this ivory-tower boardinghouse contributed to its upkeep, lights, heat, [and] the wages of a general cook (a former Cotton Club chorine)." [28] Paul Bowles has remembered the house as "well heated, and . . . quiet, save when Benjamin Britten was working in the first-floor parlor, where he had installed a big black Steinway." [29] The Middagh Street house was razed in 1947 to make way for the Brooklyn-Queens Expressway, and that June McPhee moved to another building leased by Davis, this one at 305 East Eighty-sixth Street in Manhattan. He stayed there until the following April and then drifted between various hotels on West Twenty-second, in the vicinity of the Hotel Chelsea. [30]

During these years of roaming from apartment to apartment, Henry and Sidney Cowell's house in Shady, New York, became a stable retreat. Repeatedly, in letters to the Cowells (especially Sidney), McPhee thanked them for their kindness, exclaiming at one point: "I hope you realize how wonderful it has been to have Shady to work in—a lovely piano, country-house, friends, and sympathy." [31] He did much of the writing of both *A House in Bali* and *Music in Bali* there and most often stayed in the house alone, while the Cowells were in their New York apartment.

A WRITER EMERGES

After leaving Bali McPhee turned increasingly to prose as his chief creative outlet, and the island's culture became his principal topic. He had planned a book on Balinese music from the very beginning of his stay there. While in New York during the mid-1930s, he had written Marc Blitzstein asking if his wife, Eva Goldbeck, "would consider working a bit with me on my Bali book." [32] Then in January 1939, when he was barely off the island, he again discussed the project, which was well underway, in a letter to Margaret Mead: "I don't know in what key to pitch my book, whom to address it to.

I think a purely technical analysis dooms the book to an audience of sticks, and yet I hold the literary approach in suspicion." [33] By the summer of 1941 at Yaddo, the two approaches had become independent:

> I'm doing a book on daily life in Bali, as a relaxation from the one on music. It has gone very well—18000 words in three weeks, and I am really happy in doing it. I can allow my romantic libido to find expression in a way it can't in the other thing. I write so much better than I compose that I wish a miracle might happen, even at this late date, and that I could express that something that I feel within, that has never found satisfactory utterance. [34]

That fall he called his book on daily life "an emotional outlet against the cold analysis of the book on Balinese music." [35] And during the same period he claimed to have "fallen under the spell" of Carson McCullers, a fellow Yaddo resident:

> I am just reading her new Ballad, which is my idea of beautiful writing. . . . She has urged me to write my memoirs of Bali, and said a few days ago that if I had ten pages done by Saturday she would give me a party. Well, I shall have at least twenty by then, and I am anxious for her to read them and see her reaction. [36]

The book, which was to become *A House in Bali*, took several more years to complete (a draft was finished in the fall of 1944). [37] It was McPhee's first foray into a large-scale writing project, and it brought more joy than any other activity during this period. He took care with his prose, going through "at least" three revisions: "Writing the book has been like making bread—You let the dough rise, cut [it] down, let it rise again." [38] He told Mead not long before its publication:

> I daresay I was a fool to be so fussy about what I thought was style, but I've always had ambitions as a writer, and at last when I had a subject, I could not resist playing with it self-indulgently. At the same time I was trying to make a complex experience crystal-clear. [39]

According to Sidney Cowell, McPhee puzzled over the organization of the book, wondering how to structure such an episodic story. He turned to at least two volumes for inspiration. The first was Isak Dinesen's *Out of Africa* (1937), in which a continuous, forward-moving narrative is strung on a series of anecdotes: Dinesen's years as a manager of a coffee plantation in Kenya are described through vignettes of places, people, and events. In the fourth section of her five-part book, Dinesen abandons any attempt at a unified story and breaks the work down into short sketches, similar to a series of minute operas.[40] McPhee was also influenced by Cora Du Bois's *The People of Alor* (1944), which he reviewed for the *New York Times*. Du Bois's book was a personal memoir with a scientific twist, and McPhee was "fascinated by the organization of material."[41]

McPhee felt confident writing *A House in Bali* and was proud of the final result. He worked closely on the book's format with his publisher, John Day Company, a division of Asia House, and contributed the photographs reproduced in the back. After a long session over its layout, he wrote Sidney Cowell a letter that sounded as spontaneous as a late-night chat over the kitchen table:

> Really, I'm pleased with the book. It's a snobbish book, in a way, for what I've withheld, and where I've placed the accents. And yet it has a wide appeal, I know, from the variety of readers who have enjoyed the pieces. The only effect that counts in the long run is one of mystery, of what you imply rather than say. Perhaps I feel that way because I've been trained as a musician, and feel words the way I feel tones. The sentence must float, if you know what I mean. Not be weighted down. Just as the music of Mozart floats, while Beethoven, my god, and Bach too at times, sinks, sinks to the bottom of the glass. That's what comes of being too insistent about being sincere, or putting yourself into it. Chopin floats; Schubert too. What is it, exactly? Something like wind, gentle or wild—I can't put my finger on it.[42]

The "pieces" to which McPhee referred were an eight-part serialized preview of *A House in Bali* entitled "In This Far Island," published in the magazine *Asia and the Americas* between December 1944 and July 1945. It was an abridged version of the book, with only parts of the story told, but it used the same structure and some of the same language.

The release of *A House in Bali* was first planned for spring 1946, but because of a war-related paper shortage it had to be delayed until fall.[43] Once the book appeared, however, it was a success, receiving consistently glowing reviews in music journals, such as Music Library Association *Notes* and *Musical Courier,* as well as magazines and newspapers with a wider circulation—*Saturday Review, The New Statesman,* the *New York Times,* and the *New York Herald Tribune.*[44] Most reviewers commented on its atmospheric quality. Henry Cowell wrote in *Notes,* "Almost nothing is explained, only incidents and sense-impressions are delicately described and sensitively reported."

McPhee had great hopes for the book, just as he did for *Tabuh-Tabuhan.* But again he faced defeat. For one thing, if sales were good he planed to quit a job he then held at the Office of War Information: "The moment, if it comes, I have a thousand dollars in the bank from my book, I shall stop [working at OWI] and take a chance on what will follow in my life."[45] By mid-December of 1946 the first press run (of unknown size) had been sold, and McPhee was disgusted with the publisher for delaying the production of more copies: "To let a book die after the reviews it got seems to me outrageous. I was not seeking to make my fortune, but I had at least hoped to gain some self-respect."[46] He had a well-known literary agent, Harold Ober Associates, the same firm that represented William Faulkner and Langston Hughes (Ivan van Aauw was the person who handled McPhee's work).[47] *A House in Bali* was published in 1947 in London and in 1951 in Italy.[48]

A House in Bali, although highly praised by writers, anthropologists, and musicians, never brought McPhee the acclaim and money he sought. By the late 1940s he reported to Copland, "I had hoped *House in Bali* would have helped open some doors. I don't know why, but I might just as well have never written it."[49]

Two years after *A House in Bali* McPhee published *A Club of Small Men* (again, a John Day imprint), a delightful children's story about the *gamelan angklung* he had established for the boys in Sayan. The book is dedicated "To Cathy" [Bateson], Margaret Mead's daughter, with whom he spent a great deal of time during the forties. He contributed not only photographs but also the line drawings that introduce each chapter.

▌ ▛ ▌ Unlike *A House in Bali,* work on *Music in Bali,* McPhee's major literary opus, was long and fitful. Begun while he lived in Bali, the book was not published until 1966. Over the years, as he fluctuated between periods of productivity and total inertia, his energy level and financial state paralleled progress on the book. The work was difficult for two main reasons. First, had McPhee been able to maintain his status as a gentleman-scholar, the project would have been a pleasant diversion, albeit a substantial one, in a life of comfort. But as he continually scraped along, trying to eke out a living through grants and occasional free-lance writing, the book became a millstone. As McPhee acknowledged:

> To do the book on Balinese music as a sort of pastime, in a life of freedom from shabbiness, would be a pleasure. But to do it as a duty, for the sake of science and knowledge, on a miserable allowance, is nothing but sheer drudgery, unrewarding and humiliating. I did not live in Bali to collect material. I lived there because I wanted to, for the pleasure of it.[50]

Another problem was his lack of academic training. Sometimes he felt impeded by it, especially in writing sections such as the one tracing the historical background of Balinese music: "I find this all very hard, since I am no scholar."[51] At other times he was disdainful of scholarship's rigors. At one point, for example, he wanted to purge the book of "all stupid jargon-like aeophones [*sic*], idiophones, [that are] beloved [by] Sachs and Hornbostel."[52] Minna Lederman, who watched McPhee struggle with the project for years, believed he had "a terrible feeling of not being able to handle the material."[53] Yet despite occasional bouts of insecurity, he certainly acted like a scholar, especially in his fastidious approach to interpreting research and refining language. Once, in the midst of a successful work stint, he confessed to Sidney Cowell: "Little, trivial things seem able to disturb me for hours. You'd think I was James or Flaubert."[54]

A graph of McPhee's yearly progress on *Music in Bali* would be wildly

161

jagged. Already in June 1941 the ups and downs had started: "I'm at Yaddo for the summer, to finish the book on Balinese music, but it is hard work, as my heart is no longer in it." [55] That October, by contrast, he was "getting on well with the book." [56] And so it went as the years passed and the book remained unfinished. In August 1944 McPhee wrote Mead in a fit of guilt because he had not completed the book during the period of a Guggenheim grant (1942–43):

> As you were the key sponsor for my Guggenheim project, and the one perhaps most interested, I feel you ought to know that it is now clear to me that the book will not materialize. I have to admit defeat for a number of reasons, the main one being that I have not the background to put it together the right way. I was able to kid myself that I could overcome this somehow, while the experience was still fresh and I had the enthusiasm. But I seem to have rather gone to pieces, and it has shown to such an extent in my work that I realize that it is useless to think further about it. [57]

McPhee always saw *A House in Bali* as a diversion from what he called "the *real* book." [58] By September 1945, when *House* was finished, *Music in Bali* was "still only half done. I may go back to it now with fresh enthusiasm, now that I've said farewell to romance." [59] Around the same time he wrote David Diamond,

> I'm back at That Other Book—purely music (Bali and Java) which I am trying desperately to finish by spring, so that I can get away somewhere else. I don't know why it has taken me so long, since I know what I know, except that some outer confusion as far as America is concerned seems to retard work in general. [60]

The excitement of publishing *A House in Bali* and waiting for reviews preoccupied McPhee during much of the summer and fall of 1946. He mentioned the music book little during those months. By December he sounded carefree and almost indifferent, with far more enticing diversions at hand.

I got myself a Christmas present which is and will be more than I can afford in the shape of a young man named Vincent. We don't have much in common, but I like to look at him and have him around. He works on some construction job, carrying bricks, I believe. . . . I don't see myself getting started on another book—I have nothing to write about. As for the book on music—that tome—I've simply decided, in the words of Vincent, Aw, fuck it! It really is not worth the effort.[61]

During the next few years work on the book progressed poorly. The material became stale for McPhee, and he, in turn, was enervated by an increasing need for money. In 1949, suddenly his energy revived with the help of a Bollingen grant. He had done "a lot of revision and rewriting, and the whole thing has gained a great deal from having been put away."[62] By December 1949 he was immersed once again in the project.

I'm in a state of deepest concentration, for I've picked apart and had to reorganise the whole chapter on Balinese scales. I'm not out of it yet, and I mustn't let what I have almost got hold of slip. . . . I nearly lost my mind over this, and may still do so, but there's no use getting panicky.[63]

By the early fifties the pendulum had swung back in the other direction. Again, the project seemed "so hopeless to complete."[64] Several bouts of near-completion and reediting lay ahead.

At the same time McPhee undertook other writing assignments, especially reviews and articles for *Modern Music*. His first article on Balinese music had appeared there, and during his tenure with the magazine, from 1931 to 1946, his work filled approximately 140 pages. Like Aaron Copland, Virgil Thomson, and other composers of his generation, he received important journalistic experience in its pages. McPhee wrote four special articles, all relating to Bali, and also took on two regular columns—"Scores and Records" (1939–45) and "The Torrid Zone" (1943–46). According to Lederman:

He had a natural literary gift—he wrote with ease, with a very personal style. He had such a brilliant way of making musical life in Bali, and in other places, clear to all of us. . . . His reviewing was also quite brilliant. He would go to a concert—he had a great deal of wit—and review it and give you the essence of it very well indeed. He was a born story-teller.[65]

McPhee's first feature column, "Scores and Records" had been started in 1936 by Copland. There McPhee reviewed a wide variety of music—from Bach, as played on a new organ at Harvard, to Chávez's arrangement of a *Chaconne* by Buxtehude; from a recording of Edward MacDowell's *Second Suite* to one of African music made by Laura Boulton. He could be quite critical when he disliked a work. He called Charles Ives's *Sixty-Seventh Psalm,* as recorded by Lehman Engel's Madrigal Singers, "three minutes of the most horrible sound it has ever been my lot to hear" and dubbed Robert McBride's *Jingle-Jangle* "a sort of Nola rewritten to glorify the vibraphone, that insipid American version of a lovely Javanese instrument."[66] Each installment covered a large number of newly issued scores and recordings, with vivid descriptions of the music. Here, for example, is his review of the Mercury publication of Virgil Thomson's Third Piano Sonata of 1930:

Adventure in C might better describe this chaste and Lilliputian work where a sharp would be as disturbing as a coarse word at a church social. The frame is further restricted, for the melodic line is bounded by the octave. Within these narrow confines the music manages to have an amusing vitality that is not completely guileless.[67]

McPhee seemed to evaluate each new work of a composer individually, with little false loyalty to someone whose earlier music he might have admired—or to a friend. McPhee's writing about Copland is a good example. He liked the early pieces, such as *Music for the Theatre,* but had trouble with the *Lincoln Portrait* ("the eloquent simplicity somehow does not ring quite true to my ears"[68]) and especially the Violin Sonata of 1942-43:

> More robust, more taut and co-ordinated than the *Piano Sonata,* its vigor is, nevertheless, ambiguous. We are confronted with a style which by now is almost too familiar and perfected, a style that can be both recherché and baffling in its simplicity, under-statement, and Stein-like syntax. For some this style will be warm and revealing, but to many it must remain an enigma.[69]

The politics of criticism did not escape McPhee. Right after his negative review of *Lincoln Portrait,* he wrote Copland, trying to smooth things over, "[I] was so glad you bore no grudge regarding Lincoln."[70] McPhee discussed the ethical issues of criticism quite frankly with Copland on several occasions. In 1941, for example, when he was waiting for word about an application to do fieldwork in South America, a decision in which the composer and ethnomusicologist Charles Seeger would have some say, McPhee confessed that he was playing a bit with his journalistic power:

> This column get more and more a pain in the neck. . . . See what I said about Carl Engel, and see what I shall say about Ruth Crawford, wife of Sieger [*sic*] and so involved in the SA project. I can no longer be what I once called honest, but then, when you've reached forty you find that you are no longer shocked to find your tongue in your cheek at times.[71]

McPhee's other regular feature for *Modern Music,* "The Torrid Zone," began in May-June of 1943 and grew naturally out of his longtime fascination with Harlem and its jazz. His forays there had begun in the 1920s and continued to satisfy an unrelenting appetite for anthropology. McPhee once told Sidney Cowell just how much Harlem affected him:

> I don't know why it is, but the moment I am among Negroes, I feel strangely at peace and happy, and always wish I lived in Harlem, desperate Ghetto even that it is. It is only the feeling

that a white must remain an outsider and unwelcome that keeps my [*sic*] from looking for a place there.[72]

McPhee had brought his jazz records to Bali, revealing in *A House in Bali* that Louis Armstrong, Duke Ellington, and Ethel Waters were the only Western musicians to whom the Balinese responded.

By signing "The Torrid Zone" with the pseudonym "Mercure," McPhee may have been acknowledging his erratic temperament. Lederman admits that a column about the Apollo Theatre and jazz "was rather outstanding in *Modern Music.*" The column guides readers through the newest jazz releases and suggests clubs for the hottest listening. All the reviews show a long and intimate acquaintance with the music. In 1945, for example, McPhee wrote, "Stuff Smith's fiddle sound[s] very much the way it did ten years ago."[73] Another section of the same issue shows that his writing in "The Torrid Zone" was as opinionated as his reviews of concert music:

> Josh White's plaintive voice, his clear diction, and his beautiful
> and restrained guitar playing combine to make the Asch album of
> songs by this folk-blues artist one of the events of the season.
> The success of one song, *One Meat Ball,* has been a sensation. . . .
> But if you want an object-lesson in the degradation of a Negro
> tune, once it falls into the hands of white musicians, listen to two
> subsequent recordings rushed out to cash in on the success—the
> Bay Ridge interpretation by Louis Prima and his band, and the
> sexy and goonlike voices of the Andrews Sisters, those Rhine
> maidens of the jukebox.[74]

During these years McPhee did other free-lance writing, principally for *Mademoiselle.*[75] He also published a group of Balinese recipes in *Harper's Bazaar* (1949) and elsewhere two substantial essays—"Dance in Bali" (*Dance Index,* 1948) and "The Five-Tone Gamelan Music of Bali" (*The Musical Quarterly,* 1949). The composer Lou Harrison, who in the ensuing years would become so closely connected to Asian muscial traditions, has remembered being deeply affected by the latter article and copying out all the musical examples.[76]

THE SEARCH FOR AN INCOME

In the 1940s McPhee pursued several means of earning money and re-establishing himself professionally. Very soon after his arrival in New York he began looking for lecture engagements, and by the fall of 1939 he had his first speaking date. His topic, of course, was the music of Bali. After one of these appearances he wrote David Diamond, "The lecture went very well. The place was simply jammed to the doors, their largest crowd, and the new movies [of Balinese gamelans] are really good."[77] The Boosey and Hawkes Artist Bureau managed his lectures and produced an illustrated eight-panel pamphlet promoting a series of eight talks.[78] Engagements were hard to obtain, as McPhee wrote Mead in October 1941:

> I feel very well, and chastened. There would be nothing the
> matter with me if I could only get some lecture engagements. Try
> as I may, I can get no results. My agent has got me nothing. . . . I
> can't understand it except that I am not good enough, and in all
> seriousness I can't believe it. Don't give it much thought, but for
> gods sake if you see any chance let me know. I really need it for
> my morale, and also a little bit for my budget.[79]

Mead responded immediately, telling him not to take the lack of response personally:

> About lectures. I'd put it down to the times. If your agent had
> got you a lecture in a given spot one year and failed the next
> year—you could say it was you. But I don't see how no bids for
> lectures on the basis of lecture bureau folder can be interpreted
> as you. I find that I am being asked to lecture less and less on the
> South Seas and more and more on the present emergency.[80]

In the spring of 1942 McPhee went on at least one lecture tour that included Chicago, Urbana, and Boston; other cities may also have been on his itinerary.[81]

During the 1940s McPhee made repeated attempts to get funding for fieldwork abroad. None succeeded. In April 1941 he proposed an expedition to South America, especially Peru and Bolivia, to Carleton Sprague Smith, then chief of the music division of the New York Public Library. McPhee described his Bali fieldwork in some detail and went on to suggest that his new project would focus mostly on vocal music: "Work songs, recreational and ritualistic music would occupy the greater part of the program, although where interesting instrumental music was found it would be dealt with in the same way as in Bali." [82] He requested a recording machine and motion picture camera, as well as one or two assistants. Charles Seeger and George Herzog were also involved in planning the project and helped McPhee refine his goals. Seeger was enthusiastic and proposed that McPhee "go down to Peru and Bolivia for a year, record, take movies, and collaborate with the anthropologist [Luis Eduardo] Valcarcel." [83] McPhee confided to Chávez just how much the project meant to him:

> I have no right to count on this thing at all, and yet I have been
> rather counting on it for the last two months, for it means much
> to me both financially and morally. I shall be at very loose ends if
> I am in New York next autumn, and shall have to look for some
> kind of job, and god only knows what I can do. [84]

The proposal never took off. By June McPhee was beseeching Copland, "If you can push [the proposal] in any way, *please* do," and told him that an offer of three thousand dollars had been made, which was unacceptable (McPhee had asked for eight thousand): "I *have* to be paid, as I have no money to do it on myself." [85] Soon after, he wrote Mead, asking what she knew of the project's success. McPhee was impatient to know the outcome so he could start preparing: "The one snag (not impossible, however) is that Smith and Seeger are primarily interested in the popular folkmusic—you know, that dull hybrid of Indian and Latin copulation, while George and I would like to get the real stuff, which is much harder to find." [86]

Eventually Seeger wrote McPhee that he would never "entirely give up the project, but. . . ." [87] Earlier in the summer, when McPhee had told Chávez that the project was at a "standstill," he added: "I am not surprised, because it is just one more disappointment in a series that I am long resigned to. Life has been incredibly dull and empty since I returned [from Bali], and now I must add to all that financial problems."[88]

In 1942 McPhee's luck changed when he was given a grant by the Guggenheim Foundation "for preparation of a book on Balinese music." The grant was renewed in 1943.[89] Mead wrote a strong letter of recommendation for him, which sympathetically pinpointed the problems of his ill-defined standing:

> I am intimately acquainted with Mr. McPhee's work in Bali; I
> have worked with him in the field, I have observed his handling
> of informants, the skill and persistence with which he has adapted
> his research methods to local possibilities, the imagination and
> constructiveness which he has used in interpreting his material.
> He has been working on this project for several years, with very
> slight funds and without the status which his abilities and the
> importance of his research justify.[90]

Her most perceptive plea came in the penultimate paragraph: "A fellowship would . . . confer dignity upon the scholar-artist who is doing the work."

All this time McPhee was obsessed with the idea of returning to the East. After A House in Bali was published in 1946, he began to develop plans for travel that would lead to a similar book, evocative of culture and landscape and directed to a general reader. In 1947 he proposed the first of these schemes to the John Day Company, publisher of A House in Bali, which offered him an advance for a book on Java. McPhee, in turn, sought another Guggenheim grant to supplement his travel expenses (this one for three thousand dollars).[91] He hoped to borrow recording equipment from the Library of Congress. To McPhee, despite postwar political turmoil in Indonesia (or perhaps because of it), there was great urgency in doing fieldwork there as soon as possible. He wanted to return to Indonesia to make recordings, the part of his mission that had failed previously.

> One thing IS clear in my mind. The next ten years will be ab-
> solutely the last chance for a recorded collection to be made of

Indonesian music. With the changes coming, it will go just like
that. . . . Nostalgia for the East is so strong right now that I am
growing a bowl of ginger. It's up six inches and looks rather nice.[92]

This time the Guggenheim Foundation turned him down, and Harold
Spivacke wrote from the Library of Congress, "It goes without saying that
we are interested in obtaining recorded music of Java. . . . At the moment
we have no recording machines available since they are all out in the
field."[93] Spivacke thought the American Council of Learned Societies, to
which McPhee was planning to apply for funds, would not help him out
because they were in the midst of reorganization.

In 1949 McPhee won another fellowship to support his work on
Music in Bali—this one from the prestigious Bollingen Foundation. The
stipend totaled $3,600 ($300 per month for a year, beginning March 1949).
He later received a six-month extension until August 1950.[94]

Even before the Bollingen fellowship, McPhee had begun attempting
to organize an expedition to Burma. Again he wanted to produce a book
like *A House in Bali,* although "less precious, more close to life."[95] In 1950 he
received a Fulbright grant for work in the northeast Shan states, but once
more the Library of Congress denied him recording equipment, this time
because political conditions were too dangerous. McPhee was forced to
decline the Fulbright and conceded to the commission that indeed Burma
was risky at the time: "I can get no confirmation that I can venture much
further north than Mandalay; even further south, my most direct information stresses restrictions of movement and inevitable limitations in field
work."[96] In 1949 he also considered doing fieldwork for a book on Haiti or
Mexico.[97]

In May 1945 McPhee began his first nearly full-time job, which lasted
for a year and a half. The position, with the overseas branch of the Radio
Program Bureau of the Office of War Information (OWI), a propaganda
arm of the State Department, seems to have been secured for him by
Henry Cowell.[98] The OWI had been established in 1942, and McPhee's
starting salary with the organization was $8.88 per hour.[99] According to
sketchy references in letters from the period, he designed radio programs—mostly of jazz, spirituals, and folk music—and made some re-

cordings. He prepared a three-part series on the history of jazz, for example, for which he wrote the script and narrated: "When I heard the first record, I was pretty revolted by my voice, for I did not realize I had such an affected drawl, and really it sounded like some dreadful Museum of Modern Art fairy." [100] By June he was reporting a positive response to the shows:

My jazz programs are really a success. All the offices—I mean English, French, Italy, and Czech use them and the scripts, and I have correspondence on their magnificence from Porto Rico and Panama. And all this comes of not having once put on a record which I did not consider most beautiful—and in time anywhere from 1924 to 1946. I have held out for no Sinatra, Woody Herman, James or whatnot, and the results show. [101]

One of McPhee's more spirited accounts of work at the OWI arose from an expedition to Harlem in July 1946, where he recorded the Camp Meeting Choir of South Carolina. He had heard the group a month earlier at a Battle of Song in Madison Square Garden and was delighted with himself when he coaxed the singers into a "brilliant" performance: "It took my best anthropological technic." [102]

Besides radio shows on jazz, he recorded a half hour program "of new two-piano arrangements" with the pianist Maro Ajemian, who later was to make the first recording of John Cage's *Sonatas and Interludes for Prepared Piano.*

The arrangements I did either at the office with machines playing full blast, or at home at three AM without so much as a look at the piano. Result; absolute fresh effects, new, completely charming. A fine pianist, an Armenian girl, Maro Ajemian, who plays exotic concertos, etc, and is intelligent and a fine musician. We really did well. Much too good for the archives of OWI. [103]

As in other aspects of his life, McPhee's spirits vacillated with the job. Initially he found it interesting—"It's remarkable how less tired you feel if you've done a full day's work"—and was rising at six to write prose for an hour before going in to the office.[104] He seemed to enjoy much of the work, yet depression frequently took over. At one point he wrote Chávez: "Government work is exhausting and sordid; there is nothing left of one by the end of the day, no urge to do anything creative, no desire to comment on anything. I come home and fall asleep at nine, to wake next morning and set out once more."[105] He gave up the position at OWI in December 1946.[106]

A COMPOSER IN CRISIS

All the while McPhee struggled to compose. The first sign of such activity came in December 1940, when Chávez wrote asking, "How is the score of the Piano Concerto going?"[107] No such piece seems to have been completed. The first known work from this period resulted from a commission for incidental music to a revival of Eugene O'Neill's *The Emperor Jones,* which ran for one week at the Westport (Connecticut) Country Playhouse and a second week at the McCarter Theatre in Princeton, New Jersey, in August 1940.[108] O'Neill's play, which dates from 1920, was set in the West Indies and charted the fall of a black leader, Brutus Jones, an ex–Pullman porter from Harlem. The role of Jones was a famous one for black actors. Charles Gilpin had first played it, and then in 1924 Paul Robeson assumed the part. Robeson starred in the revival for which McPhee's music was written.

Once again the score has been lost.[109] Yet it is intriguing to contemplate what kind of music McPhee might have written for a West Indian setting with black characters, especially since his interest in African-American culture was so strong. He wrote the score for Hammond organ, played by Max Marlin. The instrument was rewired for the performance.[110] Robert Lawrence, a critic for the *New York Herald Tribune,* enthusiastically reported on McPhee's music, calling it "subtle," "insistent," "masterly."[111] He most appreciated two aspects: a sympathy for dramatic detail ("his treatment aims not at dominating the drama but at supporting it") and effective use of rhythm. McPhee wrote no prelude and left the opening scene stark, without music. The second scene began with "a haunting melody, built upon shifting rhythmic figures." At one point the part for drum, used in addition to the organ, rapidly increased in speed, building to "an elaborate scale of metronomic markings." McPhee incorporated at least one "Negro melody" and a passage "in cakewalk rhythm." He also wrote short interludes to connect scenes. The score had no Balinese material.

Probably on the strength of his work for *The Emperor Jones,* McPhee was again asked to write incidental music in 1940, this time for the opening of a new play by the young Tennessee Williams. The play was *Battle of Angels,* which starred Miriam Hopkins and was produced by the Theatre Guild in Boston. In Williams's own words, the play was "a disaster." It opened around Christmas of 1940 and was forced to close two weeks later. Williams claimed his work "was pretty far out for its time and included, among other tactical errors, a mixture of super religiosity and hysterical sexuality coexisting in a central character. The critics and police censors seemed to regard this play as a theatrical counterpart of the bubonic plague surfacing in their city."[112] McPhee's score to this play also is lost. For him the sudden closing of the production was devastating: "It has depressed me all week, and I am trying to forget it with rye and Javanese records."[113] Ten years later he told Chávez it had been an "unhappy experience. . . . The music started out well but ended dismally. It broke me up for six months. . . . That was the last time I ever tried to compose."[114]

And, indeed, although McPhee made a few attempts at writing music during the next twelve years, he did so infrequently and often unsuccessfully. Composing became ever more "oppressive" as the balm of Bali passed. During the summer of 1941, soon after the Tennessee Williams disaster, McPhee began a series of arrangements of other people's music. Once again, as composition grew painful he turned to preexistent music. He made three arrangements of works by Dietrich Buxtehude: *Ciacona* [*sic*], *In dulci jubilo,* and *Nun komm der heiden Heiland.* All are for two pianos.[115] *In dulci jubilo* is dated December 7, 1939, just months after McPhee reviewed Chávez's orchestral arrangement of a chaconne by Buxtehude for *Modern Music.*[116] For a time it looked as though Boosey and Hawkes would publish the scores, but they decided not to.[117] Ethel Bartlett and Rae Robertson did perform the works, however, at a New York concert on December 9, 1941.[118]

In the spring of 1942 McPhee arranged Benjamin Britten's *Variations on a Theme by Frank Bridge* for two pianos under the title *Jinx*. Eugene Loring and his Dance Players used the score in a ballet about the circus that was choreographed by Lew Christensen.[119] During that summer McPhee proposed to make a two-piano arrangement of Copland's *Billy the Kid*. Boosey and Hawkes again expressed interest in publishing the score, and McPhee was eager to do it. He wrote Copland, "It would frankly be a piano-transcription; not a note-for-note extraction, but a piano orchestration. You know I admire your music enough to respect every grace-note, and this would be a labor of love (paid by B&H)."[120] The arrangement was never made. During the same period McPhee wrote Chávez that he was thinking of orchestrating Liszt's *Mephisto Waltz:* "I think it is a fine piece, but the orchestral version does not do the music justice. I would do something very sensuous and mysterious for the middle part, and the finale with the hard brightness of Petrouschka [*sic*]."[121] No trace of this arrangement exists either. In the summer of 1943, he was at work on "a boogie-woogie piece," also now lost.[122]

In 1944–45 McPhee completed *Four Iroquois Dances,* his first orchestral work since *Tabuh-Tabuhan* (see Chapter 9 for a discussion of the music). It was commissioned by the Instituto Indigenista Inter-Americano of Mexico City for broadcast to Latin America and published in *New Music* in July 1945.[123] The piece drew upon transcriptions, although more literally than *Tabuh-Tabuhan*. Curiously, it was based on American Indian sources. McPhee had done no fieldwork among native Americans and had even been disdainful of their music when he reviewed a field recording made by Laura Boulton in 1941: "I have never felt that the American Indian had any intense musical urge. Compared with the exuberant musicality of the Negro this is thin stuff. Most noticeable is the lack of rhythmic interest and energy."[124] Yet here he was, just a few years later, pulling together transcriptions of Indian music for an orchestral suite.

With *Iroquois Dances* came further disappointment. Just a few months after the piece appeared in *New Music,* McPhee acknowledged to Chávez that it was "rather chaste after Tabuh-Tabuhan" and went on to call it his "sole creative effort in five years," a revealing choice of words.[125] By 1945 McPhee's compositional activity had slowed down so completely that transcriptions such as these, with so little material of his own, stood out as being creative. Yet, rather than reviving his confidence as a composer, they came to represent yet another failure.

Two years later McPhee wrote even more harshly of them: "I really detest those pauky [*sic*] little Indian Dances of mine that New Music published. No one has ever so much as looked at them, and why Henry wanted to publish them is beyond me!"[126] In the 1960s, when Theodore Presser took over the *New Music* catalogue, McPhee withdrew the *Dances* because he "was not pleased with them."[127]

During the next few years McPhee continued to compose, even though he found the process increasingly difficult. In 1946 he scored a group of Javanese transcriptions for chamber ensemble: *Babar Layar, Gending Luang, Suduk Maru,* and *Ramayana.* They were performed at a Ballet Society concert in January 1947, together with the "Nocturne" from *Tabuh-Tabuhan.*[128] Lincoln Kirstein, secretary to the Ballet Society, of which George Balanchine was director, engineered the commission; he seems to have been inspired by the publication of *A House in Bali,* but he had heard McPhee's transcriptions as early as 1941, when he and Chávez listened to the Schirmer recording with McPhee.[129] The three dancers on the program were Javanese, and McPhee supervised the dances and sets. The instrumentalists sat behind "a series of copper-gold scrims," perhaps to lend an exotic touch.[130] The works were scored for three pianos, glockenspiel, xylophone, celesta, four cellos, and two basses. All the manuscripts are at UCLA, with two Balinese transcriptions added: *Gambangan* and *Pemungkah,* both expanded scorings of the Schirmer publications of 1940.

McPhee's final attempt at composition, before what seems to have been a six-year hiatus, was music for a CBS radio documentary, "Arrows in the Dust," about the plight of American Indians. It was aired on May 22, 1948.[131] Oliver Daniel, who worked for CBS at the time, has remembered that McPhee was hired to do the music because of his *Four Iroquois Dances*. "Colin was a not a fast worker," says Daniel, but his score was "extraordinarily beautiful." [132] Unfortunately, no score or transcription of the broadcast exists. McPhee wrote Mead: "It turned out somewhat different to what I had expected—not so much music, less Indian material, and so on, and I found myself composing in a style rather unexpected. . . . It was fun to do." [133]

By 1950, when McPhee was asked to write music for a play by Clare Boothe Luce, he declined. [134] He no longer had confidence in his ability to compose. The assignment was for a score using folk material, which he felt competent to handle, but he confided to Chávez, "The parts which called for composed music I don't feel I could manage at all. I simply don't think in terms of music any more—never hear a single musical sound in my imagination." [135]

Central to McPhee's declining productivity and dampening spirits was the problem of getting his music performed. Otto Luening, a fellow composer who had known McPhee for some time and even played some of his flute and piano transcriptions in the early 1940s, has viewed McPhee's state of mind sympathetically:

> Through the thirties and forties, American composers were pretty much ignored. McPhee had a reason to feel depressed; the only thing is he probably thought he was the only one being ignored. The lack of performances, in general, was depressing. Another composer, Charles Naginski, committed suicide at Yaddo because of it. [136]

Minna Lederman has concurred: "Composers were a species under attack in America." [137]

In this struggle some composers, such as Copland and Cowell, fought indomitably for recognition and performances, for dignity to be granted the status of "composer." Yet others, such as McPhee and Naginski, lacked the spirit for battle. McPhee's problem, in addition to spirit, was a combination of spoiled self-indulgence and good, old-fashioned pride:

> Long, long ago, long before I met Jane, I decided the most im-
> portant thing in life was immediate pleasure, and how many
> times have I thrown aside the work which was my "career"
> deliberately, partly for its sake, partly for contempt of what I was
> supposed to be taking seriously. I was too lazy to practise piano
> every day, for a life devoted to Chopin and Bach seemed pretty
> dull; I took composing seriously, but I was too proud to sell my
> symphonies by going the rounds.[138]

McPhee saved few letters or clippings from the past, yet among his papers at the time of his death was an article by Ashley Pettis from the *New York Times* (April 21, 1940): "Composers' Livelihood: Survey Shows that Few Americans Earn Living from Creative Work." Pettis described the difficulties of getting music performed in the United States and called for some form of patronage. McPhee may have derived comfort in knowing he was not alone in this struggle, yet it had a debilitating effect on his creative life. He did take one practical step, though, by joining the American Composers Alliance in 1944, but he resigned on January 1, 1946.[139]

For McPhee the cruelest stroke was that *Tabuh-Tabuhan,* his supposed masterpiece, had never been played in the United States. One sign of hope came in 1941 when Chávez performed it in Mexico City that August. McPhee was delighted, especially since Chávez's enthusiasm for the work continued. Soon after the performance, Chávez wrote McPhee:

> It gave me real pleasure to restudy and revive this work. There is
> nothing but music in it, and music of the most musical nature.
> The logic and continuity and the integration of the score is thor-
> oughly amazing. The performance itself was much better than
> the premiere you heard in 1936.[140]

McPhee replied, "You can't imagine how happy [your response] made me."[141] In his letter Chávez had launched into a litany that he was to reiterate in the ensuing years: "It is unpardonable that you have not written more, that there are not more scores coming from you and of course I do not mean necessarily from Balinese sources." But McPhee was paralyzed creatively. The ideas no longer flowed, and his confidence was shaken. As he observed in a 1941 review of a work by Carl Engel: "The urge to create music is a mysterious one that comes and goes." [142]

Finally, in November 1947, *Tabuh-Tabuhan* was heard in America— not in the concert hall but on the radio, as part of the CBS "School of the Air" series. McPhee pared down the orchestration for the occasion. Oliver Daniel, who directed the series, has recalled:

> I hired him at CBS. The orchestra I had was simply a 35-piece orchestra, and I could augment it by maybe four players. But to do *Tabuh-Tabuhan,* which was for a huge orchestra, we had to reduce the score, and Colin was then hired to make a smaller version. That was the first time I met him. [143]

Only the second and third movements were performed.

McPhee was overwhelmed at confronting *Tabuh-Tabuhan* once again and confided the intensity of his reaction to Chávez, who had been so close to the work's creation.

> I've just had a shattering experience. NBC [*sic*] did Tabuh-Tabuhan over the air a couple of days ago. I got recordings— wonderful—and have been playing them over and over. You are right. I should have been composing all this time. I can't think what I've been doing with my life, except nothing at all, de- liberately, to torture myself, I suppose. Actually, it all boils down to economics; I've been so humiliatingly poor since I came back to America that I did not have the energy and exuberance it takes to compose. I gave up years ago, when I had to sell my piano. . . . Forgive this rather lamentoso note. . . . It is the climax in the last movement of TT which has brought this on. I simply can't believe I wrote it. [144]

McPhee still had some years to wait before a live performance of the full work would take place in the United States.

Few of McPhee's other compositions were heard during this period except for *Balinese Ceremonial Music,* which attracted some attention. After making the Schirmer recording with McPhee, Benjamin Britten took the score back to London and performed all three transcriptions on at least one concert there on March 29, 1944, at Wigmore Hall.[145] In February 1942 Béla Bartók and his wife Ditta Pasztory performed the works at Amherst College (see the program on page 153).[146]

As McPhee waited for the American concert premiere of *Tabuh-Tabuhan,* as he wrestled with *Music in Bali,* and as his compositional output grew sporadic, he suffered increasingly frequent bouts of depression. He poured out his woes in letters to Sidney Cowell and Elizabeth Mayer, and he also confided, although less frequently, to Margaret Mead and Carlos Chávez. In August 1941, midway through a long stay at Yaddo in Saratoga Springs, McPhee wrote Mayer a letter that was to become typical:

> I feel very well and rested after this pleasant summer, but have
> never felt so completely invaded with hopelessness and lack of
> any direction whatsoever. I think it is the feeling that there has
> been *something* within that cried for expression, but in what form
> I have never really known, and it is too late to worry about any-
> way. I know this is a familiar symptom, but it does not make
> it any the less poignant. And it is all the more baffling when it
> goes together with a perfectly sound body, indestructably good
> health, and the general inclination to enjoy the simple pleasures
> of life.[147]

McPhee suffered from "spells" in which isolation seemed to be his only cure. "I seem to lose all sense of identity and nothing but solitude will help me recover." Life had become "an empty desolate affair—I have these crises of terrific weeping that are utterly exhausting." [148] For a time during the 1940s he was treated for depression by Dr. William Mayer, husband of Elizabeth Mayer and director of the Long Island Home in Amityville, a psychiatric hospital. Mayer prescribed Benzedrine, but McPhee was reluctant to become dependent on medication and took it for only a short time. In the mid-1940s McPhee confided his frustration to Sidney Cowell: "If I thought the doctor with his pill would be of some use, I'd go very soon, but really, I doubt it. You can do nothing for Celtic melancholia, and I wish to god someone would transform me into a seagull flying around some misty rock in the Hebrides." [149] In January 1943 McPhee wrote to Elizabeth Mayer:

> Feeling so wretched, and tired during the day, in spite of Benze-
> drine, and only waking up around eight at night. Then I work
> till one, fall asleep, only to wake again at three precisely. Now
> only the blue pills take effect. How topsy-turvy it all is, and what
> a bore. [150]

In the midst of his depressions McPhee occasionally threatened suicide. To Sidney Cowell he repeatedly confided his waning hold on life:

> You can't combat with any weapons the state of one who no
> longer has any desire to live. This of course has gone on since I
> returned to America, and although I've made occasional attempts
> to get out of it, each one has been a failure. . . . Ten years ago, I
> could see this time with so much clarity . . . even before then.
> And never did I have a feeling of hope, nothing, nothing, but the
> conviction of approaching doom. Well, here we are. [151]

On several occasions McPhee described the genesis of his depressions as lying deep in the past, as he wrote Dr. Mayer:

> I remember that at nineteen I was filled with the idea I had
> something precious to say, and that at twenty-three I no longer
> believed it. I already felt lost, filled with despair, and took refuge
> in living completely for the moment. Many times there was a
> decision to make between some important opportunity and a
> sexual (homosexual) relationship which was purely sensual.
> I never hesitated to choose the latter. . . . The Balinese period
> was simply a long extension of this. [152]

In a letter to Sidney Cowell from 1945, McPhee confessed to ripping up old Toronto concert programs, an act that seems to have been a metaphor for killing the musician in himself. Here, too, he talked of his condition as having a long history: "Knowing that I've had a certain talent has always made me all the more determined to destroy it. I don't know when this perverse feeling began, but I know that when I went to Paris to study I was already half-hearted about a career." [153]

Although McPhee described his problem as one rooted in youth, he may also have found difficulty in readjusting to Western life. Watching him weave through *A House in Bali,* we sense a man lost in the mysteries of this distant land. Not only did he respond to the island's music and food; something about the very temperament of the place seemed to mesh with his own. He described completely losing track of time, often even of contact with the West, and of being sympathetic to the "sudden depression and boredom that can descend on a Balinese without a moment's warning." [154] He also found comfort in the island's acceptance of homosexuality.

The Balinese are a people for whom time is in some ways suspended, and the progression of daily life has few climaxes. The anthropologist Clifford Geertz has described these traits:

> It amounts to the fact that social activities do not build, or are not permitted to build, toward definite consummations. Quarrels appear and disappear, on occasion they even persist, but they hardly ever come to a head. . . . Daily life consists of self-contained, monadic encounters in which something either happens or does not—an intention is realized or it is not, a task accomplished or not. . . . Balinese social life lacks climax because it takes place in a motionless present, a vectorless now. [155]

McPhee functioned for six years in this timeless warp. Pressure was removed, and life flowed evenly forward, with little competition. He later acknowledged how calm and leisurely his work in Bali had been:

> I did nothing while I was there except live, look and listen, until the time came when I felt I had to write about the music. . . . It had so many qualities, abstract, sensuous, anonymous, formal—

it seemed to contain some lesson, and reminded me of the time
when I thought music a mysterious art. I envied [the Balinese]
their impersonal life.[156]

Jane Belo also went through troubled times after her return from Bali. Like
Colin, she spent some years turning her Bali research into a book, and she
too faced psychological difficulties. Belo's papers at the Library of Congress
contain a large group entitled "Hospital Notes: 1944–55," which are
essentially field notes documenting her experiences during repeated stays
in a psychiatric hospital. The exact nature of her illness is not given.

❦

▌〢▌ Central to McPhee's depression was not only his tenuous standing as
a composer but also his depleted financial condition. His life seemed to
grow bleaker as the 1940s drew to a close. He had occasional odd jobs, such
as hosting radio programs on Javanese and Balinese music for WNYC
(New York), and he sold some of his Balinese transcriptions and many of
his personal belongings, all in desperate attempts to raise cash.[157] Perhaps
the biggest disappointment came when a plan to do a film version of *A
House in Bali* failed. An unnamed Hollywood film company, together with
the Indonesian Ministries of Information, Education, and Finance, considered the project for a while. McPhee was filled with expectation:

> To do [the film] would turn me into a different being. Apart
> from the financial relief, there would be that wonderful feeling
> that here was something I *could* do, with ease and confidence, and
> apart from anything else, there [sic] mere composing a score could
> easily return me to writing music again, even at this late date.[158]

Nothing ever came of the plan.

McPhee had other wild ideas for earning a living: starting a restau-
rant in Oregon ("a self-respecting lunch wagon . . . [with] a superb view")
and getting a contract for a cookbook ("a trivial idea, but amusing").[159]
They were passing fantasies.

Beginning in 1946, as McPhee's financial situation became increasingly strained, he started borrowing money from friends, loans that he

always paid back. Margaret Mead and Aaron Copland were among those who helped out in the 1940s; by the 1950s Oliver Daniel was chipping in too.[160] Part of the problem was family related. McPhee's mother had a stroke in 1948 and required nurses' care, forcing Colin and his brother Douglas to support her. Colin's share came from royalties on *A House in Bali* and from the generosity of Jane Belo.[161] For Colin this situation meant not only an added financial burden but also renewed contact with a family from which he had distanced himself. His mother died in 1949.

McPhee drank heavily during this period, mostly privately, although his friends were aware of the problem. He had also done so in Bali. I Madé Lebah has recalled that McPhee and Walter Spies frequently partied together and that McPhee had an ugly temper when he was drunk.[162] By the late 1940s and early 1950s, McPhee's weight fluctuated a great deal, also because of liquor.

As Colin McPhee moved into his fifties, many dreams remained unrealized. In 1949, on the brink of a new decade, he looked back on the previous few years in a letter to Sidney Cowell and turned his disappointments into a wistful metaphor:

> It is always very warming to hear that I'm liked; you have an
> instinct for the right time for giving me these little confirma-
> tions. . . . I suppose anyone who refuses to do anything except
> what he believes in is worth the effort—actually a superior
> tramp—[and] will always have the magic charm of Tao. The
> beautiful mystery is this: that my few friends admire or love me,
> not for what I've accomplished, but what they think I might have
> done. A work of art which does not exist is the most beautiful of
> all. I stand for all the things which might have been done—a
> rich blend of nostalgia, Puritan stoicism and futility. Shake well,
> add fresh ginger and pour through a fine sieve.[163]

8

CHANGING FORTUNES

 **1952–59**

An event in the fall of 1952 heralded a new beginning for Colin McPhee: the arrival of the *gamelan kebyar* from Peliatan, Bali. The troupe of approximately twenty-five musicians and fifteen dancers came over under the aegis of John Coast, a British manager, for the first appearance of Balinese musicians in the United States.[1] At New York's Fulton Theatre it played to a full house and received rave reviews. McPhee wrote two preview pieces about the group for the *New York Times* and eagerly looked forward to visiting with old friends—especially Sampih, who was a principal dancer with the ensemble. He also hoped that *Tabuh-Tabuhan* might get some residual attention. Early in September he expressed that hope in a letter to Oliver Daniel, then at CBS radio, who in the years ahead would do much to promote McPhee's music:

> I'm writing, naturally, to ask a favor. As you know, a Balinese
> company will be here for a month, which promises to be a sen-
> sation. Sampih, the kid in my book, is one of the stars, and the
> gamelan is one of which I was once an honorary member. . . .
> There is terrific interest already among musicians, dancers, and I
> was wondering if there would be any way you could think of to
> get the recording of Tabuh-T on the air on some program at CBS

during the month they are here. There's a legitimate tie-up, and
of course you know how I've felt about it's [*sic*] never having
been played elsewhere in US.[2]

No such broadcast came about, but McPhee did receive some notice in the
press. He took Virgil Thomson, then music critic for the *Herald Tribune*,
backstage after the performance to "meet the stars," and although he later
made it clear to Thomson that "I certainly don't want any secondary
gleanings of publicity from this affair," he was happy when Thomson's
review acknowledged his connection with the troupe.[3]

In addition to Sampih, two of McPhee's old Bali friends, I Madé
Lebah and Anak Agung Gedé Mandera, came to New York with the
gamelan. Lebah and Mandera both have remembered being given a grand
tour of the city by McPhee, and he also brought Lebah to a bookstore
where *A House in Bali* was on display. Despite continuing poverty, he
offered Lebah a share of the book's royalties in recognition of the drummer's role in assisting McPhee's fieldwork. Lebah recalls that checks
arrived periodically during the ensuing years.[4]

While McPhee's life as a composer seemed to be over, in his early
fifties he continued to work on *Music in Bali*. His financial woes remained
unrelieved, and he had few emotional or professional rewards, only a
feeling of being neglected and somehow not fulfilling his potential. The
depressions and mood swings of the 1940s continued, as did the drinking.
In 1951 or 1952 he moved again, this time to a single room in a cheap
rooming house at 473 West Twenty-second Street (with a rent of six
dollars per week). He would remain there for most of the decade.[5] McPhee
was ashamed of the place and at first told only the inner circle about it—
Sidney Cowell, Minna Lederman, Marian Eames, and his literary agent.
His room had no phone, but he could be reached by calling the desk, which
contacted him by buzzer. When he moved there he reassured Sidney
Cowell, "I'm not fleeing debts, as I don't owe anyone a cent."[6] Oliver
Daniel has recalled that McPhee seldom let friends see his room. "He
became terribly depressed when, on one CBS telecast, they were showing
different slums in the city and showed his street and the actual house he
lived in."[7]

By the time he settled on West Twenty-second Street, McPhee had divested himself of most personal possessions, including many of the artifacts he had brought back from Bali, as well as his musical scores and piano. Both Sidney Cowell and Minna Lederman have remembered him giving away and selling batiks, gongs, drums, shadow puppets, and masks. This was done partly out of necessity, for his small room could hold very little, and partly out of a desire to eliminate painful memories of the past. But the process was disheartening, as he wrote Sidney Cowell:

> Of course I'm unhappy, with practically all I own in the world in three suitcases. It's a strange feeling. You know how eagerly I've been getting rid of belongings in the past year. Now that they have dwindled to nothing (which I barely regret), and with my mother dead, I feel so utterly unsubstantial. I've put so much value in home and possessions, and especially after the elaborate set-ups in Bali and New York, this contrast is at times hard to take.[8]

All of McPhee's friends remember poignant stories about him from these years: threatened suicides, a New Year's Eve spent alone with a bottle of gin and a jar of herring, bouts of living on beer because he believed it nutritionally sustaining.[9] All were sympathetic and tried to help. McPhee continued to use the Cowells' house in Shady as a retreat; he even had his own cat there, Ketut (a name traditionally given to the fourth child in Balinese families). As Sidney Cowell recalls, "Ketut was a very sharp cat with whom Colin used to do tricks. They liked to go for walks together."

Although McPhee could be difficult and demanding of friends ("petulant" is a word both Oliver Daniel and Sidney Cowell have used), he still managed to keep people close. Again, Sidney Cowell's memories are vivid:

> If things didn't go right, or if you served something he didn't like, he was just like a spoiled child. He was a very spoiled man in many ways because he had had such triumph and been at the top with money. Yet he always did something so charming and delightful that everybody would do anything he possibly wanted.

McPhee realized how difficult he could be and often complimented Cowell on her valor in putting up with his turbulent spirit. He was well aware of his effect on others, as revealed in this story about an evening with Margaret Mead and Gregory Bateson:

> Margaret and her husband Gregory were here a few nights ago,
> and Margaret, tight as usual on a thimble of Sherry, began to ask,
> first, what I understood by the word bitch, (not meaning canine
> variety) to which I said Katherine Anne Porter, and after we had
> worried that she said, what was the male version, and what was
> the name. This we mulled over for an hour, as I cooked a perfect
> paprika chicken, with asparagus in a perfecter mousseline sauce,
> and although I felt the conversation was directed towards me in
> a covert way, I did not let it curdle the sauce.[10]

McPhee prepared many a delectable dish for eager friends. Indeed, one of his more irresistible charms seems to have been his skill in the kitchen, a talent remembered by almost everyone who has written or talked about him. He had studied at the Cordon Bleu in Paris, and, according to Sidney Cowell, "He could cook Javanese, Chinese, Indian, Japanese, Balinese, French, Italian—and then he'd make cornmeal mush and fried potatoes." His resourcefulness was boundless; as he once put it, "I believe I'd find a way to make a souffle in a lifeboat."[11] Before McPhee moved to West Twenty-second Street, Cowell recalls,

> He loved to give dinner parties for just two or three people, not
> more. He felt that the flavors, the delicate and exotic flavors that
> he liked, had to blend or to marry, just so. And they wouldn't
> do so for large amounts of people. He would set Balinese and
> Javanese records going in the background and then bring out
> things, like sarongs, for the guests to play with. He always wore
> his sarong when he was cooking.

According to Paul Bowles, Colin came to visit him and his wife Jane at a house they rented on Staten Island in the 1940s. He cooked in a sarong there, too.[12] Occasionally in the 1950s Colin would go to a friend's house and take over the kitchen, as Minna Lederman has recalled: "He often came to cook at our house, and we would ask people in. Virgil Thomson was a great addict of the McPhee cuisine, and I recall one evening, Colin decided to make scallops in at least a thousand different ways. I think Virgil demanded still more." [13] Another time, when Colin was staying in Shady, he sent Lederman a "very charming letter with little cats on the paper" that demonstrated just how far his resourcefulness in the kitchen could go:

He was very good with cats, and one night a cat came in with a bird it had found. Colin examined the bird and thought it a rare and edible creature. He decided not to waste it on a cat and prepared it for himself. 'Couldn't have been better!' said he.

A U.S. PREMIERE

Despite occasional festive dinners and a group of caring friends, McPhee led a life of solitude as he moved into his fifties. But a second major event occurred to relieve the bleakness that had begun to seem unremitting: *Tabuh-Tabuhan* finally received its American concert premiere in New York on October 16, 1953. [14] The performance probably was inspired by the successful visit of the Peliatan gamelan and dancers one year earlier. McPhee had waited nearly twenty years for this event, and it triggered a chain of important opportunities for him. Leopold Stokowski conducted, and ironically—since McPhee had virtually renounced his homeland—the premiere took place in a program of works by Canadian composers sponsored by Broadcast Music Incorporated. When first approached about the performance, McPhee had said no, but Henry Cowell talked him into participating. [15] McPhee remained apprehensive as the evening approached. For years he had been complaining about the debilitating effect of having *Tabuh-Tabuhan* ignored. Now the piece would be exposed to public scrutiny.

Although McPhee worked closely with Stokowski in rehearsals, he grew increasingly uneasy as the evening approached. [16] Two days before the concert he wrote Copland,

> I certainly don't recommend you come to the concert on *my*
> account. I'm really shocked by Stokowski's change in standards.
> The work depends on the rhythmic coordination of two pianos.
> I have two indifferent dray horses who apparently have never
> heard of syncopation. In addition, instead of grand pianos, to give
> essential resonance in many passages, I have two tiny Baldwins.
> All the ensemble is incredibly ragged, and it will be a real floperoo.
> When I think of the time and loving care Carlos gave it. . . . It
> will simply be the last nail, establishing me publicly as a com-
> pletely incompetent composer. . . . I'm going with Minna, some
> comfort, for I'd rather be shot.[17]

McPhee's fears were groundless. The performance went splendidly, and critics praised the work. Carnegie Hall was decorated with Canadian colors and filled with United Nations representatives. Oliver Daniel and Don Ott remember the Soviet delegate, Andre Vishinsky, sitting in the box right over their seats.[18] Virgil Thomson called *Tabuh-Tabuhan* "the evening's most brilliant and striking work," and he featured McPhee's photograph with a review in the *Herald Tribune*: "[*Tabuh-Tabuhan*'s] themes and rhythms are all authentic (and very beautiful), its sound and structure very nearly so. . . . The whole piece is a delight for bright sounds, lively rhythms and lovely tunes. It may be the ending-piece that all conductors are looking for."[19] Olin Downes of the *New York Times* was more moderate in his enthusiasm but made some of the same observations: "This score is fascinating for its timbres, for the use of over-lapping rhythm groups and the dramatic accumulating power of its deep pulse and its super-imposed rhythms."[20]

McPhee rejoiced. The day after the concert he sent notes to both Thomson and Downes, thanking them for such generous treatment.[21] But to Chávez he confided his true reaction:

> Stokowski at long last played Tabuh at a concert of 'Canadian
> Music' at Carnegie Hall last Friday, when I re-emerged as an
> exotic Canadian and Tabuh had terrific success. . . . Stokowski
> played the work quite superbly in places, but almost tripped in

several passages. Fortunately the work has repeats in every
passage, and should be titled The Second Chance Symphony.
I couldn't forget the loving care and beautiful performance you
gave the work.[22]

Suddenly McPhee was in demand. Associated Music Publishers contacted
him immediately about publishing *Tabuh-Tabuhan* (for which McPhee
received a three hundred dollar advance), Artur Rodzinski called the
morning after the concert asking to see the score, and within the next
six months three possibilities for commissions emerged—from the
Koussevitzky Foundation, the Louisville Orchestra, and Lincoln Kirstein.
Again McPhee's friends stepped in to help. Copland seems to have assisted
in obtaining a commission from the Koussevitzky Foundation, Chávez
worked on both the Louisville Orchestra and Kirstein, and Daniel aided
with all three.[23]

The morning after *Tabuh-Tabuhan,* even before these commissions
became a possibility, McPhee talked about returning to composition.
"There is music it seems I should like to write at this period in my life, but
only orchestral."[24] Over the years he had become increasingly convinced
that his strength lay in that medium, a conviction that he had clearly
articulated to Sidney Cowell in 1947: "Only music done in the grand
manner, which I do extremely well, appeals to me; no songs or violin
sonatas for me, thank you. The Balinese have a special word for what I
mean—ramé—festive noise. Only a symphony or piano concerto!"[25]
During the next several years McPhee clung fast to that statement.

CREATIVE REBIRTH

McPhee secured the first of these commissions in 1954 from the Koussevitzky Foundation, which asked him to write a work for cello and orchestra. He responded: "I know nothing about the cello and couldn't care
less."[26] The foundation's board reconsidered and agreed to an orchestral
piece of approximately sixteen minutes, to be written for the twenty-fifth

anniversary of the Vancouver Symphony. Again there was a Canadian connection. McPhee began the work in August 1954 and finished it by that December.[27] (Ironically, about the same time that McPhee received this assignment—his first in some time—he was writing the libretto for a cantata titled *The Commission,* with music by Henry Cowell. It parodied a composer's woes in negotiating such a deal.)

Considering that nine years had passed since McPhee's last or-chestral composition, he seems to have been relatively undaunted at facing manuscript paper again. While in early October he confessed to Chávez that composing brought with it "many difficulties," he attributed them largely to "writing on transparent sheets for quick duplication, something I've not done before."[28] By early November, though, he told Copland that the work was going better.

> I find the more I write the easier it is, and I hope there will be no snags near the end! I found I did not make good progress unless I began scoring. I wrote Tabuh in complete score form from start to finish, with only a few pages in reduced score, and practically no changes in orchestration. It's rash, but I seem to think that way. . . . If this work comes out satisfactorily I shall be very happy. I've enjoyed doing it, and only wish I had more time.[29]

Yet problems remained, mostly because he had been so far removed from active music making—not just composing but playing the piano. "It was hard to get back into writing. I have no back log of material, absolutely no scores—of mine or anyone else's. Bought a volume of Schumann to practise, . . . for literally I hadn't *touched* a piano key in five years."[30]

McPhee completed *Transitions* on December 6, 1954, and it received its premiere by the Vancouver Symphony on March 20, 1955. Irwin Hoffman conducted, and the concert was broadcast throughout Canada.[31] During the same fall McPhee finished an article entitled "Children and Music in Bali" for *Childhood in Contemporary Cultures,* edited by Margaret Mead and Martha Wolfenstein.

Despite McPhee's optimism while composing, *Transitions* in some ways shows a composer out of touch with his craft (see Chapter 9 for a discussion of the music). Significantly, he was unsure about the title. On October 22 he wrote Chávez: "I don't know about a title, but in my mind is the image, Marine Horizons. How would that strike you, if you were a stranger?" [32] And to Copland he mused: "I wonder if I dare call it Atlantis!" [33] Both titles appear on various versions of the score, as does "Symphonic Transitions." McPhee finally settled on "Transitions," which, as he said in a program note, "refers to the changing moods and tempos of the music, and to the musical structure, which consists of a series of thematically related episodes." [34] Curiously, and perhaps not coincidentally, his Toronto mentor Arthur Friedheim had written a symphonic poem entitled *Transitions* in 1924, Colin's last year at home. Friedheim later commented, "I based it on the main dogma of the esoteric Hindu religion which appealed to me as an excellent subject for such a composition." [35]

Although McPhee seemed pleased with *Transitions* immediately after it was completed, there is no record of his later evaluation of the work.

In January 1955 McPhee wrote Chávez an energetic letter full of news about his recent musical activities. Recordings of the Concerto for Piano with Wind Octette and *Tabuh-Tabuhan* were planned, the premiere of *Transitions* was imminent, and a second New York performance of *Tabuh-Tabuhan* was scheduled. "All in all, I'm happy at the moment, in a subdued sort of way. I have you to thank first of all, for much of this, and secondly Aaron." [36]

Tabuh-Tabuhan received two performances during those years. The first occurred on February 18, 1955, by the National Orchestral Association, conducted by Leon Barzin with McPhee at one of the pianos, in a concert of music by composers who had won grants from the National Institute of Arts and Letters the previous year. [37] The second took place at the United Nations on October 24, 1956, conducted by Hugh Ross, McPhee's old friend from the Schola Cantorum. [38] But perhaps McPhee's biggest triumph was having the work recorded by Howard Hanson and the Eastman Rochester Symphony Orchestra. By the 1950s recordings had become a major vehicle for gaining acceptance of a composition. Mercury released the disc in the spring of 1956 under a subsidy from the American Composers Alliance,[39] and McPhee seemed happy with Hanson's interpretation—with some reservations. He shared his reaction with Chávez immediately after the record appeared:

> Tabuh, recorded by Hanson, is out. He seems to have done it with enthusiastic attention. They play for all they are worth. It sounds wonderful. But I could not go up for the recording, and tempos here and there are devastatingly wrong. As far as I'm concerned, nothing can ever be too fast, and anything can be too slow. Hanson chooses the latter course.[40]

This recording gave McPhee and *Tabuh-Tabuhan* some long-awaited national exposure. It was enthusiastically reviewed in *High Fidelity* by Alfred Frankenstein and in the *American Record Guide*.[41]

During this same period another early McPhee work, the Concerto for Piano with Wind Octette, was revived in a Composers Forum concert at Columbia University on November 6, 1954; a recording appeared in 1956.[42] On both occasions Grant Johannesen was the pianist and Carlos Surinach the conductor. The Composers Forum concert also included McPhee's *Sea Shanty Suite,* in its first performance since 1929. Peggy Glanville-Hicks organized the event, and Virgil Thomson moderated the discussion afterwards.

Again McPhee met success. There were nearly a thousand people in McMillan Theatre at Columbia University, including many composers: Aaron Copland, Henry Cowell, Wallingford Riegger, Virgil Thomson, Alexei Haieff, and Arthur Berger.[43] Both the *New York Times* and the *Herald Tribune,* especially the latter, lavished praise on McPhee:

> The McPhee Concerto is surely one of the classics of the '20s; its three movements expound instrumental and acoustic originality that—though colored by the era—is highly personal, highly expert. Its first movement, the most interesting thematically is perhaps the least perfect in form; its slow movement is a dream: A choral of Gothic calm is veiled, yet magically transcends a

pointillated modern surface texture. The Finale, as all the movements, demonstrates the composer's mastery in elaborative pianism that remains organic. 'Sea Chanteys' . . . ended the program with a bang, and is a tour de force of arrangement and instrumentation.[44]

A review of the recording by Edward T. Cone was far less complimentary, however. Cone went on at length about the glories of Roger Sessions's Second String Quartet, which was on the other side of the disc, and then turned to the McPhee concerto, which he called "trivial and eclectic." Cone's association with Sessions had been long and close. Aesthetically the two held attitudes very different from those of a composer such as McPhee:

> If I have devoted most of my space to the Quartet at the expense of the McPhee Concerto, it is because the former is obviously the more important composition. . . . [The McPhee concerto] strongly suggests Les Six in its use of simple diatonic or modal melodies accompanied by irrelevant dissonances, in its immediate juxtapositions of distant keys, and in such devices as chordal counterpoints of parallel triads.[45]

He found the finale to be "a brilliant toccata" with "quite a bit of rhythmic excitement," yet its ending was "characteristically 'cute.'"

In the midst of this rush of attention, McPhee's spirits rose and he became more productive. Yet some of the old problems remained. He stayed at the West Twenty-second Street rooming house and survived from one commission to the next. Both Copland and Daniel continued to help out with occasional loans or outright cash gifts. In March 1955, for example, three months after *Transitions* had been submitted to the Koussevitzky Foundation, McPhee still had not been paid. He wrote Copland asking if anything could be done to "speed up" the process. Copland responded with a check. Others followed.[46] Oliver Daniel gave similar help, and there were other small boosts—a $250 Benedict Grant in 1956 from the Museum of Natural History, a $300 advance on a commission from the National Institute of Arts and Letters, and occasional pick-up jobs, such as preparing a filmstrip on Indonesia for *Life*.[47] McPhee described how precarious his financial situation continued to be:

> I'm back at my old game of touch and go, with money in bank
> to barely last me through March, starvation rates, my standard.
> However, god intervened momentarily, as I thought, in terms of
> a small assignment from Life mag[azine] . . . with the result that
> I don't have to take the revolver from the drawer till May.

He concluded: "What amazes me, of course, is my general instinct for steering, which has enabled me to survive all this time, doing nothing I was trained to do, and taking no job I did not feel fairly sure I could tackle."[48]

A big blow came in May 1954 when Sampih, McPhee's "child," was murdered in Bali en route to a performance for President Sukarno of Indonesia. McPhee thought that jealousy over Sampih's stardom and newly acquired riches lay behind the killing; only two years before, Sampih had traveled with the Peliatan gamelan to New York. McPhee was devastated: "I feel depressed and hopeless more than ever before. I've been in bed almost a week with chills and fever." (The "chills and fever" were symptoms of malaria, which McPhee had contracted in Bali and which continued to plague him after returning to the United States.[49])

During these years McPhee fantasized at least once that he and Jane might reunite. In October 1952, not long after the Balinese troupe visited the United States, the two ran into one another "by a mystic accident" at the Museum of Natural History. Colin had not seen her "since she rashly became engaged to FT [Frank Tannenbaum]." He told Chávez,

> She looked beautiful, sad, aged, nervous, and everything that
> would break your heart. We had a wonderful twenty minute
> reconciliation, and she has much to forgive, and I hope to help
> her to emerge from the utterly tragic mess she is in by going over
> past Bali film material with the idea of making a short documen-
> tary, under the aegis of Margaret Mead. . . . Whether [Jane and
> I] join forces again for the finale is a matter of delicate chance.[50]

They seem to have had little further contact. McPhee thanked her in 1954 for a copy of one of her latest publications (probably *Bali: Temple Festival* of 1953): "It is really so much more than bare anthropology—a poetic approach [that] after all I could only expect. . . . I do hope you'll publish more very soon." [51]

█ 𝕄 █ Throughout these years McPhee continued to work on *Music in Bali,* announcing its completion every now and then. As before, his pace vacillated with his moods. In the early 1950s, for example, he wrote Sidney Cowell, "I must work like mad to finish book by March, which seems very likely as page succeeds page. I'm not happy with it, as you know, but some days it seems worth my effort and the Bollingen investment, others a tale told by an idiot." [52] By June 1952 he claimed to be done with the book; a similar point was reached in February 1954. [53] However, in May 1956 he delivered a completed manuscript to the Bollingen Foundation so that they could recommend a publisher. After all the years of anguish, he experienced a bit of postpartem depression when he finally had a draft in hand. "I feel lost with the end of the book, suddenly too aware of the time devoted to it." [54] By July Yale University Press was considering the manuscript. It would be expensive to produce, with (as McPhee first conceived it) four hundred musical examples, one hundred photographs, and about sixty Balinese scales shown in relation to Western tuning. [55] The press held the manuscript for two long years and finally accepted it for publication in 1958, after the Bollingen Foundation decided to contribute a twelve thousand dollar subvention. [56]

Meanwhile, in a modest way McPhee was also flourishing as a composer. On November 3, 1953, right after the American concert premiere of *Tabuh-Tabuhan,* Chávez had written McPhee: "I was . . . delighted to read about the success of Tabuh. I hope this means that you really reemerge as a composer. Probably a commission from Lincoln or from the Louisville Orchestra. Would you like me to mention it to them?" In 1956 the latter commission was finally realized. At the same time Chávez also helped McPhee obtain a residency at the Huntington Hartford Foundation in Los Angeles. There McPhee wrote Symphony No. 2 ("Pastorale") to fulfill his Louisville commission.

McPhee took a bus cross-country and arrived in Los Angeles on June 30, 1956. It was a "grim" trip. But he was delighted to be in a new climate viewing new landscape. His arrival was not auspicious, however.

> When I got here around 10 at night, I looked at the inviting bed with pleasure. I had barely sat on the edge when crash! down came mattress to the floor. I slept nine hours, however, in a well upholstered armchair, with feet on coffee table. The bed was fixed at once, of course, a slight business of supports.[57]

Despite the commission and Huntington Hartford residency, McPhee's financial situation remained shaky. Immediately before leaving New York he wrote Copland, thanking him for a loan ("I want you to know I couldn't have made out . . . without your help. I still have no idea when I can hope to return it"[58]). And Oliver Daniel advanced him some money against the Louisville commission.[59] McPhee stayed in Los Angeles for six months.

While at Huntington Hartford, McPhee made a new friend, Mantle Hood, a fellow composer and specialist in Javanese music, who was soon to play an important role in McPhee's life. McPhee contacted Hood to talk about *Music in Bali,* and Hood went to McPhee's room for drinks before dinner.

> Huntington Hartford had these marvelous, big, private studios, quite elegant, and he had a grand piano there with the lid up. I saw two things at once when I entered: one was the complete, handwritten orchestral score to *Tabuh-Tabuhan,* the other was a sizable jug of martinis without ice.[60]

McPhee was at Huntington Hartford principally to write his Second Symphony, but unlike the work on *Transitions,* his pace was slow. In September he confided to Chávez, "My own work goes badly, I'm sorry to say, and this is between us. I feel I am bleeding to death through time and loss of self. No one here would know this, and I must keep it hidden."[61] One month later he had progressed no further. This time he turned to Copland, sarcastically saying he was writing "a so-called symphony."

I find it hard to take up threads, especially trying to break free of Bali cliches. Perhaps I shouldn't bother, but just accept fate. I'm so near calling it a day, at least musically, and going on with this particular work is just a struggle, to be renewed each morning. All the comforts, and there are many, of HHF are of little avail, which just goes to show how perverse the creative spirit can generally be.[62]

By the end of that month McPhee panicked about meeting the commission deadline and wrote Oliver Daniel asking help. "I'm simply nowhere with the Symphony, having worked and rejected for the last three months until I'm no longer sure of a single phrase."[63] He had asked Robert Whitney, conductor of the Louisville Orchestra, for an extension until November but felt that he could not meet this deadline either. To Daniel he said:

I now don't know what to write or do. Ask for further postponement? Keep on slugging at what seems so futile? Or face it and give up the commission altogether. . . . And believe me, I *want* to write it, and *should*. . . . In many ways I feel more secure than when I saw you last, and do not feel that my creative life is necessarily over. But the present block now daily assumes greater proportions as time passes.[64]

McPhee must have put the score away for some months after returning to New York in late December 1956.[65] He wrote music for two United Nations films and then returned "with fresh enthusiasm" to the Louisville commission in the fall of 1957. He delivered the finished score in late December 1957 for a premiere on January 15, 1958—"a close shave!"[66] The work was recorded in April, and the recording released in early 1959. Reviews in local Louisville papers were favorable.[67]

By the time he wrote the Second Symphony, McPhee's relationship to Bali was dramatically different from what it was in 1936, when he composed *Tabuh-Tabuhan*. The clangorous sounds of the gamelan had been muted with the passing years and now were part of a distant memory. McPhee's personal circumstances had changed as well. The self-assured man of 1936 had been humbled by poverty. His standing in the music world was tenuous, and his productivity shaken. In many ways, the Second Symphony reflects these changes (see Chapter 9). It is a subdued work, without the exultant joy of *Tabuh-Tabuhan*. But it is a sublimely beautiful one in which the sounds and structures of the gamelan have thoroughly imbued the substance of McPhee's language. As McPhee told Copland: "[The symphony] was meant to be as much understatement as T-T was the reverse."[68] Once again, he was a fully functioning composer.

Meanwhile in 1957, when work on the Second Symphony had ground to a halt, McPhee had composed two scores for films made for the United Nations. Doing so restored his self-confidence. The first, *Air Skills,* was written between February 12 and March 20; the second, *The Blue Vanguard,* between August 10 and September 17. After taking nearly twenty years to write *Music in Bali* and not being able to meet the deadline for the new symphony, he was delighted with himself. "This last job shows me I still can deliver efficiently, on time, and I hope will lead to others. . . . The music is all done, and was recorded Tuesday. Really a success from all angles. Everyone loves it, even me."[69]

McPhee was recommended for the first U.N. job by Virgil Thomson, who advised Thorald Dickinson, a film producer then living in the Chelsea Hotel, of local composers for various projects.[70] Thomson's generosity backfired a bit, for McPhee wrote him in January 1957,

> Saw Dickinson yesterday and all seems set, though will not
> be confirmed till Monday. The film sounds attractive, and I'm
> offered five hundred. I have a problem, however, in finding
> money for getting a piano. The man I rent from always wants
> cartage both ways and three months in advance—about $75.
> I daren't pay this out right now, and if you could possibly ad-
> vance this for the present, I could pay it back as soon as paid for
> UN score.[71]

There is no record of whether or not Thomson lent McPhee the money.

Again there was a Canadian connection, for *The Blue Vanguard* was produced for the United Nations by the National Film Board of Canada. It was a fifty-five-minute documentary about the United Nations Emergency

Colin McPhee in the 1960s.

Force set up during the Suez Canal crisis by Lester B. Pearson, former Canadian prime minister. McPhee must have finished the score at the last minute, because it is dated September 17, and according to a preproduction schedule the first recording session was scheduled for the sixteenth.[72] He went to Montreal in late September to help with the mixing. True to his fitful luck, tensions in the Middle East prevented the film from ever being released.

In 1958 McPhee received yet another commission, this one from the Contemporary Music Society, an American organization, for a piece called *Nocturne*, which was given its premiere at the Metropolitan Museum of Art on December 3, 1958, with Leopold Stokowski conducting. The program featured Western works with ties to Asia.[73] McPhee's friend Oliver Daniel had founded this society and brought in Stokowski as its conductor. He also had much to do with engineering McPhee's commission. The connection between McPhee and Stokowski went back at least to 1936, when McPhee showed him the score of *Tabuh-Tabuhan* in hopes of getting a performance. And in 1953, after finally conducting the American premiere of the work, Stokowski had written McPhee: "What would you think of composing another composition, perhaps to last about ten minutes and to be in one movement, of your memories of Balinese music? A composition of this length would be enthusiastically welcomed by listeners all over the country, and, eventually, all over the world."[74]

No letters survive to document McPhee's work on the *Nocturne,* only an entry in Don Ott's diary for October 1958, six weeks before the premiere: "Colin played the first part—finished—of his new composition for the Stokowski concert. . . . The piece was beautiful even on the piano."[75] As with the Second Symphony, McPhee continued to achieve a comfortable and highly successful mode of expression in the *Nocturne.* It is a luxuriant piece, with the shimmering energy of the gamelan transformed into a profound personal statement (see Chapter 9). Again reviews were positive and a recording resulted, this time on the CRI label with David Van Vactor conducting.

An interesting sidelight to this concert involved another composer, Chou Wen-chung, whose *To A Wayfarer* was heard alongside McPhee's *Nocturne.* Chou has recalled meeting McPhee around 1949, after arriving in New York from mainland China, and has credited Colin with recommending that he study with Edgard Varèse. According to Chou: "McPhee thought Varèse could help me because of Varèse's interest in sound. On the other hand, he felt that Varèse's music involved the process of going from one explosion to another, and that my personality and tradition would not lead to the same thing."[76] Over the years McPhee kept up with Chou's progress and advised the younger man about promoting his music, suggesting that he go to see Stokowski. Chou, in turn, has recalled being "a great admirer of *Tabuh-Tabuhan.* Today it might seem outdated, but at the time, I thought it was one of the most distinguished scores of that nature, using the Western orchestra to express the music of another culture."

Just as McPhee seemed to be launched once again, after his success with the Second Symphony and *Nocturne,* he stumbled into 1959, which in his own words was a "dismal" year. He grappled with the "final" manuscript of *Music in Bali,* [77] and once again he fell into a foul mood: "As far as composing is concerned I give up. I don't expect to continue. I'm nowhere in the least demand, nor hope to be. I'm fundamentally embarrassed by the music I've written with recent commissions, and long ago was ready to call it a day." [78] That fall the lament continued: "Everything is so financially hopeless . . . . I'm more destitute than I've ever been, with not even clothes. I could not go any place this hot summer because I had only a winter suit. . . . I'm very weary of it all, I can tell you." [79]

At some point in the midst of this misery, McPhee had received a commission from Robert Boudreau's American Wind Symphony in Pittsburgh and had begun writing a piece that would become the Concerto for Winds. [80] Given his financial and emotional state, work did not progress smoothly. In November he reported to Oliver Daniel that although he had been composing he could "see no way to finishing [the piece]. . . . I really don't know how to carry on any further. I'll be without money again before Christmas." [81] Daniel proposed another small commission, which McPhee declined, and there was also talk of writing a work for the Joffrey Ballet, which never happened. [82] McPhee was eager to do the Boudreau work, however, and promised Virgil Thomson, "No Oriental ambience in any sense this time." [83]

McPhee's deadline had been April 1960, and again, as with the Louisville commission, he did not meet it. In early March he wrote Boudreau asking to be released from the assignment because he had been sick much of January: "Perhaps through fatigue or other preoccupations I found I had lost all contact with the work as far as it had gone, and in which I no longer have any confidence." [84] He sent a carbon of his letter to Oliver Daniel, with a cover note confiding, "I have not known a day or night free from tension and anxiety for months." [85] In February Jane Belo seems to have gotten word of his difficulties, for she wrote Margaret Mead, "Here is the check with the money for Colin's 'advance.'" [86] It is not known if Colin was aware of her generosity. Meanwhile, though, he tackled the concerto once again and in June submitted a completed score, which "took me six weeks to write." [87]

In spite of his promise to Thomson, McPhee filled the concerto with

Balinese themes, many of which were drawn directly from *Tabuh-Tabuhan*. Yet this time his references to the earlier work were bald, even tired, by comparison to the imaginative recollection that had pervaded both the *Nocturne* and the Second Symphony. The Concerto for Winds would not be McPhee's most compelling work, but at least he continued to compose. Besides, another twist of fortune, this one resoundingly good, lay just ahead.

9

COMPOSITIONS AFTER 1940

Colin McPhee's conflicted attitude toward composing during the 1940s, 1950s, and 1960s yielded uneven results. Because of this and because access to his scores remains difficult, McPhee's entire output from this period has been largely ignored, allowing works of extraordinary beauty and invention to be eclipsed by less successful ones.

McPhee was caught between historical currents. By the 1950s, when *Tabuh-Tabuhan* was finally performed and recorded in America, much musical interest had shifted to serialism; even Aaron Copland, McPhee's close colleague, began incorporating the technique. While Asian ideas were affecting American composers more deeply with each passing year, some of those composers, such as John Cage, were attuned to the philosophies, not the sounds, of the East. Others, such as Lou Harrison, followed McPhee in drawing directly upon the musics of Asia but emphasized traditional instruments rather than transferals to the Western orchestra. If George Gershwin sat between "two stools" representing the hardened categories of popular and concert music, as Virgil Thomson once defined his status, Colin McPhee was in a room cluttered with chairs, none of which quite fit.[1] After the late 1920s he always seemed to be too early or too late: preparing gamelan transcriptions long before the arrival of the minimalists, with their similarly conceived "pattern" music; composing a huge orchestral work such as *Tabuh-Tabuhan* when American symphonies were reluctant to perform such fare; and returning in the 1950s to a musical language that seemed conservative, even old-fashioned, but that twenty years later was coming back in vogue.

Perhaps because of this curious posture, as well as because of its intrinsic worth, McPhee's music deserves serious attention. He stands with other twentieth-century American composers, such as Marc Blitzstein, Paul Bowles, and Harold Shapero, whose work has been unjustly marginalized. McPhee was important first as a neoclassicist and later as a prophet of East-West integration. By the final decades of his life, as both compositional focuses remained critical to his music, he worked to fuse them in new ways. In fact, his work during these years can be seen as a pursuit of some ideal balance between free composition and transcription, as a way of taming the Western ego through Eastern methods. The following passage, written by McPhee in Bali, tells much about concerns that continued to occupy him in the United States:

> I feel that the artist must strive more and more for anonymous expression, to be first of all a good craftsman, and try and negate all that cries from within for self-conscious and egotistical declaration. I am sure that this is the only way that one can find one's true self. . . . What a marvellous thing would be a program made up of new works by composers whose names were not included in the program.[2]

It was a revolutionary idea, especially for a composer whose musical language remained fairly conservative. And so in the years ahead McPhee's mission would be to reconcile "anonymous expression" with personal creativity—in short, to adopt the Balinese attitude toward composing as much as to integrate its musical language.

Since a chronicle of McPhee's composing activity has been given previously, this chapter will focus on extant compositions from the final decades of his life. Information about recordings and scores (e.g., publishers and current locations of copies) is given in the music catalogue (Appendices A and B).

GAMELAN TRANSCRIPTIONS

McPhee's gamelan transcriptions took multiple forms, and many of them—indeed, most of them—reach back to the 1930s. In the early 1940s, however, right after returning from Bali, he polished off some transcriptions for Western instruments and had a few published. Later in the decade he also arranged a new set for chamber ensemble. And in the years ahead he continued to return to them—refining details, making fresh arrangements, and keeping the music of Bali a living part of his experience. These pieces are among the most significant and least explored aspect of his output.

The body of transcriptions made by McPhee in Bali is large. It now fills twelve notebooks and many randomly stuffed folders at UCLA and includes transcriptions of two sorts: direct notations in score of actual gamelan instrumentations and arrangements for Western instruments. Of the latter group, nearly forty separate titles for piano and two for flute and piano have been located (a number of them including several variants).[3] All the transcriptions, whether notated for Balinese or Western instruments, are products of the same working process. Notation was the only means available to McPhee for documenting gamelan repertories, and he regularly used the piano as a transcribing tool. While he traveled a good deal around the island, much transcribing seems to have been done at his Sayan home, where musicians gathered for long sessions. He later recalled, "I wrote down melodies as they played them, [then I] played them back on the piano, while they patiently corrected my mistakes."[4] Some of the pieces emerged as arrangements for piano; others did not. Many exist in several forms. But most were literal renderings of the music as he heard it. Here the focus will be on the transcriptions for Western instruments.

Since McPhee transcribed at the piano, it was only natural that some of his pieces should end up as works for that instrument. But there were other reasons for his decision. McPhee had a long and intimate history with the piano, which had been at the heart of nearly all his compositions. He also had some experience reworking music for the instrument, with arrangements of the *Rákoczy March* and Gershwin's *The Man I Love*. McPhee claimed that he was inspired to transfer the sounds of the gamelan to piano by hearing "the little duets at the piano by the children [of Sayan]. . . . The clear, incisive tones of the gamelan seemed to find a natural echo in the tones of the piano, and so I began to make a few experimental arrangements."[5] But he had a predecessor, Walter Spies, who by the time McPhee arrived in Bali had already spent several years transcribing gamelan music for two pianos.

McPhee's first transcriptions were drawn from the *gendér wayang* repertory, music for the enchanting nighttime shadow play performances. It was a repertory he dearly loved, calling it "perhaps [the] most perfect expression" of Balinese music,[6] and it was a good place for a newcomer to begin understanding the complexities of the music. The *gendér wayang* ensemble is compact: a quartet of *gendér,* with two small instruments doubling two large ones at the octave. The music is divided into individual parts that change as the action of the shadow play unfolds.

Lagu délem, a piece from the *gendér wayang* repertory, illustrates McPhee's varied approaches to the transcription process. At least eight different versions of this composition are extant at UCLA—four for solo piano (one of the earliest is shown in ex. 33), two for two pianos, and two for traditional instruments (see table 1). These various arrangements were prepared over the course of thirty years, and a solo piano version of *Lagu délem* was recorded by Sylvia Marlow in 1959.

Although there are slight differences among these versions, all are renderings of the same piece, transcribed from I Lotring's *gendér wayang* in Kuta. The earliest date given on a *Lagu délem* manuscript is 1933 (version G); the latest reworking of the piece was in 1962 (version F). McPhee included more dynamics and phrasing indications in the solo piano and two-piano scores (there are almost none in the ones for *gendér*), and he seemed to change his mind about tempo (going from "Andantino" in versions A and B, to "Moderato/pesante" in version E, to "Commodo" in versions C and D).

While *Lagu délem*'s various texts are all direct transcriptions—that is, not recomposed in any way—their musical characteristics correspond to McPhee's own interests as a composer. The scale collection (*sléndro,* roughly translated into Western pitches by McPhee as F♯, G♯, B, C♯, E) is constant, but the tonic changes from the first eight-bar section to the

TABLE I.   Extant versions of *Lagu délem*

A. Solo piano. Dated "Bali, 1935." Andantino. Holograph (see ex. 33).

B. Solo piano. Dated "Bali, 1935." Andantino. Holograph.
Comment: Some fuller voicings than version A, especially Part II
where the left hand is doubled at the octave.

C. Solo piano. Dated "Amityville, June 9–41." Commodo. Holograph.
Comment: Rhythm of the left-hand ostinato is notated differently
from versions A, B, E, F, and G; phrasing is given in Part II of right
hand only.

D. Solo piano. Dated "Bali 1934"; reworked in 1950s or 1960s.
Commodo ♩ = 80. Holograph.
Comment: Much like version C (including left-hand rhythm);
phrasing included for Part I (all phrasing is different from versions
A and B).

E. Two pianos. n.d. [1931–35]. Moderato/pesante. Holograph.
Comment: Part I with repeat and second ending; no Part II; first
piano doubles second at the octave.

F. Two pianos. [1956 or 1962]. Moderato. Holograph.
Comment: Includes Part II with figuration; much more varied voicing
than E (e.g., opens with Piano II alone, then Piano I adds octave
doubling in the right hand at measure 4).

G. Gendér quartet. Dated "Lotring—Kuta Village, 1933"; included in
Music of the Balinese Gendér Wayang (transcription of a complete set of
pieces for the shadow play that was compiled by McPhee in 1962).
Deliberato. Holograph.
Comment: No phrasing; upper score of Part II is beamed to show
interplay of two voices.

H. Gendér quartet. n.d. ♩ = 69. Found in *Music in Bali* (exs. 219–20),
"Kuta Village."
Comment: No phrasing; upper score of Part II is beamed as in
versions A through F.

EXAMPLE 33   *Lagu délem*. Transcription arranged for piano by McPhee (version A).

second (see ex. 33, mm. 9–16), where the opening material is restated, with slight modifications, one step higher. Another trait sympathetic with McPhee's personal style is found in the right-hand ornamentation of the reprise, which essentially forms a shifting ostinato (measures 17–33).

Perhaps the best-known body of McPhee's transcriptions, however, is that published as *Balinese Ceremonial Music* by G. Schirmer in 1940 and recorded immediately afterwards by McPhee and Benjamin Britten. When McPhee released these transcriptions, recordings of actual gamelan playing were still rare in the West, and live performances occurred only occasionally at world fairs. Transcriptions, therefore, served a practical as well as an artistic purpose. *Balinese Ceremonial Music* includes three separate arrangements for two pianos, each illustrating a different facet of the gamelan repertory. *Pemoengkah,* like *Lagu délem,* is from the shadow play (in this case an overture), *Gambangan* comes from the ancient music used in cremation ceremonies, and *Taboeh Teloe* from the feast music played by the *Gamelan gong gedé* (Gamelan of the Great Gongs). Each has an opening description by McPhee, conveying the atmosphere of the piece, its function and original tuning (given in a chart), and concise but detailed performance instructions.

Pemoengkah will serve as an example of how McPhee's transferals to Western instruments relate to his direct notations of gamelan scoring.[7] In the introduction to *Pemoengkah,* McPhee describes the quartet of *gendér* used for the original Balinese piece and suggests how pianists might achieve a similar effect:

> It is difficult to convey by words an impression of the strange beauty of the sound from these instruments. Sweet, yet acid, soft, yet metallic, the four *gendér* are in perfect accord with the nature of the performance. The clear-cut design of the music and the delicate arabesques are reflected in the transparent lacework of the puppets, whose gestures, miniature and heroic, nervous and menacing, are in turn retranslated into sound by the sensitive and, at times, vaguely sinister nature of the music.
>
> The music must be played lightly and transparently, *not expressively,* with just enough pedal to attain a good legato.[8]

He goes on to point out that *Pemoengkah* was included on the 1928 Odéon recordings but that his transcription reflects "actual playing," a statement corroborated in *Music in Bali:*

> The following step by step account of this composition [*Pemoengkah*] is based on the version played by the *gendèr wayang*

ensemble of Kuta village, of which the composer, I Lotring, was the leader. The composition was obtained through musical dictation. Lotring and a second *gendèr* player remained for two weeks at my house in Sayan while the music was transcribed.[9]

Comparing the two-piano version of *Pemoengkah,* as published in *Balinese Ceremonial Music,* with the various sections of gamelan scoring reproduced in *Music in Bali* shows that McPhee treated the two forms of transcription symbiotically—they share much material, and at the same time each illuminates elements missing from the other.[10] The full *Pemungkah,* as discussed in *Music in Bali,* is a multisection composition, with a tonic that shifts to different degrees of a five-note scale. *Music in Bali* gives excerpts from all the sections, together with descriptive commentary. In the two-

EXAMPLE 34   *Pemungkah,* closing section. Transcription by McPhee from *Music in Bali* (ex. 208, mm. 1–12).

EXAMPLE 35   *Pemungkah* from Suite of Gamelan Transcriptions arranged for chamber ensemble by McPhee, mm. 1–10 (Pianos I and II are drawn directly from *Balinese Ceremonial Music*).

(*continued*)

piano version, however, McPhee includes only the closing portion of the piece. Not only is it more compact for performance within the context of a Western concert; it represents the same section of the piece that appeared in the Odéon recordings.

While the substance of the two transcriptions is similar, there are differences in details. In the introduction to this closing section of the piece, McPhee notates only two voices in *Music in Bali,* explaining in the text that each voice is doubled at the octave (ex. 34, mm. 1–5). In the two-piano score, however, he indicates the doublings (ex. 35). Similarly, when the principal part of this section begins, the version in *Music in Bali* again

EXAMPLE 35 (*continued*)

(*continued*)

provides the basic outline of the material while the two-piano score is more elaborate, reflecting performance practice. McPhee stated of the transcription given in *Music in Bali:* "[This passage] illustrates the breadth and suppleness of the melodic line in this final section of the *pemungkah,* but it does not reveal how the melody is divided between the two *gendèr* players," and he went on to illustrate two ways in which the line was broken up and elaborated—one from Kuta village, the other from Mas.[11] The two-piano version of *Pemoengkah* provides yet a third variant of the basic material (ex. 35, mm. 6–10).

The transcriptions for Western instruments, therefore, are an extension of McPhee's research. Often, as with *Pemoengkah,* they convey infor-

EXAMPLE 35 (*continued*)

mation about performance practice that is not present in the direct notations for traditional instruments. While these transcriptions remain consistently faithful to their sources, they represent a kind of binding link between fieldwork and creative composition. McPhee assumed two roles as he made them. Most of all, the transcriptions made it possible to hear music that was otherwise unavailable in the West.

In 1946 McPhee returned to two pieces from *Balinese Ceremonial Music* (*Pemoengkah* and *Gambangan*) and added three transcriptions of Javanese court dances. He then arranged the entire group for a chamber ensemble of three pianos, glockenspiel, xylophone, celesta, four cellos, and two basses (all instruments were not used in every section). The pieces were performed with choreography by George Balanchine in January 1947. A reconstruction of the full score (ex. 35) shows how McPhee amplified the ensemble.

While McPhee's other transcriptions for Western instruments often have parallel versions in gamelan scoring, found in either *Music in Bali* or his field notes (or both), two of them represent a mingling of literal transcription with free composition: *Lagu ardja* and *Kambing slem,* both scored for flute and piano. Years later McPhee wrote about these pieces:

> I now come to the next step in my arrangements of Balinese music. I had already made a collection of little melodies which boys delighted in playing on the *suling*. . . . Out in the ricefields or under a tree, they would spend hours improvising on these little tunes. As these had no accompaniment, I tried composing light, percussive accompaniments for the piano, choosing tones that would suggest gongs and other Balinese percussion instruments.[12]

TABLE 2.   Form of *Kambing slem*

Section A (measures 1–9): Unaccompanied flute solo.

Section A1 (measures 10–21): Extended repeat of opening solo over piano ostinato.

Section A2 (measures 22–33): Flute an octave higher with increased ornamentation over new piano ostinato.

Section A3 (measures 34–48): Piano only with melody (taken from flute) over shifting ostinato.

Section A4 (measures 49–61): Flute an octave higher with little ornamentation; melody doubled in piano bass (some heterophony between the two); shifting ostinato in piano treble.

EXAMPLE 36 *Kambing slem*. Transcription and arrangement by McPhee for flute and piano, mm. 10–24.

Lagu ardja is quoted in the middle movement ("Nocturne") of *Tabuh-Tabuhan* and has already been discussed in connection with that piece. *Kambing slem*, from 1935, is similar. It is essentially a series of variations on a *suling* (bamboo flute) melody, taken from the *gamelan arja* repertory, a popular theater form with singing in which the *suling* is often an "obligato [*sic*] instrument, weaving ornamental figuration around the voice in the octave above."[13] McPhee uses ornamentation as the basis for variation and claims to have set the nine-bar melody "in relief" with his piano accompaniment.[14] The work is structured as shown in table 2.

The flute part is based on a six-note scale, which is usual for *suling arja,* and the piano draws from the same pitch group, with one notable exception—section A2. (In example 36, compare section A1, beginning at measure 10, and A2, beginning at measure 22.) At section A2 McPhee's own compositional style shines out of an accompaniment filled with Balinese gestures. The flute melody continues to revolve around its tonic (A) while three ostinatos are layered below. Although the use of such interlocking ostinatos is traditionally Balinese, it is also a longstanding trait in McPhee's work and is employed here with a characteristic touch: multiple tonal centers. The piano bass sounds a shifting pattern of C and F. Above it, two mirrored ostinatos are heard, one in augmentation of the other. Both center around focal pitches of the flute scale (A and E) but are approached by semitones (G♯ and D♯), notes outside the flute's realm. Another notable feature is the heterophonic ornamentation of the flute melody by the piano right hand in A4 (ex. 37). Such a device occupies the ground shared both by authentic *suling* practice (compare with McPhee's transcription of ornamentation for another *suling* melody in example 38) and by McPhee's own musical sensibility.

EXAMPLE 37   *Kambing slem,* mm. 49−52.

218

EXAMPLE 38   *Pererén arja.* Transcription by McPhee from *Music in Bali* (ex. 287).

FOUR IROQUOIS DANCES

As in his gamelan transcriptions and *Tabuh-Tabuhan,* McPhee once again united composition with ethnomusicology in his *Four Iroquois Dances* of 1944–45. Although he had once expressed disdain for American Indian music (see Chapter 7), he seems to have had a change of heart. He certainly was scrupulous in research for the composition, for his papers at UCLA contain a large group of articles on American Indian repertories. Most prominent among them are studies by George Herzog, with whom

McPhee seems to have maintained a professional connection until at least 1948, when Herzog moved from Columbia University to Indiana University. McPhee was already exploring general literature on the subject in the fall of 1941, when he wrote Margaret Mead asking about the reliability of Clark Wissler's *American Indian* of 1922.[15]

McPhee scored the *Dances* for woodwinds, horns, trumpets, strings, timpani, maracas, and tom-tom and introduced the published score with a statement clearly describing the sources and his role in arranging them:

> The musical material was taken from records made by William N. Fenton and published by the Library of Congress in an album titled Songs from the Iroquois Longhouse. . . . The melodic structure of each chant is left intact; the stanzas are repeated several times with a different orchestration. Only in the final Medicine Dance, . . . have I found it necessary to resort to a construction, however simple, of my own.[16]

In the first three movements—"Corn Dance," "Eagle Dance," and "Scalping Dance"—McPhee adheres fastidiously to the traditional sources. He makes some alterations in structure (for example, his "Eagle Dance" closes with a return to the opening material, a symmetrical device absent from the recording) and injects other touches of his own, yet generally he transfers the originals to a new medium. Unison writing abounds (the recordings feature solos or unison singing by two performers), and instruments often alternate to imitate dialogue between singers. Even when McPhee imposes his own ideas, they in some way relate to the Iroquois songs. In "Corn Dance," for example, the final section diverges from a mostly unison setting to present the Iroquois melody heterophonically (ex. 39); heterophony, in turn, is a principal characteristic of this repertory.

The *Iroquois Dances* give insights into McPhee's methods as a transcriber. In "Corn Dance," for example, he shapes the form of his instrumental version to highlight a particular nuance in the Iroquois singing. "Corn Dance" repeats one section from the original song (itself with an internal repetition), the first time (measures 1–10) with G, B, C♮, and D as the principal tones, the second (measures 36–38) with G, B, C♯, and D.

EXAMPLE 39   "Corn Dance" from *Iroquois Dances,* mm. 51–56.

(*continued*)

EXAMPLE 39 (*continued*)

Perhaps McPhee was trying to represent both alternatives, for on Fenton's recording the C is neither sharp nor natural but somewhere in between.

As McPhee acknowledged, his transcription of "Medicine Dance," the final movement of the suite, takes more liberties than any other with the Iroquois material. It is based on two rhythmic patterns, one of sixteen measures and the other of four (as McPhee transcribes them). McPhee retained the melodic shape that accompanies the first pattern in the Iroquois original, but the actual intervals are different (exs. 40 and 41). He also made rhythmic changes. As in previous movements, McPhee imposes a meter on free-flowing material. He also inserts a favorite rhythmic pattern ♩. ♩. ♩, which is found later on in the field recording of "Medicine Dance" but not in this particular spot.

EXAMPLE 40   "Medicine Dance" from *Iroquois Dances*. Rhythm of mm. 1–2 in timpani.

EXAMPLE 41   Corresponding rhythm from recording of "Medicine Dance" in *Songs of the Iroquois Longhouse*.

McPhee begins his "Medicine Dance" by stating the entire first motive in the timpani and strings. The second motive is then superimposed in the woodwinds over a fragmented version of the first (ex. 42). Adding a C♮ in the strings at measure 21 produces simple, open harmonies that tug, in typical McPhee fashion, against the C♯ in the woodwinds and horns.

Yet on the whole *Four Iroquois Dances* is not a successful composition. Obsessed with authenticity, especially with representing the unison singing style on the recordings, McPhee produces arrangements that come off as too literal. The piece lacks the rhythmic drive of *Tabuh-Tabuhan* and timbral pungency of the Concerto for Piano with Wind Octette as well as

EXAMPLE 42   "Medicine Dance" from *Iroquois Dances,* mm. 17–22.

(*continued*)

EXAMPLE 42 (*continued*)

some of his other engaging compositional traits: layered textures, cross-rhythms, and bimodal juxtapositions (the latter meekly present in parts of the *Iroquois Dances*). And it has none of the balanced blend of authentic traditional material with effective reshaping found in both the *Sea Shanty Suite* and *Tabuh-Tabuhan*. Perhaps the root of the problem lay in transporting the Iroquois melodies so far from their native setting and timbre yet not properly outfitting them for the voyage. In the *Sea Shanty Suite* McPhee kept voices as the principal medium and added a lightly scored accompaniment that gestured toward British folk instrumental styles. In *Tabuh-Tabuhan* he centered the work around the timbre of its native source by using a percussive "nuclear gamelan." With *Iroquois Dances,* however, he leaves behind the original scoring—voice and tom-tom or rattle—and employs an alien sound world. In a way, *Iroquois Dances* fits into a lineage of orchestral music by Americans that draws upon traditional sources—works such as Arthur Farwell's *Navajo War Dance* for piano (1905), Daniel Gregory Mason's *String Quartet on Negro Themes* (1918–19), or John Powell's *Negro Rhapsody* (1918). But it shows a significant change of attitude. Rather than appropriating the music of another culture and completely transforming it into a Western concert idiom, McPhee bears greater reverence toward the originals. While in *Iroquois Dances* he did not find a completely satisfying balance between composition and transcription, he was heading in an important direction.

TRANSITIONS

In 1954, after a nine-year hiatus from composition, McPhee completed his next major work, *Transitions* for orchestra. Although it contains no Balinese material, *Transitions* fits a pattern that had begun to emerge for McPhee: composing in the Balinese manner by drawing upon preexistent musics. Unlike *Iroquois Dances,* however, he poured more of his own invention into this composition. McPhee saw *Transitions* as "really a marine piece, an evocation of some legendary coastline, flooded with Arctic sunlight or lost in tropic fog,"[17] and the sea setting was inspired by a British shanty, "Lowlands Away," which is not quoted until the very end of *Transitions* (in the horns at measure 368). But the interval and rhythm of the shanty's opening two notes serve as the basis for much of the work. McPhee claimed he turned to "Lowlands Away" because it had "long remained fixed in my mind for its nostalgia and special sea atmosphere, and I had always intended to use it some time as [the] point of departure for an orchestral work."[18] Indeed, there was reason for reminiscence: he had already set the song in his *Sea Shanty Suite* of 1929, and he was in close touch with that piece while *Transitions* was being composed because he was rehearsing it for performance at a Composers Forum concert on November 6, 1954.

Transitions is essentially built of three large sections—or, as McPhee put it, "three connected movements"[19]—and a coda. McPhee's own formal analysis subdivides each section into several parts and shows that the work has a kind of crazy-quilt character. Although McPhee does not indicate them as such, recurring sections are all variants of their first statements (see table 3).

Many traits from McPhee's early works surface again in *Transitions*. He had played with thematic connections between movements in both his Concerto for Piano with Wind Octette and in *Tabuh-Tabuhan*. Here, as his formal scheme shows, themes A, B, C, E, F, and G all recur, making the piece one interconnected whole. Again the piano is prominent in the orchestra, joining occasionally with the glockenspiel (measures 35–44) and timpani (measures 242 and following) for a percussive effect much like that of the "nuclear gamelan" of *Tabuh-Tabuhan,* although here used more sparely. And the influence of the gamelan is occasionally present, even though there are no overt Balinese references (McPhee reported to Aaron Copland in the midst of composing, "So far, no Bali themes or treatment, you'll be glad to know"[20]). The section beginning in measure 164, for example, is built on a three-pitch ostinato pattern in the piano, which is augmented in the flute above (ex. 43). Also, the gong is used to punctuate several major divisions in the work—for example, in measure 181, at the end of the middle section.

Perhaps the most striking characteristic of the work is its relationship to McPhee's earlier choral setting of "Lowlands Away." His two-piano accompaniment there used many quartal and quintal harmonies, the latter

TABLE 3.   Structure of *Transitions*

Themes	
A (mm. 1–32); B (mm. 33–50);	
C (mm. 51[?]–74); D (mm. 75–97);	
A (mm. 98–114)	first section
E (mm. 115–29); C (mm. 130–63);	
E (mm. 164–81)	middle section
F (mm. 182–216); G (mm. 217–23);	
F (mm. 224–93); G (mm. 294–307);	
F (mm. 308–18)	main last section
A (mm. 319–31)	climax and link to
B (mm. 332–67)	coda
H (mm. 368–72)	key motif
	(quotation from
	Lowlands Away)
E (mm. 373–end)	closing phrase

Note: This diagram is McPhee's own, taken from a typescript program note. Measure numbers have been added by the author.

EXAMPLE 43   *Transitions,* mm. 164–66, piano and flute.

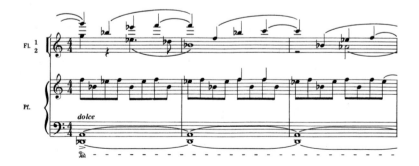

EXAMPLE 44 *Transitions,* mm. 1–4. Trombone, tuba, timpani, and string bass are tacet here.

EXAMPLE 45   *Transitions,* mm. 9–13, strings only.

often with an added second. In *Transitions* he employs the same practice from the outset, where the piano, strings, and woodwinds sound C and G, with D interposed and, for added flair, a B♭ anticipation to the C (ex. 44). Also, the opening rhythmic gesture of the "Lowlands" melody (♩ ♩) occurs frequently in both the choral setting and *Transitions.*

Other aspects of *Transitions* are consistent with McPhee's previous works. He returned to asymmetrically accented rhythmic patterns, frequently focusing them on a single pitch. Soon after the opening of the work, for example, the strings hammer out triplet Cs that are jolted by shifting accents and a varied quarter-note placement in the string bass (ex. 45). Other instances of cross-accents can be found throughout the work— for example, in the opening of the middle section, where the piano's steady eighth notes on D sound in the midst of an uneven A and D pattern in the flute and where the familiar 3 + 3 + 2 rhythm enters in the bassoon at measure 118. Also the scoring has become much thinner than in earlier compositions, with the rhythmic patterns carried mainly by strings.

Yet while *Transitions* stands tall next to the *Iroquois Dances,* it is a tentative piece, showing the long years that McPhee had been out of touch with his craft. Ironically, its greatest problem comes in the transitional passages. Each of the three principal sections and several of the inner subsections are linked by a sudden, subdued hush that heralds the entrance of new material. These junctures serve to darken the stage for perhaps too long before a new scene begins. Rather than surging forward, the piece sinks during these moments.

But the work helped McPhee regain confidence as a composer. By the time of his next opus, written three years later, the results would be quite different.

SYMPHONY NO. 2 ("PASTORALE")

With his Second Symphony, written in 1957, McPhee returned once again to the sounds of Bali. He did so with assurance and imagination, producing a work that began to move his Balinese experience in new directions. Whereas *Tabuh-Tabuhan* was filled with the flash and fire of the gamelan, Symphony No. 2 recalls the island's music through a scrim—distant, hazy, seductively mysterious. In program notes for the symphony, McPhee acknowledged the presence of Balinese materials:

> It is primarily a lyrical work, based largely on pentatonic scale
> forms, and making considerable use of Balinese melodic material
> collected during the years I spent on the island of Bali. The
> various melodies employed here no longer retain their original

Balinese character. They serve primarily as motifs, as points of departure for the creation of a broader and more personal melodic line. All have continued to hold strong nostalgic associations in my memory, and one or two I have used in other works, but always treated in an entirely different fashion.[21]

The Second Symphony is "nostalgic" in several ways, not just in calling upon Balinese materials but in using compositional methods that reached back even to earlier, pre-Bali days. As McPhee returned to writing music, first with *Transitions* and then with the Second Symphony, he seemed suffused with memories of the past. The very act of composing probably brought this on, as did renewed acquaintance with his early works through performances and recordings. In the Second Symphony he drew upon the formal structure of *Transitions,* as he outlined in typescript program notes:

The symphony is cyclic in form, consisting of three movements, which might be described as exposition, interlude, and transformed restatement. The work is framed by the opening section of the first movement, which not only terminates the first movement, but forms the conclusion to the complete symphony.[22]

As with the Concerto for Piano with Wind Octette and *Tabuh-Tabuhan,* the three movements of the symphony have thematic connections but even more internal cross-references than previously. Each of the symphony's movements is sectional, another longtime McPhee practice. The opening movement, for example, is built in five parts, the first of which returns as the fifth. Here, however, the individual parts have more strength and vitality than in *Transitions.* They pull together into an organic whole.

Another tie to McPhee's past is found in the way he breaks down the gamelan material into small pieces, often alluding to a melody rather than clearly stating it. The beginning of the symphony, a critical section that, as McPhee said, "frames" the composition, provides a good example of this technique. At measure 5 (ex. 46) the combined winds imply a melody yet never fully articulate it. The outer interval (B–F♯) sounds in the clarinet, followed by the oboe (measure 7) and flute (measure 9), and the inner

EXAMPLE 46   Symphony No. 2, first movement, mm. 1–9. Bassoon, trumpet, trombone, tuba, glockenspiel, and harp are tacet here.

(continued)

EXAMPLE 46 (*continued*)

(*continued*)

EXAMPLE 46 (*continued*)

pitches are in the flute (measure 6) and strings. The motive suggested here was to be forthrightly stated by McPhee later that same year as the principal theme in his next composition, the Nocturne for Chamber Orchestra.

Throughout the Second Symphony allusion reigns. McPhee describes the first movement as "impressionistic—color is withdrawn from what seems to be a mist-shrouded tonal painting." [23] He goes on to call the final movement "vigorous," one that builds up and then "sink[s] back into the mist, and the end reverts to the veiled quality of the opening." He was intrigued, as both a prose writer and a composer, with suggestively conjuring up sensory images of Bali.

In his notes to the Second Symphony, McPhee wrote: "Certain passages, notably toward the middle of the first movement, derive from Balinese *gamelan* methods of orchestration." Indeed, the material in that section recurs throughout the work and is based, as Richard Mueller has termed it, on the "*jobog* principle" of Balinese orchestration, which is central to the repertory of the *gamelan pelégongan*. [24] McPhee had drawn upon this gamelan style frequently in *Tabuh-Tabuhan*. Two basic elements inspired him: (1) ornamentation of a central ostinato with passing or connecting tones and (2) use of a concurrent bass ostinato that shifts regularly between a low and high chord. [25] The middle section of the symphony's first movement employs the latter characteristic; there the strings and piano together form a pendulum of recurring high-low chords (ex. 47). A similar procedure occurs beginning at measure 112 in the first movement, measure 32 in the second, and measure 28 in the third.

McPhee prunes down the orchestration from what it had been in *Tabuh-Tabuhan,* but it is by no means as lean as in his next work, the Nocturne for Chamber Orchestra. Like *Tabuh-Tabuhan,* the symphony has a "nuclear gamelan" of piano, glockenspiel, xylophone, and marimba. It functions as a unit, often when accompanying wind solos. Throughout, individual instrumental lines are often exposed; the parts weave in and out and often do not sound simultaneously.

McPhee's use of pitches adheres mostly to his practice in *Tabuh-Tabuhan.* He employs many four- and five-note Balinese patterns, although in the symphony more areas stay solely within the focal pitch group of the

EXAMPLE 47   Symphony No. 2, first movement, mm. 71–72. Flute, piccolo, bassoon, trombone, tuba, timpani, and glockenspiel are tacet here.

moment. The opening of the first movement (see ex. 46), for example, draws exclusively from one five-note collection (E, F♯, G, B, and D). But the first section of the second movement is the most unusual for McPhee for it is written solely in white notes and uses dancelike supporting rhythms and wide textural spacing—all reminiscent of Aaron Copland's *Appalachian Spring* of 1945. McPhee had kept up with Copland's work over the years, as was evident in his reviews for *Modern Music,* and may have been inspired by *Appalachian Spring* not only in this section, where the opening gesture of the violin melody even suggests "Simple Gifts," but also in the atmospheric quality and instrumental counterpoint of theme fragments at the beginning.

With Symphony No. 2, then, McPhee managed to draw fruitfully upon his compositional style of the past at the same time that he began a new stage in his relationship to the music of the gamelan—one in which the borrowed materials were more subtly and deeply integrated.

NOCTURNE FOR CHAMBER ORCHESTRA

The next year (1958) McPhee wrote his Nocturne for Chamber Orchestra, a lovely and successful work that is an outgrowth not only of his stay in Bali but also, like the Second Symphony, of *Tabuh-Tabuhan.* Its starting point is the middle movement of *Tabuh-Tabuhan,* also called "Nocturne," to which it is closely related in mood, shape, and texture. *Tabuh-Tabuhan's* "Nocturne" featured a *suling* flute melody in a rounded form of four parts, the first returning at the close. Its scoring was mostly lean, often for two pianos, marimba, xylophone, celesta, and woodwinds, with plucked strings used percussively. The Nocturne combines these elements within smaller dimensions. It is shorter and uses fewer instruments (no brass and only one piano). But perhaps the principal difference lies in its composer's increased maturity; as in the Second Symphony, Balinese elements have been comfortably imbedded into McPhee's vocabulary. The Nocturne has less raw energy than *Tabuh-Tabuhan* but more of a gentle swing, and its scoring resonates with the metallic sonorites of the gamelan.

Although the Nocturne has only one movement, like *Transitions* it is divided into many sections. At its core is the familiar "nuclear gamelan": piano, xylophone, glockenspiel, celesta, and a small gong. And as in so many other works by McPhee, the concerto principle is a shaping force. Sections with a limpid flute solo alternate with ones featuring the nuclear gamelan. The opening section is heard at three different pitch levels, with the flute solo centering first on C (measures 3–6), then B♭ (measures 8–10) and C♯ (measures 13–17). A contrasting section beginning at measure 20 is largely percussive, without a woodwind melody, and presents several irregular ostinatos heterophonically, with the glockenspiel elaborating a pattern in the piano and strings. A third section begins in measure 38 with the flute reentering to paraphrase the opening melody, which is tossed between oboe (measure 46) and flute (measure 48). Another heterophonic ostinato section starts at measure 53, with glockenspiel, celesta, and piano again at the fore. A celesta-piano duet (measure 90 and following), again heterophonic, leads to the return of the opening material at its original pitch level in measure 101.

In the Nocturne McPhee draws largely upon Balinese pitch collections but in a simpler way than previously. At the opening, four-note patterns reminiscent of the *gamelan angklung* (compare ex. 48 with ex. 49) sound alone, with no other pattern juxtaposed. Yet in other instances, such conjunctions occur. The second statement of the flute theme in measure 8, for example, combines the pitches of B♭ minor with a raised third degree (D♮).

Several characteristics stand out in the piece. First is the effective use of heterophony found in all the sections featuring nuclear gamelan. In some instances this technique, so central to the multilayered texture of Balinese music, is employed simply, between glockenspiel and piano (ex. 50). In others, especially the final transition to the opening material, heterophony becomes the focal point, with the role of elaborator bandied between the two principal instruments for a beautifully layered exchange (ex. 51).

Perhaps the most successful aspect of the Nocturne, however, is its orchestration. Using a chamber ensemble with no brass and employing the

EXAMPLE 48 Nocturne for Chamber Orchestra, mm. 1–2. Flute, oboe, clarinet, bassoon, percussion, and celesta are tacet here.

EXAMPLE 49 *Gamelan angklung.* Transcription by McPhee from *Music in Bali* (ex. 239).

EXAMPLE 50 Nocturne for Chamber Orchestra, mm. 20–21, glockenspiel and piano only.

EXAMPLE 51   Nocturne for Chamber Orchestra, mm. 90–97. (Crayon markings in the score were made by Stokowski for the premiere performance.)

strings with a light hand makes the textures shimmer and the rhythms bounce. McPhee exploits a wide timbral palette, varying themes as much through instrumental color as through heterophony. In *Tabuh-Tabuhan's* "Nocturne" the flute carried the *suling* melody, perhaps out of McPhee's rigorous respect for the Balinese original. Here, however, various woodwind instruments share the melody for effective changes in tone color. The melody's second entrance, at measure 8, begins in the piccolo and then is elaborated by the clarinet. In the third statement, at measure 13, there is similar polyphonic interplay, this time between the flute and clarinet. Likewise, the reprise features first flute (measure 103), then oboe (measure 111), clarinet (measure 115), and finally clarinet and bassoon with flute

EXAMPLE 52   Concerto for Wind Orchestra, first movement, mm. 21–28.

242   (continued)

EXAMPLE 52 (continued)

(continued)

EXAMPLE 52 (*continued*)

(*continued*)

EXAMPLE 52 (*continued*)

(measure 125). With similar clarity and contrast the timbres of the nuclear gamelan stand out from the ensemble and often combine for variety in both sonority and textural density.

With both the Second Symphony and the Nocturne, McPhee was growing as a composer, devising new ways of absorbing the sounds of Bali into the substance of his musical language. Neither work is simply a recycling of *Tabuh-Tabuhan* but a fresh approach to material long admired.

CONCERTO FOR WIND ORCHESTRA

The Concerto for Wind Orchestra of 1960 would be McPhee's last completed work. While writing it, he was sick and even more spiritually depleted than had become the pattern. As a result the piece is only moderately successful.

Again he returned to the music of Bali, although this time he quoted directly—in some instances, almost desperately—from *Tabuh-Tabuhan*. Much of the concerto's first movement, for example, is culled from the earlier piece. The second section (see piano in ex. 52) is taken from the third section of *Tabuh-Tabuhan*'s first movement (ex. 53) and transposed down a tritone. This is followed by another borrowing.

The Wind Concerto has many other parallels to *Tabuh-Tabuhan* and follows what by now had become a familiar McPhee mold: three movements (fast, slow, very fast) sharing thematic relationships. The concerto principle dominates once again, although here in a freely structured way. The solo role, first taken by the trumpet, moves throughout the wind

EXAMPLE 53   *Tabuh-Tabuhan,* first movement, second piano, mm. 90–93.

ensemble. And the scoring, although new in eliminating strings (string bass and harp are present), falls back on a nuclear gamelan of piano, glockenspiel, marimba, and xylophone. Even McPhee's program notes for the piece seem a little hackneyed, using much the same language as those for the Second Symphony. However, he incorporates two new elements: the middle movement quotes "a type of romantic song popular in Sunda [Java]," and both the first and second movements use a melody by I Madé Lebah, McPhee's devoted musical comrade.[26] The Wind Concerto, sadly, marks a weary conclusion to four decades of composition.

Of the works composed during McPhee's musical renaissance of the 1950s, the Second Symphony and the Nocturne for Chamber Orchestra stand out as most successful. In them McPhee extended the techniques of neoclassicism through the use of traits from the Balinese gamelan and, by aiming for "anonymous expression," succeeded in finding a compatible synthesis between composition and transcription. In doing so he took part in one of the most significant movements of the twentieth century. As the "world's peoples" increasingly mingle, to use Henry Cowell's phrase, so does their music. McPhee stands among those open-minded explorers who have attempted to distill a new essence from such global interconnections. As fruits of this process and as beautifully conceived works of art, the Nocturne and Second Symphony—together with *Tabuh-Tabuhan,* the transcriptions for Western instruments, and his earlier compositions—deserve to be revived.

10

THE YEARS IN CALIFORNIA

 1960–64

           The 1960s opened with two important break-
throughs for McPhee. Within days of completing his Concerto for Wind
Orchestra, in June 1960, he received a large commission and an advance of
one thousand dollars from Broadcast Music, Inc. (BMI) for an orchestral
work in celebration of its twentieth anniversary. Even more significant was
the offer of a teaching position at the University of California in Los
Angeles.

           Mantle Hood, who was responsible for bringing McPhee to UCLA,
has recalled the genesis of the appointment:

> In 1958, when I came back through New York, after being in
> Indonesia for two years, I went to see him. He was living in very
> modest quarters—with a quick look around you could tell
> things weren't all that good financially. I said 'Colin, why don't
> you come out to UCLA and do some teaching?' Well, he couldn't
> stand the idea of teaching; he would hate the idea of teaching.
> I persisted in a soft way, and when I got back to UCLA I phoned
> him and finally talked him into trying it.[1]

So in September 1960 Colin McPhee took the step that was increasingly
providing financial security for many American composers: he became a

university professor. He was apprehensive about leaving friends in New York ("friends I never see, but feel at least geographically close to") and a bit daunted by the challenge of teaching ("the courses seem as unpredictable to me as a cadenza").[2] Before moving he stored many of his belongings but remarked to Sidney Cowell how whittled down his possessions had become: "I can't help smiling when you mention things to leave behind. Do you realize I have nothing—no clothes, no books, no nothing at all. All my clothes and belongings you could put into a zipper bag, after records and films are packed."[3]

Upon reaching Los Angeles McPhee settled in the Dracker Hotel in Westwood Village—quite a contrast from conditions on Manhattan's West Twenty-second Street. His apartment was comfortable, close to campus, and contained a rented piano. During the fall semester he taught ethnomusicology and composition under a part-time appointment. At first he found teaching difficult, especially the composition course. In December he wrote Oliver Daniel, "The composition class, though only elementary, throws me, for lack of experience. The really advanced Ethnomusicology course goes better, though far from smoothly."[4] But by February 1961 he was happily reporting, "I have found my level, I think, and am beginning to enjoy it. It is too bad that it all must end in May, so soon, so soon."[5] That summer he enthusiastically described his ethnomusicology students to Sidney Cowell: "The class was truly *brilliant*. Most having done work already in Persia, Greece, India, Mexico, and Thailand. Am reading papers now, and very touched by the accurate and painstaking answers."[6]

Despite the stimulation of students and the peace of a paycheck, McPhee felt lonely in Los Angeles: "No one my age to make friends with—and the friendly students so separated by time."[7] Yet it was preferable to the abject poverty of New York. From all accounts McPhee was a gifted teacher. According to Mantle Hood, "A great delight and sadness simultaneously was the discovery during those 3 years at UCLA that he loved to teach, and the students loved him. He gave so much. It was sad that he hadn't discovered it earlier." A longtime friend of McPhee and associate of Margaret Mead, the anthropologist Rhoda Métraux, visited him in Los Angeles in late 1963 and saw a striking change from the man she had known in New York:

It was almost as if darkness turned to light and he found himself living in a sunny world. He had an admiring, affectionate group of students, he discovered himself as a teacher, a role that to his own surprise, he enjoyed immensely, and he had solid academic backing and new, mature friendships. He also knew that his most important work on Balinese music would be published in great style.[8]

Alongside this new-found career, McPhee continued to compose and work on production of *Music in Bali,* which had been inching forward since Yale University Press accepted the manuscript in 1958. He also made one last trip to Asia—to Tokyo for a conference entitled "East-West Music Encounter" held April 17–24, 1961. McPhee at first declined the invitation because of financial concerns. But he finally accepted and went with five other Americans: Elliott Carter, Henry Cowell, Lou Harrison, Mantle Hood, and Virgil Thomson.[9] McPhee spoke on April 19 on the topic "Problems of Indonesian Musical Tradition Today (The Music Crisis in Bali Today)."[10] He reiterated the belief that had shaped much of his writing about Balinese music—that the old styles were being replaced by a flashier, less musically interesting repertory: "Balanced form and metric breadth have given way to restless fantasias in which short excerpts from traditional melodies follow each other in purely arbitrary succession." McPhee described his efforts during the 1930s to convince musicians of the importance of preserving their musical heritage, and he went on to propose a comprehensive project: "to record every type of music still to be found on the island, and to revive, if possible, traditional styles of the past. Copies of the recordings could be [made] . . . readily available to Balinese musicians." McPhee was calling for a continuation of his own work in the thirties, for a chance to record ensembles on the island before the old traditions died away.

For nearly twenty-five years McPhee had dreamed of returning to Bali to resume his work. While he had also proposed trips to various other locales, Bali remained the spot he most wanted to visit. In 1962, probably not long after the East-West Conference, Mantle Hood drew up a proposal for a five-man team to spend fourteen months in Bali. He and McPhee were to head it, working with a professional photographer, a sound engineer, and an anthropologist. Hood has recalled: "We tried and tried but we couldn't get the funding. As I recall it was a little under $100,000. . . . That same year the National Science Foundation gave one-and-a-half million dollars to find a fish they thought was off the shores of Madagascar."

In February 1962, while the Bali proposal was pending, McPhee made the first of several stays in the hospital. Others followed in December 1962 and April and June 1963. He had cirrhosis of the liver, a condition that steadily worsened: "Years of malnutrition and too much alcohol in proportion finally undermined me."[11] Margaret Mead visited him in the hospital in December 1962 and reported to Sidney Cowell, "I saw him last week. He's frail—a little less pleased with life than usual! But he quickly fires with enthusiasm again. What he really wants to do is to go to Indonesia once more and look at the music."[12]

McPhee persisted in looking for funds to take him to Bali, even after Hood's proposal fell through. In January 1963 he began plans for a solo expedition and consulted Virgil Thomson for advice about funding:

> I am writing to ask if you have any idea where I could turn for an
> independent grant to take me East for a year. I'd spend part of
> the time in Bali noting cultural changes that had taken place
> since I left, interviewing musicians. . . . I would also like to
> explore the musical situation in one or two nearby islands such
> as Madura, Lombok, and Celebes, where little musical research
> has been undertaken. . . . I've talked in the past to Rockefeller
> about this, but have always been turned down, in spite of my
> knowledge and experience.[13]

Perhaps his plans were given impetus by a proposal from Stanford University Press for him to undertake a new book on Balinese music from a "completely different angle."[14] By June 1963 Margaret Mead had collected two thousand dollars for the trip.[15] But by September McPhee told her that he was not well enough to travel alone: "I'm far from strong, need occasional transfusions, and frequent doctor's check-ups."[16]

The commission McPhee had received from BMI in June 1960 called for an orchestral work "with or without soloist." Once again, Oliver Daniel helped McPhee obtain the assignment. McPhee had asked Daniel to play his Second Symphony for Carl Haverlin at BMI and to "persuade him a BMI commission for another work would be both encouraging and literally life-saving." [17] After the commission was in hand, McPhee worked on the piece intermittently during the early 1960s. For some time it seemed as if he was going to write another piano concerto, but eventually the work took on the title Symphony No. 3. [18] In the summer of 1960 McPhee promised that the score would be ready "by early fall, at the latest," a promise he was unable to keep. [19] Little seems to have been accomplished on the piece in 1961, and McPhee returned to it in the summer of 1962 while he was in residence at Huntington Hartford. That fall a publishing agreement was signed with C. F. Peters. [20] But with repeated trips to the hospital, classes to prepare, and *Music in Bali* in production, he worked on the piece only sporadically. Yet it remained on his conscience. In the spring of 1963 he closed a letter to his old friend Marian Eames with a poem that had been floating through his head when he woke up that morning:

> Little nips of brandy
> Little spots of tea
> Help the great composer
> Write his symphony. [21]

Although the symphony was never completed, McPhee continued teaching at UCLA for the next two and a half years until failing health forced him to resign in November 1963. [22] He had recovered from repeated attacks of cirrhosis of the liver and had been given loving attention by friends and students alike. During his first bout, for example, which entailed two full days of transfusions, students responded by donating blood, and he received "loads of mail from N.Y., and a steady stream of visitors here— once twelve in one day!" [23] He was also helped by UCLA colleagues, especially Mantle Hood and his wife Shirley, who took him into their home after he was released from the hospital in late March, and from John

Vincent, who made arrangements for McPhee to stay at the Huntington Hartford during the summer of 1962.[24]

During these years McPhee kept working with Yale University Press on production of his book. The copyediting and proofreading dragged on as interminably as had the writing. Most delays came from McPhee himself. According to Hood, "He was meticulous. I first saw the manuscript [in 1956] and in my judgment it was not too far from ready for the press then. But he went on and did a great deal to it."

While McPhee was at UCLA, the book repeatedly seemed near release, only to be held back by another delay. In January 1960 McPhee wrote Chávez that it was going into production and would be out "around September [1960]."[25] By September, however, he was writing Sidney Cowell, "The amount of unforeseen last minute work on the book, to prevent costly misunderstandings, is unbelievable. . . . I hand in the [revised] ms. for better or worse tomorrow."[26] In June 1961 he was "going through the edited ms. . . . which I've had for three months" and hoped the book would be out the following spring.[27] One year later he had finished correcting proofs of music examples, an early stage in production.[28] By December 1962 galleys were arriving daily: "I'm literally snowed under."[29]

Despite steady physical deterioration, McPhee earnestly read proofs. Jane Olson, McPhee's editor at Yale, reported to Sidney Cowell in late October of 1963:

> Unfortunately, although we have done everything possible to speed up the appearance of the book, it is still a long way from publication. He [McPhee] is, as you must know if you are a friend, a perfectionist, and every time he has proofs to check, he seems unable to release them.[30]

Finally, late in the fall of 1963, Olson asked Rhoda Métraux, who was traveling to Los Angeles, to get the last set of galleys from McPhee. Métraux recalls her meetings with McPhee:

So for a period I worked with Colin, went over the galleys with
him again and again—it seemed he could not let them go, he
was a perfectionist and a little obsessed with this work—and
finally I suggested that on a certain day, at a certain hour, he
would hand over the proofs, and so free himself. On that day, at
that hour, I had a friend stop by the apartment and she picked up
the package of proofs and took them away; I stayed and Colin
talked at length, as he had each day, about the discoveries he had
made [through teaching] about living happily. . . . It was as if,
having sent the galleys on, he had voluntarily resigned from
living.[31]

By the fall of 1963, as McPhee's health worsened, his handwriting became a
spindly scratch. Few letters were typed, and the sentences often were
disconnected. Shirley Hood Hawkins took him into her home for a time,
but in December he was placed in the Crescent Bay Convalescent Hospital. On January 7, 1964, he died.[32]

In death, as in life, there was recognition of a respectful but subdued
sort. A memorial concert was held at UCLA on January 14, 1964, and was
attended by a large crowd of students. William Melnitz, dean of the
College of Fine Arts at UCLA, spoke, as did Roy Harris and Charles Seeger.
Some of McPhee's compositions were played, and telegrams were read
from Jane Belo, Sidney Cowell, Claire Holt, Mantle Hood, Otto Luening,
Margaret Mead, Rhoda Métraux, and Leopold Stokowski.[33] On February
4, a gathering of McPhee's old friends took place in New York. According
to Oliver Daniel, "We played two tapes—his Nocturne and his Pastorale
[Second] Symphony. . . . Everyone told little anecdotes and stories
about Colin, and it was all very warm and filled with affection and
remembrance."[34]

In 1966, two years after McPhee's death, Yale University Press finally
published *Music in Bali*. Some thirty years had passed since McPhee began
writing the book, and thirty-five since he first set sail for the island.[35] *Music
in Bali* is monumental in every sense of the word. A massive volume (430
amply sized pages with 358 musical examples and 120 photographs, all by

McPhee), it is a lasting chronicle of a complex musical culture. Reviewing *Music in Bali* in 1968, the ethnomusicologist Judith Becker called it "one of the most carefully written, complete and precise descriptions of any musical style outside the Western world."[36] Mantle Hood's foreword to the volume pinpoints the dimensions of McPhee's achievement:

> This is a book which could have been written by only one man—a sensitive composer with a deep musicological interest, a man whose musical ear and musical integrity could not be content with a superficial examination. How very few composers in the Western world have afforded themselves the considerable time and profound experience of learning to comprehend another musical language! For the Western composer, performer, and teacher of music, Balinese music is here described in its own terms and clearly evaluated and explained. For the humanist, the social scientist, and the anthropologist, McPhee has placed Balinese music within the proper context of society. For present and future generations of Balinese musicians *Music in Bali* will stand as a record of their most sacred heritage.[37]

Today, Western musicians and scholars turn to the book to learn about Balinese music as practiced during the 1930s, and Balinese musicians consult it as a record of musical styles that have either changed or vanished. I Madé Bandem, director of the Arts Academy of Indonesian Dance in Denpasar, Bali, says that McPhee's book is a basic text for his students.[38]

Throughout the book there is a beautiful balance of penetrating musical analysis with readability. The prose artist of *A House in Bali* is ever present. His tone may be less poetic, yet within the constraints of scholarship he uses imaginative language to color descriptions vividly. In addition, each chapter is lavishly illustrated with McPhee's own musical transcriptions, many of which represent whole sections of gamelan compositions. Every page reveals his years of reflection on Balinese music.

Music in Bali will live on, together with McPhee's other writings and musical compositions, as a tribute to his lifelong commitment and passion. Henry Cowell succinctly summarized McPhee's contribution in a eulogy written after his old friend's death, and his message continues to resonate:

Colin McPhee, before he went to Bali, was one of the most
prodigious young composers in America. While in Bali he
became a world-authority on every detail of Balinese music.

He was a great pioneer in composing for Western instruments so
that they sounded completely and astoundingly Indonesian in his
hands.

He was unique.[39]

Despite the years of poverty and despair, McPhee did indeed make a
unique contribution to forging a link between East and West. He foresaw a
time when musics of the globe would become increasingly more inter-
twined, and he laid a foundation for the cross-cultural exchanges that have
intensified with each passing year. In 1973 the composer Steve Reich wrote
that "non-Western music is presently the single most important source of
new ideas for Western composers and musicians."[40] Colin McPhee was
among the pioneers to explore that potential. By living in two worlds, he
helped shape the future.

APPENDIX

CATALOGUE OF THE MUSIC
OF COLIN McPHEE

This catalogue includes all the known compositions of Colin McPhee, whether extant or not. Transcriptions are listed in Appendix B. Since lists of McPhee's works, including those that he compiled, are filled with errors, users will find that dates here often differ from those published elsewhere. McPhee himself confirmed that Reis-47, for example, has misinformation, including a piece he did not compose: "The Reis material is not very exact, and list[s] one work of mine, entitled *Bali,* which is an error, for there is not such a piece. In addition, certain scores listed there have long since been destroyed" (McPhee to Ruth Watanabe, March 28, 1955, Sibley Music Library).

Unless otherwise indicated, all sources are found in the McPhee Collection at UCLA. Most programs for his Peabody student recitals are located in the private collection of Sylvan Levin in New York.

Finally, the catalogue numbers here supersede those in my dissertation on McPhee.

ABBREVIATIONS FOR SOURCES

ACA-55   "Confidential Report for ACA [American Composers Alliance] Negotiating Committee." April 25 [1955 or 1956]. Filled out by McPhee in application for ACA membership.

AMP   Associated Music Publishers, New York

CaOONL	Music Division, National Library of Canada, Ottawa
CFP	C. F. Peters Corporation, New York
CLU	Music Library, University of California, Los Angeles
CM-CLU	Colin McPhee Collection, Ethnomusicology Archive, University of California, Los Angeles
Ms	Manuscript
NN	Music Division, Performing Arts Research Center, New York Public Library
OD	Collection of Oliver Daniel, Ardsley, New York
Reis-30	Claire Reis, *American Composers of Today*. New York: The United States Section of the International Society for Contemporary Music, 1930.
Reis-47	Claire Reis, *Composers in America: Biographical Sketches of Contemporary Composers with a Record of Their Works*. New York: The Macmillan Company, 1947.
Schwerké-25	McPhee to Irving Schwerké, Paris, [May 20, 1925]. Schwerké Collection, Library of Congress.

Also, standard bibliographic abbreviations for instruments and performers are used here; see list on p. xix.

1912

1. [Piece for Children's Percussion Band with Strings]. Score lost.
SOURCE: McPhee to Dr. William Mayer, Monday [postmarked September 2, 1942], collection of Beata Sauerlander.

Pre-1915

Source for nos. 2–5: untitled Toronto newspaper review of the Hambourg Conservatory's annual concert, May 27, 1915; also in *Musical Canada* 10 (July 1915): 67. No. 4 was the only work actually performed on the concert. All the scores are lost.

2. *Album Leaves*. Pf.

3. *Caprices*. Pf.

4. *Polonaise.* Pf.

5. *The Robin.* Voice, pf (one of a group of songs); text by Pauline Johnson.

1916

6. *Four Piano Sketches,* op. 1. Pf.   MOVEMENTS: "April," "Prelude," "Water Nymph," and "Silhouette."
   PUBLICATION DATA: Toronto: Empire Music and Travel Club, 1916; copy at CaOONL. "Water Nymph" was also published in the *Canadian Journal of Music* 2 (February 1916): 177 and reprinted in *Canadian Musical Heritage,* vol. 6 ("Piano Music II"), ed. Elaine Keillor (Ottawa: Canadian Musical Heritage Society, 1986).

1917

7. *Arm, Canadians! March to Glory!* "Dedicated to Canada's Heroic Army." Voice, pf; text by Victor Wyldes.
   PUBLICATION DATA: Toronto: Whaley, Royce, & Co., 1917; copy at CaOONL.

1919

Source for nos. 8–14: Program, Peabody student recital, May 7, 1919. The scores are lost.

8. *Habanera.* Pf.

9. *Intermezzo.* Pf.

10. *Lumière.* Pf.

11. *La Mère au berceau.* Pf.

12. *Il Neige.* Pf.

13. *Prelude.* Pf.

14. *Regret.* Pf.

15. *Sonata.* Pf. Score lost.
    SOURCE: Program, Peabody student recital, May 12, 1919; only the first movement was performed.

1920

16. *Death March of King Pendragon.* Sop, pf. Score lost.
    SOURCE: Program, Hazel Bornschein, sop, and McPhee, pf, May 20, 1920, Stieff Hall, Baltimore.

17. *Le Mort d'Arthur.* "Symphonic Poem for Piano and Orchestra" (McPhee referred to this work as his first piano concerto). Score lost.

SOURCE: Program, Peabody Students' Orchestra, Gustav Strube, cond, McPhee, pf, May 26, 1920.

1921

Source for nos. 18–21: Program, Peabody student recital, Mary Spence, sop, Colin McPhee, pf, May 20, 1921. The scores are lost.

18. *Il Danse.* Pf.

19. *Poème.* Pf.

20. Sonata in E♭ Minor (in one movement). Pf.

21. *Three Songs:* "At Night Thy Voice Is Like the Nightingale," "La [*sic*] Silence de Mnasidika," "Music, When Soft Voices Die." Sop, pf.

22. *Two Hymns for a Sunset.* Pf. Score lost.
    SOURCE: Undated newspaper clipping [Baltimore, April 1920], CM-CLU.
    PERFORMANCE: "Henri," dancer, McPhee, pf, April 9, 1920, Little Lyric Theatre, Baltimore.

23. *Two Preludes.* Pf. Score lost.
    SOURCE: Program, Peabody student recital, McPhee, pf, April 6, 1921.

1922

24. *Elegy.* Pf. Score lost.
    SOURCE: Program, piano recital by McPhee, February 16, 1922, The Canadian Academy of Music, Toronto.

25. Incidental music to *Euripides,* by Hippolytus. Soprano solo, women's chorus, string trio, ob, fl, hp. Score lost.
    SOURCE: Undated newspaper clipping, CM-CLU; also E. R. Parkhurst, "Personalia," *Toronto Globe* (November 25, 1922).   PERFORMANCE: November 1922, Hart House Theatre, Toronto.

26. *Rákoczy March.* Arrangement of the piece by Franz Liszt. Pf. Score lost.
    SOURCE: Numerous Toronto programs, beginning with McPhee's solo recital, December 4, 1922, at the Hart House Theatre in Toronto.

27. Improvisation. Pf. Score lost.
    SOURCE: Program, piano recital by McPhee, January 4, 1923, Hart House Theatre, Toronto.

28. Polonaise in A♭ (1922–24). Arrangement of the piece by Frédéric Chopin. Pf with orchestral accompaniment. Score lost.
    SOURCE: Schwerké-25.

29. *Sea Legend.* Pf. Score lost.
    SOURCE: Same as no. 27.

30. *Polka* (1922–24). Pf. Score lost.

SOURCE: Program, piano recital by McPhee, November 19 [no year], American Women's Club of Toronto, at the home of Mrs. Ralph Connable.

1923

31. *Ballad of Youth.* Pf. Score lost.

SOURCE: Announcement of McPhee's recital of March 8, 1923, on the back of the program for McPhee's recital of January 4, 1923, Hart House Theatre, Toronto. The piece is not included in the March program, however; perhaps it was never completed.

32. Piano Concerto No. 2 in B. Pf and orchestra. Score lost.

SOURCE: Program, New Symphony Orchestra, Luigi von Kunits, cond, McPhee, pf, January 15, 1924, Massey Hall, Toronto. NOTE: The following information is contained in the program notes: "The Concerto No. 2 was commenced in June 1923 and was completed in November of the same year." Listed in Reis-30 and Reis-47 as in manuscript.

33. Nocturne. Pf. Score lost.

SOURCE: Program, recital by McPhee, March 13, 1927, Greenwich Village Theatre, New York; there the piece is dated "1923."

34. *Sarabande.* Pf. Score lost.

SOURCE: Program, recital by Clara Rabinowitch, April 20, 1925, Salle Erard, Paris. NOTE: McPhee dated this work 1923 on the program for his recital, March 13, 1927, Greenwich Village Theatre, New York.

35. *The Forsaken Merman* (1923 or 1924). Musical accompaniment to a melodrama. Pf. Score lost.

SOURCE: Program, McPhee playing piano accompaniment, February 10 [no year given; either 1923 or 1924], Hart House Theatre, Toronto.

1924

36. *Three Moods.* Pf. MOVEMENTS: "Prelude," "Spring Afternoon," "Death Music." Score lost.

SOURCE: Program, solo piano recital by McPhee, March 29, 1924, Foresters' Hall, Toronto.

1925

37. *Pastorale and Rondino.* "Sonatina for two flutes, clarinet, trumpet and piano." Score lost.

SOURCE: Program, November 28, 1926, International Composers' Guild, Aeolian Hall, New York. NOTE: In ACA-55, McPhee listed both a "Pastorale

263

for 3 w.w. & piano, [performed by] chamber ensemble, Paris 1925" and
"Sonatina for 2 fl, cl, trumpet, piano, American Composers' Guild, New York,
1926." The sonatina is listed in Reis-30 and Reis-47 as being in manuscript.

1926

38. String Quartet (1926 or earlier). Score lost.
   SOURCE: Cited in program notes for a performance of McPhee's *Pastorale and
   Rondino* by the International Composers' Guild, November 28, 1926.

39. *Songs.* Sop, pf. Score(s) lost.
   SOURCE: In ACA-55 McPhee listed "songs" [untitled] performed by Jeanne
   [recte Jane] Bathori in Paris in 1926. Perhaps they included the songs listed
   as nos. 43–46 below.

40. Invention. Pf.
   PUBLICATION DATA: *New Music* 3 (July 1930). NOTE: The published score
   is dated "New York/Aug. 12, 1926." No manuscript is extant. A copy of
   the published score at CLU includes handwritten corrections by McPhee in
   red pen.

1927

41. *The Man I Love.* Arrangement of the song by George Gershwin. Pf. Score lost.
   SOURCE: Program, piano recital by McPhee, March 13, 1927, Greenwich
   Village Theatre, New York City. NOTE: McPhee played this arrangement
   (improvisation?) several times in the late 1920s. There may never have been
   a written score.

42. *Sarabande.* Orchestra. Score lost.
   SOURCE: Mentioned only in Reis-30 and Reis-47, where it is listed as being in
   manuscript. Perhaps it was confused with the *Sarabande* for piano (see no. 34).

1928

SOURCES for nos. 43–46: Program, recital by Abbie Mitchell, sop, and McPhee, pf,
April 15, 1928, Engineering Auditorium, New York, collection of Mercer Cook.
They were also performed by either Marjorie Nash or Janet Creighton in a concert
at Town Hall, May 1, 1928. All the scores are now lost.

43. *C'est la bergère Nanette.* Sop, pf.

44. *Cradle Song.* Sop, pf.

45. *Petit chaperone rouge.* Sop, pf.

46. *Theris.* Sop, pf.

47. Concerto for Piano with Wind Octette Acc. "To Jane Belo." 2 fl, ob, cl, bsn, hn, tpt, tbn, pf.
PREMIERE: The Rochester Little Symphony, Howard Hanson, cond, McPhee, pf, February 22, 1929, Eastman School of Music. PUBLICATION DATA: New Music 4 (January 1931). RENTAL SCORE: AMP. RECORDING: Grant Johannesen, pf, Carlos Surinach, cond, Columbia ML-5105; released in 1956. Rereleased in 1973 as CRI-315.
NOTE: At its premiere, the work was titled "Concerto for Piano and Seven Wind Instruments." At its second performance, by the Chamber Orchestra of Boston on March 11, 1929 (Nicolas Slonimsky, cond, McPhee, pf), the piece was titled "Concerto for Piano and Eight Wind Instruments." The New Music score is signed "Woodstock, June–October 1928." No manuscript is extant. There are parts at CLU, together with a sheet of notes and corrections by McPhee.

1929

48. *Sea Shanty Suite.* "To Hugh Ross in Friendship." Baritone solo, male chorus, 2 pf, 2 timp. MOVEMENTS: "Lowlands Away," "Billy Boy," "Stormalong," "What Shall We Do With a Drunken Sailor?" "Tom's Gone to Hilo," "Fire Down Below," "Highland Laddie."
PREMIERE: Schola Cantorum, Hugh Ross, cond, McPhee, pf, March 13, 1929, Carnegie Hall, New York City (unsigned review, *New York Times,* March 14, 1929). PUBLICATION DATA: New York: Edwin F. Kalmus, 1930 ("Fire Down Below" was not part of the published *Suite* and is now lost). NOTE: At head of page 1: "The Melody collected and Edited by Sir Richard Terry." No manuscript is extant; a copy of the published version at CLU includes handwritten corrections by McPhee.

1930

49. *Kinesis.* Pf.
PUBLICATION DATA: New Music 3 (July 1930). NOTE: The published score is dated "9 May 1930." No manuscript is extant. A copy of the published score at CLU includes handwritten corrections by McPhee.

50. Symphony [No. 1] in One Movement. Score lost.
SOURCE: Listed in Reis-30 and Reis-47 as being in manuscript. NOTE: Although McPhee never mentioned this symphony in correspondence or lists of works, it must have existed because when he wrote a symphony for the Louisville Orchestra in 1957 he titled it "Symphony No. 2" (see no. 68).

APPENDIX A

1931

51. *H₂O.* Score to a film by Ralph Steiner. Orchestra. Score lost.
PREMIERE: Copland-Sessions Concert, thirty members of the New York
Philharmonic-Symphony Orchestra, Hugh Ross, cond, March 15, 1931, Broad-
hurst Theatre, New York.   NOTE: Neither Ralph Steiner nor Hugh Ross has
a copy of the score.

52. *Mechanical Principles.* Score to a film by Ralph Steiner. Orchestra. Score lost.
PREMIERE and NOTE: Same as no. 51.

1936

53. *Revelation of St. John the Divine.* Men's chorus, 2 pf, 3 tpt, 2 timp. Score lost.
Commissioned by the League of Composers.
PREMIERE: Program, Princeton University Glee Club, James A. Giddings,
cond, March 27, [1936], Waldorf-Astoria, New York.   NOTE: Neither the
Princeton University Music Library nor the Princeton Glee Club has a score.
Reis-47 lists the work in manuscript.

54. *Tabuh-Tabuhan.* "Toccata for Orchestra and 2 Pianos." 2 pic, 2 fl, 2 ob, E hn,
2 cl, bcl, 2 bsn, cbsn, 4 hn, 3 tpt, 3 tbn, tu, cel, hp, 2 pf, strings, 6 percussionists (cymbals, Balinese cymbals, triangle, sandpaper blocks, bass drum, Balinese
gongs, tam-tam, xyl, mrmb, glock, chimes).
HOLOGRAPHS (both in McPhee's hand; OD):   1. "Tabuh-Tabuhan/Toccata
for Orchestra on Balinese motifs." Dated at end: "Mexico City, August 19,
1936." Includes red- and blue-crayon marks, presumably made by Leopold
Stokowski (as was his custom) for the 1953 performance in New York.
2. "Tabuh-Tabuhan/Toccata for orchestra and 2 pianos." On page 1: "Revised
version." Dated at end: "Mexico, June–August 1936." Revision made ca. 1956
for publication by Associated Music Publishers.   PREMIERE: Symphony Orchestra of Mexico, September 4, 1936, Carlos Chávez, cond, Mexico City.
PUBLICATION DATA: New York: Associated Music Publishers, Inc., 1960.
RENTAL SCORE: AMP.   RECORDING: Eastman-Rochester Symphony Orchestra, Howard Hanson, cond, Mercury MG-50103, also SR-90103; released
1959. Rereleased 1980 as Mercury SRI-75116.

1939

55. *Chorale Prelude "In Dulci Jubilo."* Arrangement of chorale prelude by Buxtehude. 2 pf.
HOLOGRAPHS (both in McPhee's hand; OD):   1. "In dulci Jubilo/Dec. 7/39/
(7PM-11PM)." Both piano parts are given in score.   2. "Chorale-prelude/ 'In
dulci jubilum'/Buxtehude/arranged for 2 pianos/by/Colin McPhee." Below the

title the words "To Ethel and Rae Robertson" have been erased. Both piano parts are given in score. No date. PERFORMANCE: Ethel Bartlett and Rae Robertson, December 9, 1941, New York (clipping files, NN). NOTE: At the end of both scores is a five-bar section titled "Interlude." (The word "modulation" has been crossed out.) "In dulci jubilo" is in G major; the "Interlude" begins in G minor and ends in C major.

1940

56. *The Emperor Jones.* Incidental music to the play by Eugene O'Neill. Hammond organ.
    HOLOGRAPH: Fragment for Scene 5, OD. PERFORMANCE: Program, week beginning August 5, 1940, Westport Country Playhouse, starring Paul Robeson. (McPhee's score was played by Max Marlin.)

57. *Battle of Angels.* Incidental music to the play by Tennessee Williams. Instrumentation unknown. Score lost.
    SOURCE: ACA-55. McPhee mentioned the score in letters to Henry Cowell (January 9, 1941) and Carlos Chávez (May 1, [1950]). PERFORMANCE: Boston, December 1940.

1941

58. *Ciacona.* Arrangement of *Ciaccona* in G Major by Buxtehude. 2 pf.
    HOLOGRAPH (in McPhee's hand; OD): "Ciacona/Buxtehude/arranged for 2 pianos/Colin McPhee/Edition Breitkopf & Härtel/(Spitta-Seiffert)." No date. Both piano parts are given in score. PERFORMANCE: Same as no. 55.
    NOTE: The layout of this score is much like that of the second holograph of "In dulci jubilo."

59. *Nun komm, der heiden Heiland.* Arrangement of a chorale prelude by Buxtehude. 2 pf.
    HOLOGRAPHS (both in McPhee's hand; OD): 1. "Nun Komm, der Heiden Heiland," no date. Both piano parts in score. In G minor with indication at beginning "Semi-tone higher." 2. "Choral Prelude/Nun Komm, der Heiden Heiland/Buxtehude/Arr./Colin McPhee/2nd piano," no date. Piano 2 only. In G♯ minor. PERFORMANCE: Same as no. 55.

1942

60. *Variations on a Theme of Frank Bridge [Jinx].* Arrangement of *Variations on a Theme of Frank Bridge,* by Benjamin Britten. 2 pf.
    HOLOGRAPH (in McPhee's hand, part of the Britten Collection in the Red House, Aldeburgh, England): At head of page 1: "Variations on a theme of

Frank Bridge/Britten-McPhee." Date at end: "Feb–March/1942." NOTE:
The score was used as accompaniment to a ballet titled *Jinx,* staged by Eugene
Loring and his Dance Players, with choreography by Lew Christensen, in New
York in April 1942. On March 24, 1942, Elizabeth Mayer wrote Benjamin
Britten that "[Colin] has finished the 2 piano arrangement of the Variations."

1943

61. [*Boogie-Woogie*]. 2 pf. Score lost.
    SOURCE: McPhee mentioned writing a "boogie-woogie" in letters to Chávez
    (June 14 [1943]) and Copland (August 23 [1943]). It is not known whether he
    ever completed the piece.

1944–45

62. *Iroquois Dances.* "To Sidney Cowell." 2 fl, 2 ob, 2 cl, 2 bsn, 4 hn, 2 tpt, timp,
    maracas, tom-tom, strings. MOVEMENTS: "Corn Dance," "Eagle Dance,"
    "Scalping Dance," "Medicine Dance." Commissioned by the Instituto Indige-
    nista Inter-Americano of Mexico City.
    PUBLICATION DATA: New Music 18 (July 1945). NOTE: No holograph is ex-
    tant. The parts are at CLU. In an introduction to the score McPhee states: "The
    Four Iroquois Dances were written at the request of the Instituto Indigenista
    Inter-americano of Mexico City for broadcast to Latin-America." In ACA-55
    McPhee lists under "Compositions Performed": "Four Iroquois Dances"/
    Student Orchestra for broadcast/Washington D.C. 1945." McPhee mentions a
    recording in letters to Sidney Cowell (October 22 [1945] and January 2 [1946?])
    and says that it was made by Charles Seeger; apparently McPhee never re-
    ceived a copy. Later McPhee renounced the pieces entirely: "When notified
    by Mr. Cowell and Mr. Ussachevsky of the taking over of the N[ew] M[usic]
    catalogue, I wrote them at once informing them I wished to withdraw the Iro-
    quois Dances entirely, as I was not pleased with them (McPhee to Nicholas J.
    Elsier, Jr., August 16, 1962). In an undated typescript resume, now at CM-CLU,
    McPhee also listed "Iroquois Ecologue"; the piece is also cited in Reis-47 as
    being in manuscript.

1948

63. *Broken Arrow.* Orchestra (exact instrumentation unknown). Score lost.
    PERFORMANCE: May 22, 1948, CBS radio. NOTE: McPhee's score was writ-
    ten for a radio documentary about the plight of American Indians; it was
    entitled "Arrows in the Dust." Sig Mickelson was the producer, Dr. Philip
    Eisenberg the co-producer. The show originated in Minneapolis. CBS no

longer has a transcript (Carol Parne, CBS industry librarian, telephone interview with author, January 31, 1983).

1954

64. *Transitions.* "Dedicated to the memory of Serge and Natalie Koussevitzky." Pic, 2 fl, 2 ob, E hn, 2 cl, bsn, 4 hn, 3 tpt, 3 tbn, tu, timp, pf, strings, 2 percussionists (cymbal, glock). Commissioned by the Serge Koussevitzky Music Foundation, Library of Congress.

HOLOGRAPH: There are four reproductions of the complete holograph at CLU. The reproductions have different titles, and some have pencil corrections, as noted below:

1. TITLE PAGE: "Symphonic Transitions/for orchestra/by Colin McPhee." (Title is typed and pasted on.) At head of page 1: "Transitions" (pasted on). This score includes a few pencil corrections by McPhee.

2. TITLE PAGE: "Transitions/for/orchestra." (Title in longhand; pasted on.) At head of page 1: "Transitions." "1954" added in ink beneath McPhee's name. Includes a few pencil corrections by McPhee.

3. TITLE PAGE: "Transitions/for Orchestra" (longhand; pasted in). At head of page 1: "Transitions." Title page has "1st score" added in pencil. No pencil corrections.

4. TITLE PAGE: "Atlantis/for orchestra" (longhand; not a paste-over). At head of page 1: "Atlantis." Date at end: "Dec 6 1954."

PREMIERE: March 20, 1955; Vancouver Symphony; Irwin Hoffman, cond. The concert was broadcast throughout Canada. RENTAL SCORE: AMP.

NOTE: At CLU there are also a piano score in McPhee's hand, transparencies of pages 69 and 72, and typed corrections for the parts.

1957

65. *Air Skills.* Pic, fl, hn, pf, glock, timp, gong, triangle.
HOLOGRAPH: Full score at CLU in McPhee's hand. "U.N. Film/Air Skills/18m." At head of page 1: "Music for U.N. Film/on/Aviation in the East/Colin McPhee." At end: "New York, Feb 12–March 20 [no year]." Parts are also at CLU. NOTE: Score was for a United Nations film.

66. *Blue Vanguard.* Pic, 2 fl, ob, cl, bsn, 2 hn, tpt, tbn, glock, cymbal, timp, pf, strings.
HOLOGRAPH: Full score at CLU in McPhee's hand in both ink transparencies and a reproduction. "Music for the Film, Blue Vanguard." At end: "Aug 10–Sept 17/1957." NOTE: The Blue Vanguard was produced for the United Nations by the National Film Board of Canada. Carlos Surinach was the con-

ductor. It was a fifty-five-minute documentary about the Suez Canal crisis (Marion Meadows, National Film Board of Canada to author, November 8, 1982).

67. *In Our Hands* (1957?). Fl, ob, hn, tpt, tbn, pf, triangle, glock, xyl, timp. HOLOGRAPH: Transparencies in McPhee's hand at CLU; also reproduction of full score and parts. No title page. NOTE: From cues in the score, it is apparent that this was also written to accompany a film. The score is not dated, however, and no other documentary evidence has been located.

68. Symphony No. 2 ("Pastorale"). 2 fl, 2 ob, 2 cl, 2 bsn, 4 hn, 2 tpt, 3 tbn, tu, timp, glock, mrmb, pf, hp, strings. Commissioned by the Louisville Orchestra. HOLOGRAPH: There are four reproductions of the complete holograph at CLU. One has added material on the title page: "Symphony No. 2/(Pastorale)/ Commissioned by/The Louisville Orchestra/To OLIVER DANIEL." Dated at end: "December 15, 1957." PREMIERE: Louisville Orchestra, Robert Whitney, cond, January 15, 1958, Louisville, Kentucky. RENTAL SCORE: AMP. RECORDING: Louisville Orchestra; Robert Whitney, cond, LOU-59-2; released in 1960.

69. Concerto for Piano with Wind Octette Accompaniment (1928/1957). 2 pf. PUBLICATION DATA: AMP, 1957. NOTE: At head of page 1: "Reduction of the Wind Octette by the composer." McPhee also published a piano reduction of the wind parts in the *New Music* score of 1931. No holograph exists. One published version at CLU has a few changes indicated by McPhee.

1958

70. Nocturne for Chamber Orchestra. Fl, ob, cl, bsn, xyl, glock, triangle, tamb, gong, cel, pf, strings. Commissioned by the Contemporary Music Society. HOLOGRAPH: Reproduction of holograph at CLU (both full score and incomplete set of parts). "Nocturne/for Chamber Orchestra/by/Collin [*sic*] McPhee." At end: "New York, Nov. 11, 1958." PREMIERE: Leopold Stokowski and his orchestra, December 3, 1958, Metropolitan Museum of Art, New York. RENTAL SCORE: CFP. RECORDING: Hessian Radio Symphony, David Van Vactor, cond, CRI-219; released in 1968.

1960

71. Concerto for Wind Orchestra. Pic, 3 fl, 3 ob, 3 cl, 2 bsn, cbsn, 4 hn, 3 tpt, 3 tbn, tu, triangle, timp, mrmb, glock, tamb, xyl, hp, pf, cb. Commissioned by Mr. and Mrs. Oliver M. Kaufmann for Robert Boudreau's American Wind Symphony.

HOLOGRAPH: 2 reproductions at CLU. At end: "New York City/June 9/1960."
PREMIERE: Robert Boudreau's American Wind Symphony, July 1960,
Pittsburgh.   PUBLICATION DATA: CFP [1962]. Pocket score, reduced from
McPhee holograph. In a letter to McPhee (November 2, 1962), Walter
Hinrichsen of C. F. Peters said the score was to be out "by or before the end
of November 1962."   RENTAL SCORE: CFP.

Post-1960

72. Symphony No. 3 [never completed]. Orchestra. Commissioned by Broadcast
Music, Inc., for its twentieth anniversary.
HOLOGRAPH FRAGMENTS (while unlabeled, these pages are probably from
Symphony No. 3):   (1) Short score in McPhee's hand, "Symphony in G/
Allegretto," 7 pages. Filed in CM-CLU transcription notebook: "Misc. Un-
identified Musical Ms. and Theme Jottings" (the same folder also contains
several unlabeled single sheets of orchestral scoring on transparencies);
(2) Orchestral score in McPhee's hand, unlabeled, 31 pages on transparencies.
Filed with no identification in CLU. The first fifty measures or so correspond
to the short score above.
NOTE: McPhee was offered the commission in a letter by Carl Haverlin,
June 3, 1960. He never completed the work.

[*Out of the Depths* and *Magnificat*] (1962). SATB, org.
NOTE: These two manuscripts are part of the McPhee Collection at CLU. Neither is signed by him or bears any resemblance to his compositional style, neither is in his hand, and neither is mentioned in any of his correspondence from
the period. In short, these works are most likely not by McPhee. One is signed
"8/2/62—Pacific Palisades," the other "8/6/62—Pacific Palisades." McPhee
was in residence at the Huntington Hartford in Pacific Palisades that summer;
perhaps these scores were given to him by a colleague there.

PRELIMINARY CATALOGUE OF COLIN McPHEE'S GAMELAN TRANSCRIPTIONS FOR WESTERN INSTRUMENTS

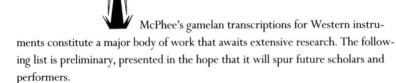

McPhee's gamelan transcriptions for Western instruments constitute a major body of work that awaits extensive research. The following list is preliminary, presented in the hope that it will spur future scholars and performers.

This catalogue is arranged alphabetically. Tune names beginning with the words *lagu* (meaning "melody" or "tune") or *gamelan* (meaning "percussion orchestra") are alphabetized under the second word of the title. McPhee's spellings of titles, many of which follow the Dutch method of the 1930s, are retained. Numberings continue from those in the catalogue of McPhee's music; they too supersede the ones in my dissertation. Since in the McPhee Collection at UCLA the Western transcriptions are interfiled with those for gamelan instruments, I have tried, wherever possible, to provide locations (notebook names appear in parentheses after "source").

ABBREVIATIONS FOR TRANSCRIPTION RECITALS

McPhee gave at least five recitals of transcriptions during the 1930s and recorded a group of them for the Schirmer label in 1941. They are abbreviated in the catalogue as follows:

NYC   Cosmopolitan Club, New York City, November 6, 1935. McPhee and Marc Blitzstein, pianos.

MC   Palace of Fine Arts, Mexico City, August 1936. McPhee and Eduardo
            Hernandez Moncada, pianos.

Bali-A   Bali-Congress/Java-Instituut; location and date not given on pro-
            gram [October 1937]. McPhee and Walter Spies, pianos.

Bali-B   Bali-Congress/Java-Instituut; location and date not given on pro-
            gram but different from Bali-A [October 1937]. McPhee and Walter
            Spies, pianos.

Bali-C   "Program of Balinese Music." No date or location; perhaps this
            is the program at the Harmony Club in Den Pasar, mentioned by
            McPhee in *A House in Bali,* pp. 222–23. Performers are not cited,
            but presumably they were McPhee and Spies.

Schirmer-17 "The Music of Bali," Schirmer's Library of Recorded Music, set
            no. 17, released in 1941. McPhee and Benjamin Britten, pianos;
            Georges Barrère, flute.

Note: A key to other manuscript and bibliographic abbreviations is found on
pages 259–60.

73. *Angar Angolar.* n.d. Solo pf.
    SOURCE: Holograph, CM-CLU (Gendér Wayang–2).   NOTE: The title is
    unclear on the manuscript.

74. *[Bandjoewangian] Lagoe Bandjoewangian (Angkloeng).* [1931–37]. 2 pf.
    SOURCE: Holograph, CM-CLU (unlabeled notebook).   PERFORMANCES:
    Bali-A, Bali-B, Bali-C.

75. *Bapang.* [1931–37]. 2 pf.
    SOURCE: Holograph, NN.   PERFORMANCES: Bali-B, Bali-C.

76. *Barong.* n.d. 2 pf.
    SOURCE: Holograph, NN.

77. *Batél.* [1931–37]. 2 pf. Score not located.
    PERFORMANCE: Bali-A.   MB: Examples 215–18[?].

78. *Bima Krohda. Gendér Wayang.* n.d. Solo pf.
    SOURCE: Holograph, CM-CLU.

79. *[Délem] Lagu Délem–Music from the Balinese Shadow Play.* 1935; 1941; [1956 or
    1962]. Solo pf.
    SOURCES: (1) Holograph, CM-CLU. Signed at top: "Transcribed by Colin
    McPhee." Dated at end: "Transcribed, Bali, 1935." (2) Holograph, CM-CLU
    (unlabeled notebook). Signed at top: "Transcribed by Colin McPhee." Dated

at end: "Bali, 1935." This is a fuller version than the preceding: many octave doublings in left hand; performance indications are written out rather than abbreviated. (3) Holograph, CM-CLU (unlabeled notebook). Dated: "Amityville . . June 9–41." (4) Holograph, CLU. This probably dates from 1956 or 1962. Copies are in a folder labeled "Cameo Music Productions" and addressed to McPhee at Huntington Hartford, where he was in residence in 1956 and 1962.

RECORDING: Sylvia Marlowe (harpsichord), Decca DL-10001/DL-710001; released in 1959.   MB: Examples 219–20.

80. [*Délem*] *Lagoe Délem.* [1931–35; 1956 or 1962]. 2 pf.

SOURCES: (1) Holograph, CM-CLU (unlabeled notebook). This score opens with both pianos and matches the first part of the Schirmer recording. However, it lacks an ornamented reprise (as the recording and the following score have). (2) Holograph, CLU. Probably dates from 1956 or 1962. Copies are in a folder labeled "Cameo Music Productions," as in no. 79 (4).

PERFORMANCES: NY, MC, Bali-A, Bali-B, Bali-C.   RECORDING: Schirmer-17.

81. *Doerga.* [1931–37]. 2 pf. Score not located.

PERFORMANCES: Bali-B, Bali-C.

82. *Gabor.* [1931–35]. 2 pf.

SOURCE: Holograph, CM-CLU (two separate copies in unlabeled notebooks).   PERFORMANCES: NY, MC.

83. *Gambangan.* 1934. "For Margaret Mead." 2 pf.

SOURCE: Published in *Balinese Ceremonial Music* (New York: G. Schirmer, 1940). DATED AT END: "Bali, 1934."   PERFORMANCES: NY, MC, Bali-A, Bali-B, Bali-C (McPhee probably performed different versions on these programs; they include *Gambangan, Gambangan Gong,* and *Gambangan Pelégongan*).

RECORDINGS: Schirmer-17; Douglas Young and Peter Hill, Cameo Classics GOCLP9018, released in 1982.   NOTE: CM-CLU copy of *Balinese Ceremonial Music* has performance indications (for cello) penciled in *Gambangan* (see also no. 115).

84. *Ganderangan–Klandis. Pedjogedan.* n.d.

(1) Solo pf.   SOURCE: Holograph, CM-CLU (notebook labeled "Joged, etc."). (2) Sketch for two-piano version (same notebook).

MB: Examples 172, 174–180.

85. *Garoeda* [1931–37]. 2 pf. Score not located.

PERFORMANCES: Bali-A, Bali-B, Bali-C.

86. [*Gendér Wayang*] *Music of the Balinese Gendér Wayang.* 1932–38; 1962. Gender Wayang Ensemble.

SOURCE: Holograph, CM-CLU. DATED ON COVER: "Transcribed by Colin McPhee, 1932–38/Copyright, 1962." NOTE: Although this transcription is not for Western instruments, it is included here because it appears to be the only full-length reconstruction of a Balinese musical event made by McPhee (58 pp.).

87. [*Jaran Sirig*] *Djaran Sirig - - - (Selat)*. 1937. 2 pf.
SOURCE: Holograph, CM-CLU (unlabeled notebook). DATE ON COVER: "March 18–37." PERFORMANCES: Bali-A, Bali-B, Bali-C (these may have been performances of this piece or the following one). MB: Example 248.

88. [*Jaran Sirig*] *Djaran Sirig*. n.d. 2 pf.
SOURCE: Holograph, CM-CLU (notebook labeled "Angklung"). NOTE: Different from the preceding piece.

89. *Kambing Slem*. 1935. Fl, pf.
SOURCES (both holographs, CM-CLU, unlabeled notebooks): (1) Flute part only (written out twice). It is part of a group of pieces titled "2 Balinese flute melodies/transcribed for modern flute and piano/Colin McPhee." (2) Flute and piano score. Dated at end: "Bali–1935." RECORDING: Schirmer-17.

90. *Kochapi Mas*. 1955. Sketch (solo pf?).
SOURCE: Holograph, CM-CLU (negative) (unlabeled notebook). DATED: "October 12, 1955."

91. [*Luang*] *Gamelan Gending Luang*. n.d. 2 pf.
SOURCE: Holograph, CLU (filed with Suite, no. 115).

92. *Merak Ngilo*. [1931–37]. 2 pf. No score located.
PERFORMANCE: Bali-A.

93. *Mésem*. [1931–37]. 2 pf. No score located.
PERFORMANCE: Bali-A.

94. [*Pemoengkah*] *Pemoengkah 13. Gen[der] Wajang. Koeta*. n.d. Solo pf.
SOURCE: Holograph sketch, CM-CLU (notebooks labeled "Gender Wayang–2"). NOTE: A variant of no. 95.

95. *Pemoengkah*. 1934; [1956 or 1962]. "For Margaret Mead." 2 pf.
SOURCES: (1) "Pemoengkah," published in *Balinese Ceremonial Music* (New York: G. Schirmer, 1940). Dated at end: "Bali, 1934." (2) Holograph, CLU. This is a variant of the published version and probably dates from 1956 or 1962. A copy is in a folder labeled "Cameo Music Productions" (together with no. 79).
PERFORMANCES: NY, MC, Bali-A, Bali-B, Bali-C. RECORDINGS: Schirmer-17; Douglas Young and Peter Hill, Cameo Classics GOCLP9018, released

in 1982. MB: Examples 181–212. NOTE: One copy of the published version at CM-CLU has pencil markings for solo performance; a second has celesta and cello parts penciled in. The recordings were made from the published score.

96. *Pemoengkah–Samban (Oeboed)*. 1937. Sketch [solo pf?].
SOURCE: Holograph, CM-CLU (notebook labeled "Angklung"). Dated at beginning: "July 9–37."

97. *Pemungkah Angklung*. n.d. 2 pf.
SOURCE: Holograph, CLU (filed with Suite, no. 115). NOTE: Different from preceding transcriptions.

98. [*Pengechét Bérong*] *Gamelan Angkloeng–Bérong, pengechét*. n.d. 2 pf.
SOURCE: Holograph, CM-CLU (notebook labeled "Angklung"). MB: Examples 244–46.

99. *. . . Pengipoek. Klandis . . . Djobok*. n.d. 2 pf.
SOURCE: Holograph, CM-CLU (unlabeled notebook). MB: Examples 130–36; 138.

100. *Rébong*. [1931–37; 1956 or 1962]. 2 pf.
SOURCES: (1) Holograph, CM-CLU, n.d. (unlabeled notebook). (2) Holograph, CLU, 1956 or 1962. In folder labeled "Cameo Music Productions" (see no. 79). PERFORMANCES: Bali-A, Bali-B, Bali-C (lists McPhee as soloist). RECORDING: Schirmer-17. MB: Examples 221–23.

101. *Seduk Maru*. n.d. 2 pf.
SOURCE: Copyist score, CM-CLU. MB: Example 120.

102. *Sekar Ginotan*. n.d. Solo pf.
SOURCE: Holograph, CM-CLU (notebook labeled "Gender Wayang–2"). MB: Examples 296–99; 302–4.

103. [*Sekar Ginotan*]. [1931–35]. 2 pf.
SOURCE: Holograph (and negative), CM-CLU, untitled score (unlabeled notebook). PERFORMANCES: NY, MC, Bali-A, Bali-B, Bali-C.

104. *Selendero. Genderwajang. Koeta*. [1931–37]. Pf.
SOURCE: Holograph, CM-CLU. PERFORMANCE: Bali-C (two-piano version). NOTE: This appears to be Piano I of a two-piano score. It is a loose manuscript, shelved together with a gamelan transcription of *Selendero*, which in turn is signed at the end: "From I Lotring, Koeta, at Sajan, Bali/Sept. 21–23/33."

105. *Selunding Bali*. 1945. 2 pf.
SOURCE: Holograph, CLU (filed with Suite, no. 115). Signed and dated at end: "Sept 14 –45."

106. [*Sesoelingan Ardja*] *Lagoe Sesoelingan Ardja.* 1936. Fl, pf.
SOURCES: (1) Holograph, CM-CLU (unlabeled notebook). Date at end: "arranged Feb 3, 1936/New York." Score of both flute and piano. (2) Holograph, CM-CLU (unlabeled notebook). Part of "2 Balinese flute melodies/ transcribed for modern flute and piano/Colin McPhee." Only the flute part is given; it is written out twice. PERFORMANCE: Bali-B, Bali-C. RECORDING: Schirmer-17.

107. *Sumbambang Djawa.* n.d. 2 pf.
SOURCE: Holograph, NN.

108. *Taboeh Teloe.* [1937–38]. "For Margaret Mead." 2 pf.
SOURCE: Published in *Balinese Ceremonial Music* (New York: G. Schirmer, 1940). DATED AT END: "Bali, June, 1938." PERFORMANCES: Bali-A, Bali-B, Bali-C. RECORDINGS: Schirmer-17; Douglas Young and Peter Hill, Cameo Classics GOCLP9018, released in 1982. MB: Examples 7, 320, and 348. NOTE: At least two of the performances listed here took place in 1937. Either an earlier version of *Taboe Teloe* was performed then or McPhee's date on the manuscript is incorrect.

109. [*Tangis*] *Lagoe Tangis deh Angkloeng Bandjaroema.* 1937. 2 pf.
SOURCES: (1) Holograph, CLU (filed with Suite, no. 115). Dated at end: "Sept. 17/37." (2) Holograph, CLU (filed with Suite, no. 115), n.d. Appears to be earlier version of preceding; largely the same through measure 39 (although this copy lacks a few accents and other details); then trails off into sketches for concluding section. PERFORMANCES: Bali-A, Bali-B, Bali-C.

110. *Tjalonarang.* [1931–35]. 2 pf. No score located.
PERFORMANCE: Bali-A, Bali-B, Bali-C.

111. [*Tjandang*] [*Lagoe Tjandang*]. [1931–35]. 2 pf.
SOURCE: Holograph, CM-CLU (notebook labeled "Pelégongan"). PERFOR-MANCES: NY, MC, Bali-A, Bali-B, Bali-C. NOTE: The Piano II part is found first in McPhee's notebook (titled); the Piano I follows (untitled).

112. [*Tjoepak*] *Lagoe Tjoepak* (*Batél*). n.d. Solo pf.
SOURCE: Holograph, CM-CLU (notebook labeled "Gendér Wayang–2"). NOTE: A solo arrangement of no. 113.

113. [*Tjoepak*] *Lagoe Tjoepak.* [1931–35]. 2 pf.
SOURCE: Holograph, CM-CLU (notebook labeled "Gendér Wayang–2"); there are two versions of the last two pages of the piece. PERFORMANCES: NY, MC, Bali-A, Bali-B, Bali-C.

114. *Wargasari.* n.d. 2 pf.
SOURCE: Holograph, CM-CLU (notebook labeled "Selundéng/Charuk/ Luang").

Following is a special set of transcriptions arranged for ensemble by McPhee in 1946.

115. [*Suite of Gamelan Transcriptions*]. [1946]. 3 pf, glock, xyl, cel, 4 vcl, 2 cb.

MOVEMENTS:

1. *Babar Layar.* 3 pf, glock, xyl, cel, 4 vcl, 2 cb.
SOURCES: Full score (holograph). Parts: Pf I/II/III, cel (played by pf I in second section only), vcl, cb, glock [no xyl].

2. *Gending Luang.* 3 pf, 4 vcl, 2 cb.
SOURCES: Full score (holograph). Parts: Pf I/II/III, vcl, cb.

3. *Seduk Maru.* 3 pf, 4 vcl, 2 cb.
SOURCES: No full score. Parts: Pf I/II/III, cb, vcl.

4. *Gambangan.* 3 pf, cel, 4 vcl, 2 cb.
SOURCES: No full score. Parts: Pf III, cb, cel. NOTE: The published two-piano score for *Gambangan* from *Balinese Ceremonial Music* was used here; the copy at CM-CLU has a cello part added in pencil.

5. *Pemungkah.* 3 pf, cel, 4 vcl, (no cb).
SOURCES: No full score. Parts: Pf III, vcl, cel. NOTE: Again, as with *Gambangan,* the two-piano score for *Pemungkah* from *Balinese Ceremonial Music* was used here.

6. *Babar Layar.* On cover sheets for the cello, bass, and celesta parts of *Babar Layar,* McPhee lists the contents of the entire suite. For no. 6, he simply indicates "Repeat #1."

SOURCES: Holograph, some full scores at CLU; also copyist's parts at CLU (as itemized above). PREMIERE: *Babar Layar, Gending Luang,* and *Seduk Maru* were performed at a Ballet Society concert on January 13 and 14, 1947, with choreography by George Balanchine. The three dancers were Javanese.
NOTE: The first three and the final transcriptions are of Javanese court dances; the last two are Balinese.

APPENDIX C

WRITINGS OF COLIN McPHEE

Several of McPhee's articles were reprinted in Jane Belo's *Traditional Balinese Culture* (New York: Columbia University Press, 1970). The book is abbreviated here as *TBC*.

"The Absolute Music of Bali," *Modern Music* 12 (May-June 1935): 163–69.

"An American Composer in Bali." Unpublished five-part script for a Voice of America radio series, ca. 1958, typescript, CM-CLU.

"Angkloeng Gamelans in Bali," *Djåwå* 17 (1937): 322–50.

"The Balinese Wajang Koelit and Its Music," *Djåwå* 16 (1936): 1–34 [offprint]; reprint, *TBC*.

"A Child's ABC of Theology," *The Hue and Cry* [Woodstock, New York] 6 (August 17, 1928): 3.

"Children and Music in Bali," *Djåwå* 18 (1938): 309–23; revised version, *TBC;* also in Margaret Mead and Martha Wolfenstein, eds., *Childhood in Contemporary Cultures* (Chicago: University of Chicago Press, 1955), 70–98.

"Clinic in the South Seas [review of *The People of Alor* by Cora Du Bois]," *New York Times Book Review,* September 17, 1944.

A Club of Small Men. New York: The John Day Company, 1948.

The Commission. Libretto to a symphonic cantata with music by Henry Cowell (for four vocal soloists and orchestra). Commissioned by the League of Composers. The Cowell score was completed in 1954, DLC.

"Dance in Bali," *Dance Index* 7 (1948): 156–207; reprint, *TBC*.

"The Decline of the East," *Modern Music* 16 (March-April 1939): 160–67.

"Eight to the Bar," *Modern Music* 20 (May-June 1943): 235–42.

The Exotic Sounds of Bali [liner notes]. Columbia ML-5845/MS-6445; released in 1963.

"Figuration in Balinese Music," *Peabody Bulletin* 36 (May 1940): 23–26.

"The Five-Tone Gamelan Music of Bali," *Musical Quarterly* 35 (April 1949): 250–81.

"Forecast and Review," *Modern Music*. Individual titles follow:

> "Winter Chronicle New York," 8 (March-April 1931): 42–45.
>
> "New York—January, February, 1936," 13 (March-April 1936): 41–46.
>
> "New York's Spring Season, 1936," 13 (May-June 1936): 39–42.
>
> "New York, Autumn of 1936," 14 (November-December 1936): 28–31.
>
> "Winter Season, New York, 1936," 14 (January-February 1937): 87–89.
>
> "Further Seasonal Note," 16 (May-June 1939): 254.
>
> "The Stravinsky Mystery," 16 (May-June 1939): 266–67.
>
> "South America Once More," 17 (May-June 1940): 245–46.
>
> "Jungles of Brazil," 18 (November-December 1940): 41–43.
>
> "Tools of Musical Culture," 18 (March-April 1941): 205–6.
>
> "The Season Opens—1943," 21 (November-December 1943): 31–34.
>
> "Winter Stars and Lesser Lights," 21 (January-February 1944): 96–97.

[Four caricatures], *Peabody Bulletin* 17 (Spring 1921): 8–9.

"Gamelanmuziek van Bali: Ondergangsschemering van een kunst (Interview met Colin McPhee)," *Djåwå* 19 (1939): 183–86.

"Gourmet in Bali," *Harper's Bazaar* (November 1949): 200–201, 203.

"The Green Earth Scorched," *Modern Music* 19 (March-April 1942): 163–66.

A House in Bali. New York: The John Day Company, 1946; reprints, New York: AMS Press, 1980, and New York: Oxford University Press, 1987. Also translated by Fabbio Caddeo as *Maghi, musici e attori a Bali*. Milano: Valentino Bompiani, 1951.

"In This Far Island," *Asia and the Americas* 44–45 (1944–45).

[Interview tape from Composers' Forum concert, 1954]. Princeton Electronic Music Center Library.

"Music and Films," [Chicago] *Musical Leader* (March 12, 1931).

Music in Bali. New Haven: Yale University Press, 1966; reprint, New York: Da Capo Press, 1976.

Music of Bali [liner notes]. Westminster XWN-2209, released in 1956.

"Musical Exploration in Bàli," *Musical America* 60 (February 10, 1940): 12, 263.

"A Musician Listens to Balinese Music," *Djåwå* 18 (1938): 50–62.

"One More for the Record," *Modern Music* 21 (March-April 1944): 195.

"Orage [A Poem]," *Canadian Magazine* 62 (December 1923): 148.

"Report on Bali's Music," *New York Times,* March 5, 1939.

"Scores and Records," *Modern Music* 16–22 (1939–45).

"Shadows in Bali," *Mademoiselle* 23 (October 1946): 190–91, 306–8.

"The Sounds of Bali," *Hi-Fi Review* (December 1958): 26–30.

"Spirituals to Swing," *Modern Music* 23 (Summer 1946): 224–25.

"They Live the Dance: The Balinese Who Appear Here This Month for the First Time Bring a Unique Art Form," *New York Times Magazine,* September 7, 1952.

"The Torrid Zone" [signed "Mercure"], *Modern Music* 20–23 (1943–46).

"Visitors from Bali," *New York Times,* August 31, 1952.

D APPENDIX

GLOSSARY OF BALINESE TERMS

All definitions used here are McPhee's own, taken from Appendix 2 of *Music in Bali*. If they are found elsewhere in his book, page numbers are given.

ANGKLUNG   archaic form of tuned bamboo rattle (see also *gamelan angklung*)

BANJAR   district or ward of a town or village

DALANG   the operator of the puppets and reciter of the dialogue in the shadow play

GAMELAN ANGKLUNG   an ensemble made up of metallophones and various small gongs, distinguished from all other gamelans by its four-tone scale. The ensemble sometimes includes a number of *angklungs* (*MB,* 234)

GAMELAN PELÉGONGAN   intended primarily to accompany the *légong* dance, [it] is actually an enlarged five-tone *Semar Pegulingan* orchestra (*MB,* 150)

GANDRUNG   popular form of dance performed by a boy

GANGSA   bronze; a name interchangeable with *saron* in indicating any one-octave metallophone with keys resting over a sound-box and struck with a single mallet

GENDÉR   metallophone having a two-octave or wider range, with keys suspended over tubular resonators, and played with two mallets

GÉNGGONG   Balinese form of jews harp, made from sugarpalm wood

JOGÉD   popular form of dance performed by a girl

KEBYAR   a modern dance, performed by a boy or youth to the accompaniment of the *gamelan gong kebyar;* the music which accompanies the dance

LÉGONG   a form of dance performed by three small girls

PELOG   the seven-tone scale system allowing for various forms of pentatonic scales

SLENDRO   the five-tone scale system having no semitones

TROMPONG   row of small, horizontally mounted gongs used as solo instrument in the *gamelan gong* and *Semar Pegulingan*

WAYANG   *wayang kulit,* the shadow play; *wayang wong,* a special form of play with living actors

NOTES

ABBREVIATIONS USED IN NOTES

ACA	American Composers Alliance, New York City
AH-DLC	Ann Hull Collection, Music Division, Library of Congress
B	Box
CaOONL	Music Division, National Library of Canada, Ottawa
CaOTMCL	Metropolitan Toronto Library
CJM	*Canadian Journal of Music*
CLU	Music Library, University of California, Los Angeles
CM-CLU	Colin McPhee Collection, Ethnomusicology Archives, University of California, Los Angeles
C-NN	Cowell Collection, Music Division, New York Public Library
CV-CtY	Carl Van Vechten Collection, Beinecke Rare Book and Manuscript Library, Yale University, New Haven
DLC	Library of Congress, Washington, D.C.
F	Folder
GB-DLC	George Biddle Collection, Manuscript Division, Library of Congress

HB	Colin McPhee, *A House in Bali* (John Day Company, 1946)
IS-DLC	Irving Schwerké Collection, Music Division, Library of Congress
Letters	Margaret Mead, *Letters from the Field: 1925–1975* (Harper and Row, 1977)
MB	Colin McPhee, *Music in Bali* (Yale University Press, 1966)
MC	*Musical Canada*
MM-DLC	Margaret Mead Papers, Manuscript Division, Library of Congress
MoMu-DLC	Archives of *Modern Music,* Music Division, Library of Congress
NN	Music Division, Performing Arts Research Center, New York Public Library
NS-DLC	Nicolas Slonimsky Collection, Music Division, Library of Congress
OD-GU	Olin Downes Collection, University of Georgia, Athens
SK-DLC	Serge Koussevitzky Collection, Music Division, Library of Congress
TBC	Jane Belo, ed. *Traditional Balinese Culture* (Columbia University Press, 1970)

To avoid repetition, notes here generally do not give manuscript locations for the following correspondents: Jane Belo (Margaret Mead Papers, Library of Congress), Carlos Chávez (Archivo General de la Nacion, Mexico City), Aaron Copland (Music Division, Library of Congress), Henry and Sidney Cowell (Music Division, New York Public Library), Oliver Daniel (Collection of Oliver Daniel, Ardsley, New York), David Diamond (Rochester, New York), Elizabeth and William Mayer (Collection of Beata Sauerlander, New York City), Margaret Mead (Margaret Mead Papers, Library of Congress), and Carl Van Vechten (Beinecke Library, Yale University).

Page numbers in brackets refer to unnumbered offprints of journal articles.

PREFACE

1. I made this trip to Bali in 1984 as historical consultant for the documentary film "Colin McPhee: The Lure of Asian Music," released by Michael Blackwood Productions in New York City. While there, I interviewed musicians with whom

McPhee had been associated during the 1930s. Pino Confessa and Andrew Toth generously helped arrange interviews and served as translators.

2. Mark Swed, "40 Years Later, But It's Never Too Late: Harold Shapero's Symphony for Classical Orchestra, Forgotten Since Its Premiere, Is Making a Comeback," *New York Times,* May 8, 1988.

3. Joseph Horowitz, *Understanding Toscanini: How He Became an American Culture-God and Helped Create a New Audience for Old Music* (New York: Alfred A. Knopf, 1987), 436.

4. McPhee to Oliver Daniel, January 18, 1963, CM-CLU.

5. McPhee to Sidney Cowell, August 25, [1945] (B38/F611). David Ewen's *American Composers Today* does not include an entry for McPhee (New York: H. W. Wilson Company, 1949).

6. McPhee to David Diamond, "Friday" [1940s].

CHAPTER 1: THE EDUCATION OF A PRODIGY

1. Much of the information about McPhee's family comes from three sources: (1) Janet McPhee, widow of Colin's brother, Douglas McPhee, to author, April 15, 1983; (2) Janet McPhee, interview with author, Toronto, May 1, 1983; and (3) *Nassagaweya: A History of Campbellville and Surrounding Area* (Campbellville, Ontario: Campbellville Historical Society, 1982). Also, an unpublished undergraduate essay by Joseph Natoli tracing McPhee's Toronto childhood has provided many valuable leads (University of Toronto, ca. 1976, under the supervision of John Beckwith; copy in CaOONL).

2. Extract of birth of Colin Carhart McPhee, issued by the Superior Court of Montreal and drawn from the register of Bethlehem Congregational Church in Montreal on July 18, 1935, CM-CLU. For some unknown reason, beginning around 1924 McPhee often gave 1901 as his birthdate.

3. McPhee to Carl Van Vechten, postmarked May 17, 1933, Hong Kong.

4. McPhee, "Scores and Records," *Modern Music* 19 (May–June 1942): 271.

5. The descriptions of Colin's parents here and in the next paragraph come from the previously cited interview with Janet McPhee and from Donald White of Red Bank, New Jersey, a distant relative of Colin's mother (telephone interview with author, November 8, 1982).

6. The records of Fern Avenue Public School in Toronto show that Colin McPhee entered there on February 10, 1913, and that he had just arrived from Montreal (Paul P. Pavlovich, vice principal of Fern Avenue School, to author, March 22, 1984).

7. Robertson Davies, *A Mixture of Frailties* (Ontario: Penguin Books, 1958), 246.

8. George Parkin de Twenebroker Glazebrook, *The Story of Toronto* (Toronto: University of Toronto Press, 1971), 196.

9. Much of the information given in the ensuing pages about Canadian musical life comes from various articles in Helmut Kallmann, Gilles Potvin, and Kenneth Winters, eds., *Encyclopedia of Music in Canada* (Toronto: University of Toronto Press, 1981).

10. Both the *Canadian Journal of Music* (hereafter *CJM*), published in Toronto from 1914 to 1919, and *Musical Canada* (*MC*), also published in Toronto but with a longer life span (1906–33), regularly reviewed visiting artists.

11. Stuart Lawson, interview with author, Toronto, May 1, 1983.

12. Lorna Hassell, "Hambourg Conservatory," *Encyclopedia of Music in Canada,* 408.

13. Luigi von Kunits, "Ernest J. Farmer," *CJM* 2 (February 1916): 173; and Ernest Farmer, "Evolution and the Teaching of Composition," ibid.: 183. The quotations in this paragraph come from the second article.

14. "A Novelty Recital," [ca. 1914], CM-CLU.

15. "Re-Opening of the Hambourg Conservatory of Music," *MC* 12 (September 1917): 80; and "Juvenile Canadian Composers," *MC* 10 (April 1916): 257–58.

16. Untitled newspaper clipping [1915], CM-CLU.

17. Hector Charlesworth, "Colin McPhee's Career," *Toronto Globe and Mail,* June 21, 1941, Clipping File-CaOTMCL.

18. Farmer, "Evolution and the Teaching of Composition." McPhee later told Carlos Chávez that his "Opus One" had been "composed at age eight" (letter to Chávez, March 21, 1955) and to another friend recalled writing at twelve "a piece for children's percussion band with a few strings, etc." (letter to Dr. William Mayer, postmarked September 2, 1942, collection of Beata Sauerlander).

19. Copies of both are in the National Library of Canada. In 1915 (March-April, November, December) and 1916 (January), the Empire Music and Travel

Club published a series of advertisements in *CJM* calling for composers to submit manuscripts.

20. Farmer, "Evolution and the Teaching of Composition."

21. In 1917 Farmer began performing frequently studied pieces at the end of each program so that students could hear the works interpreted "with high artistic finish." On one recital his group of such works included "the recently published sketches of Colin McPhee" ("The Hambourg Conservatory," *MC* 11 [February 1917]: 166).

22. See two articles by Helmut Kallmann in *Encyclopedia of Music in Canada:* "Patriotic Songs," 729–30, and "Wars, Rebellions, and Uprisings," 986–87.

23. Kallmann, "Whaley, Royce & Co. Ltd.," *Encyclopedia of Music in Canada,* 994.

24. "Winners of Peabody Diplomas," *Baltimore Sun,* May 15, 1921. Interviews by author with Ann Hull, Westport, Connecticut, December 5, 1981, and Sylvan Levin, New York City, September 25, 1981.

25. Denoe Leedy, "Harold Randolph: The Man and Musician," *Musical Quarterly* 30 (April 1944): 198–204.

26. Ibid., 198.

27. Gustav Klemm, "Gustav Strube: The Man and the Musician," *Musical Quarterly* 28 (July 1942): 291–92.

28. "A New Rhapsody by Gustav Strube," *Musical America* 14 (May 20, 1911): 17.

29. Programs for these concerts are housed in the library of Peabody Conservatory and in the private collection of Sylvan Levin.

30. "Adolph Weiss and Colin McPhee," *American Composers on American Music: A Symposium,* ed. Henry Cowell (Palo Alto: Stanford University Press, 1933; reprint, New York: Frederick Ungar, 1962), 37.

31. Pupil's record for Colin McPhee, Mr. Randolph, teacher, Peabody Conservatory of Music, 1918–19 and 1919–20 (Registrar's Office, Peabody Conservatory of Music).

32. Pupil's record for Colin McPhee, Mr. Strube, teacher, Peabody Conservatory of Music, 1919–20 and 1920–21 (Registrar, Peabody).

33. "The Artist," *Peabody Bulletin* 16 (February 1920): 3.

34. *Peabody Bulletin* 17 (Spring 1921): 8–9.

35. Yenmita [pseudonym for Edward W. Wodson], "Music Notes . . . Splendid Afternoon Concert—Colin McPhee's Third Piano Recital at Hart House," unidentified clipping [March 9, 1923], CM-CLU.

36. Theodore L. Bullock, introduction to Arthur Friedheim, *Life and Liszt: The Recollections of a Concert Pianist* (New York: Taplinger Publishing, 1961), 18.

37. "Arthur Friedheim Among Us," *MC* 2 (July-August 1921): 24–25.

38. The City of Toronto directories list McPhee in 1923 as a music teacher at the academy; he was living with his parents. In 1924 his occupation was the same, but his residence had changed to 679 Spadina Avenue, where he rented a room (James A. Fraser of the Toronto City Archives, letter to author, March 5, 1982).

39. Eric Friedheim, letter to author, January 25, 1984.

40. *Life and Liszt,* 256.

41. An engraved invitation and program for this concert are in CM-CLU. Both are dated February 16 with no year, but a Canadian Academy of Music advertisement for the concert appeared in the *Mail and Empire,* February 11, 1922.

42. Charlesworth, review of McPhee's concert on December 4, 1922, *Saturday Night* (December 9, 1922), CM-CLU and Clipping File–CaOTMCL.

43. Augustus Bridle, "Colin M'Phee Makes His Pianistic Debut," *Toronto Daily Star,* December 5, 1922, CM-CLU and Clipping File–CaOTMCL. In addition to writing many reviews about McPhee over the years, Bridle included McPhee in two separate essays about new music in Canada: "Who Writes Our Music? A Survey of Canadian Composers," *Maclean's* (December 15, 1929): 20, 30, 32; and "Composers Among Us," in *Yearbook of the Arts in Canada (1928–1929),* Bertram Booker, ed. (Toronto: Macmillan, 1929), 133–40.

44. *The Globe*'s concert listing was included every Saturday under the headline "Some Dates Ahead" in E. R. Parkhurst's regular column, "Music in the Home, Concerts, and the Drama." One such listing for the 1922–23 season can be found on November 4, 1922.

45. Program, Hart House concert, Sunday, November 12, 1922. McPhee performed in a four-hand piano accompaniment to the Brahms *Liebeslieder Waltzes* (Collection of Hart House, University of Toronto).

46. Morley Callaghan, *That Summer in Paris: Memories of Tangled Friendships with Hemingway, Fitzgerald, and Some Others* (New York: Coward-McCann, 1963), 31.

47. "Euripides Modernized," unidentified clipping, CM-CLU. A brief notice by E. R. Parkhurst in *The Globe* (November 25, 1922) read: "The music for the play 'Hyppolytus' [*sic*] at its production last week at the Hart House Theatre was especially written for the occasion by Colin McPhee of the Canadian Academy of Music."

48. Announcement flyer, Bertram Forsyth's recital of poetry and prose, assisted by McPhee, Hart House Theatre, February 10 [no year], CM-CLU.

49. Program, Eighth Twilight Concert, given by the New Symphony Orchestra, Luigi von Kunits, conductor, Colin McPhee, pianist, Massey Hall, January 15, 1924, CM-CLU.

50. Bridle, "Concerto by Colin McPhee Accentuates Sheer Impulse to Create," unidentified clipping [*Toronto Daily Star,* before January 15, 1924], CM-CLU.

51. "Colin McPhee's Concerto," *Mail and Empire,* January 16, 1924, CM-CLU. In *American Composers on American Music,* Wallingford Riegger wrote that McPhee's Toronto concerto was "shocking" to the audience (p. 37).

52. Bridle, "Concerto by Colin McPhee Accentuates Sheer Impulse to Create."

53. [Bridle], "Beethoven, M'Phee and Salvi Combine . . . McPhee's Concerto as a Contrast to Beethoven Is the Last Word in Being 'Different,'" *Toronto Daily Star,* January 16, 1924, CM-CLU.

54. Photo caption: "Colin McPhee, The brilliant young Canadian pianist and composer who will give a recital at Foresters Hall on March 29th," *Saturday Night,* March 22, 1924, Clipping File–CaOTMCL.

55. These descriptions are culled from three reviews: "Colin M'Phee's Recital Proves Marked Success/Gifted Young Pianist Charms Audience Throughout Entire Evening—Representative People Present," unidentified clipping [March or April 1924], CM-CLU; Bridle, "Colin M'Phee Plays Farewell Recital," *Toronto Daily Star,* March 31, 1924, CM-CLU; and [Hector Charlesworth?], "Colin McPhee's Recital," *Saturday Night,* April 5, 1924, CM-CLU and Clipping File–CaOTMCL.

56. Program, McPhee's Farewell Recital, Foresters' Hall, March 29, 1924, CM-CLU.

57. "Colin McPhee's Recital," *Saturday Night.*

58. Bridle, "Colin M'Phee Plays Farewell Recital."

59. Edmund Wilson, *O Canada: An American's Notes on Canadian Culture* (New York: Farrar, Straus and Giroux, 1965), 82.

60. Ibid., 106.

61. Callaghan, *That Summer in Paris,* 30.

62. [Bridle], "Colin McPhee," *Toronto Daily Star,* March 15[?], 1924, CM-CLU.

63. According to the I.O.D.E.'s education secretary, Mrs. H. A. Palmer, "in Feb. of 1924, at a municipal meeting, it was decided to create a travelling scholarship of $2000.00 for Mr. McPhee for one year. However later on mention is made that there had been some discrepancy in the way the motion had been handled and it was rescinded. Later that month it was recorded that Mr. McPhee had withdrawn his request for a travelling scholarship" (letter to author, September 27, 1983).

64. In an article charting McPhee's history, Charlesworth wrote: "In his European studies young McPhee was assisted by the late Sir Albert Gooderham, the extent of whose private benefactions to music and musicians in Toronto is unknown to most of those who were his fellow-citizens" (*Globe and Mail,* June 21, 1941, Clipping File-CaOTMCL). Unfortunately, Gooderham's papers have not been located.

65. Henry Bellamann, "Isidor Philipp," *Musical Quarterly* 29 (October 1943): 423.

66. Program, Clara Rabinowitch's recital, Salle Erard, April 20, 1925, CM-CLU.

67. *Chicago Tribune,* Paris, April 16, 1925, CM-CLU.

68. Program, McPhee's recital, Salle Malakoff, May 26, 1925, "Concert Under Direction of Lysbeth Sewell Foster/Paris–New York," CM-CLU.

69. Bridle, "All Ye Who Chorally Sing/What News for Next Season?" *Toronto Daily Star,* June 13, 1925, Clipping File–CaOTMCL.

70. "Wednesday" [May 20, 1925], IS-DLC.

71. Program, McPhee's recital, Salle des Agriculteurs, November 9, 1925, "Administration de Concerts A. Dandelot & Fils," CM-CLU. For the February 10 concert no program remains, only advance notice in the November 9 program: "M. Colin McPhee donnera un deuxième Récital de Mercredi 10 Février en soirée, à la Salle des Agriculteurs."

72. J. B., "Récital Colin Mac Phee [*sic*] (9 Novembre), *Le Ménestrel* 87 (November 20, 1925): 475; and review of McPhee recital, *Paris-Soir,* November 23, 1925 (both CM-CLU).

73. Irving Schwerké, *Chicago Tribune,* Paris, November 11, 1925, IS-DLC.

74. The Bathori performance is listed in McPhee's application to the American Composers Alliance, [1955 or 1956], ACA. Among his papers at CLU is an unidentified review of his work as an accompanist that was published in a German newspaper.

CHAPTER 2: A YOUNG PROFESSIONAL IN NEW YORK

1. McPhee must have been in New York by the summer of 1926, since his Invention is dated "New York/Aug. 12, 1926" (*New Music* 3, July 1930).

2. For more information on the new music enterprises of the 1920s, see: R. Allen Lott, "New Music for New Ears: The International Composers' Guild," *Journal of the American Musicological Society* 36 (1983): 266–86; Rita Mead, *Henry Cowell's New Music 1925–1936: The Society, the Music Editions, and the Recordings* (Ann Arbor: UMI Research Press, 1981); Carol J. Oja, "The Copland-Sessions Concerts and Their Reception in the Contemporary Press," *Musical Quarterly* 65 (1979): 212–29; Carol J. Oja, "Cos Cob Press and the American Composer," Music Library Association *Notes* 45 (December 1988): 227–52; Deane L. Root, "The Pan American Association of Composers (1928–1934)," *Yearbook for Inter-American Musical Research* 8 (1972): 49–70; and Ruth Watanabe, *The Institute of American Music of the University of Rochester: American Composers' Concerts and Festivals of American Music 1925–71, Cumulative Report* (Rochester, New York, 1972).

3. Henry Cowell, undated typescript tribute to McPhee, written ca. 1964, C-NN.

4. Cowell, "Trends in American Music," *American Composers on American Music: A Symposium,* ed. Henry Cowell (Palo Alto: Stanford University Press, 1933; reprint, New York: Frederick Ungar, 1962), 4.

5. Wallingford Riegger, "Adolph Weiss and Colin McPhee," *American Composers on American Music,* 36–42.

6. Aaron Copland, "The Composer in America, 1923–1933," *Modern Music* 10 (January-February 1933): 90.

7. Program, CM-CLU.

8. In his application to the American Composers Alliance in 1955 or 1956, McPhee listed a "Pastorale for 3 w.w. & piano" performed by a "chamber ensemble" in "Paris, 1925," ACA.

9. While *neoclassicism* as a stylistic designation encompasses a broad range of composers and techniques, it is most often applied to the work of Igor Stravinsky, beginning with *Pulcinella* of 1920, and includes especially figures active in Paris during the 1920s. See: Scott Messing, *Neoclassicism in Music: From the Genesis of the Concept through the Stravinsky-Schoenberg Polemic* (Ann Arbor: UMI Research Press, 1988).

10. Louise Varèse, *Varèse: A Looking-Glass Diary, Vol. I: 1883–1928* (New York: W. W. Norton, 1972), 251, 276.

11. Lecture given at Mary Austin House, Santa Fe, 1936. Quoted in Chou Wen-chung, "Varèse: A Sketch of the Man and His Music," *Musical Quarterly* 52 (April 1966): 157.

12. W. J. Henderson, "Modern Works Given in Concert," *New York Sun,* November 29, 1926; Olin Downes, "Music: More of the Ultra-Moderns," *New York Times,* November 29, 1926.

13. "New Music Given by Composers' Guild at Aeolian Hall," *New York Herald Tribune,* November 29, 1926. McPhee retained some status in Paris, for his International Composers' Guild performance was reviewed briefly in the *Paris Times* (December 12, 1926).

14. The program at CM-CLU gives no more specific information about these pieces.

15. "First Heard Here," unidentified clipping, CM-CLU. McPhee also received a favorable review from Arthur Mendel: "Colin McPhee gave an excellent performance of a *Sonata* by Lopatnikoff, severe, logical, and vigorous" (*Modern Music* 6 [January-February 1929], 31).

16. "Give First Hearings of Chamber Music," *New York Times* (February 10, 1930).

17. "Colin M'Phee to Give Recital in Americus Hotel: Composer-Pianist Wrote Symphonic Poem at Age of 19. Coming Here Dec. 7," unidentified Allentown, Pennsylvania, newspaper, late November or early December 1927, CM-CLU.

18. All four concerts were under the management of Arthur Judson, who also handled the International Composers' Guild. The programs are in the Gauthier Collection at NN.

19. Marjory M. Fisher covered the Los Angeles concert for *Musical America,* calling Gauthier "the veritable high priestess of the modern cult of song"; McPhee's

accompanying was perfunctorily described as "able" ("Coast Forces Exchange," 47 [January 28, 1928]: 24).

20. "Debut by Mme. Pfiffer: Soprano of the Vienna Opera Gives a Successful Recital," *New York Times,* April 5, 1927.

21. "Abbie Mitchell," *Musical Courier* (April 19, 1928), 28. Program, "Song Recital by Abbie Mitchell Soprano," Engineering Auditorium, 27 West 39th Street, Sunday evening, April 15, 1928, at 8:30 P.M. (Collection of Abbie Mitchell's son, the late Mercer Cook, of Silver Spring, Maryland). Two of the songs were performed two weeks later (May 1, 1928) in a concert by the Women's University Glee Club (program, CM-CLU).

22. Kurt Schindler founded the Schola Cantorum in 1909 as a choir of forty women. One year later it was incorporated as the MacDowell Chorus and included two hundred mixed voices. In 1912 it was renamed the Schola Cantorum. See: Winifred Douglas, "Twenty Years of the Schola Cantorum," pamphlet, n.p. (1929), NN. Information about the Schola Cantorum's activities during the late 1920s is contained in several *New York Times* reviews: "Colorful Concert by Schola Cantorum: Mixed Chorus of 200 Gains in Tonal Balance" (March 14, 1929); "[Philharmonic-Symphony Orchestra and Schola Cantorum] to Cooperate in Programs" (May 24, 1929); and "Schola Cantorum Musicales" (October 27, 1929).

23. Hugh Ross, interview with author, New York City, October 4, 1982.

24. "New Schola Conductor," *New York Times,* May 22, 1927.

25. As announced by E. R. Parkhurst in "Personalia," *The Globe,* February 11, 1922.

26. The *Sea Shanty Suite* is discussed later in this chapter, and the program for McPhee's performance of *The Rio Grande* on January 29, 1931, is in CM-CLU.

27. Claire Reis, *American Composers of Today* (New York: The United States Section of the International Society for Contemporary Music, 1930), 31. Both are still listed in the 1932 and 1947 editions; they are also cited in the "Biographical Notes" at the end of Cowell's *American Composers on American Music,* p. 209.

28. The string quartet appears in Louise Varèse's program notes to the International Composers' Guild performance of *Pastorale and Rondino* in 1926. The work for chorus and orchestra turns up in an unidentified promotional piece for a performance of the Concerto for Piano with Wind Octette in 1930 ("He [McPhee] states that he now [1930] is writing a work for Chorus and Orchestra," clipping, CM-CLU) and in a 1929 letter to Nicolas Slonimsky, where McPhee writes, "At present

I am at work on a big work for chorus and full orchestra" (NS-DLC). The ballet is cited in program notes for the Women's University Glee Club performance of two McPhee songs in 1928 (Town Hall, May 1, 1928, CM-CLU).

29. Here, as with other McPhee compositions discussed in this book, complete information about publication and recordings (where applicable) can be found in Appendix A.

30. Albert Roussel, quoted in William Austin, *Music in the Twentieth Century* (New York: W. W. Norton, 1966), 419–20.

31. Program, American Composers' Series twelfth concert, featuring the Rochester Little Symphony, Howard Hanson, conducting, Colin McPhee, pianist, February 22, 1929, CM-CLU. McPhee also performed the concerto in Boston under Nicolas Slonimsky on March 11, 1929 (program, CM-CLU), in New York with Georges Barrère's Little Symphony on March 23, 1930 (announced in *New York Times,* March 23, 1930), and in New York, again under Slonimsky, on April 11, 1931 (program, NN).

32. In McPhee's notes to this piece, he renames the last movement "Finale" (typescript inserted into the Concerto score at CLU).

33. Ibid.

34. "Fire Down Below," the shanty not included in this publication, is lost. According to Hugh Ross, McPhee arranged the sea shanties "with the idea that we [i.e., the Schola Cantorum] would do it. We did not commission them" (interview with author, October 4, 1982).

35. Sir Richard Runcian Terry, *The Shanty Book,* Part I (London: J. Curwen & Sons, 1921). Part II appeared in 1926. The title page of McPhee's published score bears the following credit line: "The Melody [*sic*] collected and Edited by Sir Richard Terry" (Colin McPhee, arranger, *Sea Shanty Suite for Baritone Solo, Men's Chorus, 2 Pianos and 2 Sets of Timpani* [New York: Edwin F. Kalmus, 1930]).

36. Stan Hugill, *Shanties and Sailors' Songs* (New York: Frederick A. Praeger, 1969), 112.

37. W. B. Whall, *Ships, Sea Songs and Shanties* (Glasgow: J. Brown & Son, 1927), 87.

38. McPhee, "Scores and Recordings," *Modern Music* 17 (January-February 1940): 110.

39. Pitts Sanborn, "Schola Cantorum Presents Its Miscellaneous Program," *New York Telegram,* March 14, 1929.

40. "Music," *New York World,* March 14, 1929.

41. According to McPhee's application to the American Composers Alliance in 1955 or 1956, the *Sea Shanty Suite* was performed by the Columbia University Glee Club and Yale Glee Club in 1929; the New York Downtown Glee Club, Harvard Glee Club, and Princeton Glee Club in 1930, and the New York University Glee Club in 1931 (ACA). The Composers Forum programmed the work in 1954.

42. McPhee to Madeleine [Friedheim], [June or early July 1929], private collection, New York.

43. Riegger, "Adolph Weiss and Colin McPhee," *American Composers on American Music,* 40.

44. McPhee, "Music and Films," *Musical Leader* (March 12, 1931); also quoted in Olin Downes, "Music and Film," *New York Times,* March 8, 1931.

45. McPhee, "Music and Films."

46. Quoted in "Adolph Weiss and Colin McPhee," 40.

47. Olin Downes, "Concert of Music and Films," *New York Times,* March 16, 1931. There was at least one important precedent, however, involving an American composer. George Antheil had planned for his *Ballet Mécanique* of 1925 to coordinate with a film by Fernand Léger and Dudley Murphy. Unfortunately, synchronization of the film and music proved impossible. McPhee did, however, perform in the New York concert premiere of *Ballet Mécanique* in 1927 (without film).

48. Program, CM-CLU. The orchestra was made up of members of the New York Philharmonic Symphony.

49. McPhee, "Music and Films." Ralph Steiner writes of their collaboration: "No cooperation—he saw film & composed" (Steiner, letter to author, January 30, 1984).

50. Gilbert Seldes, "Films and Music: The Work of Ralph Steiner," *New Haven Times,* April 3, 1931.

51. "Concert of Music and Films."

52. McPhee to Van Vechten, postmarked "4 [blurred] 1932, Paris."

53. Ralph Steiner, *A Point of View* (Middletown, Connecticut: Wesleyan University Press, 1978), 13.

CHAPTER 3: ASIA BECKONS

1. McPhee, *A House in Bali,* 2. The two books that he mentions are early histories of Java and Indonesia: John Crawfurd, *History of the Indian Archipelago,* 3 vols. (Edinburgh: Archibald Constable, 1820), and Thomas Stamford Raffles, *The History of Java,* 2 vols. (London: Black, Parbury, and Allen, 1817).

2. Edward Leuders, *Carl Van Vechten and the Twenties* (Albuquerque: University of New Mexico Press, 1955), 5.

3. Minna Lederman, interview with author, New York City, October 12, 1981.

4. Biographical information for Jane Belo is given in a one-page, undated sheet (which reads like a resume) and on a New York driver's license issued on May 21, 1935. Both are housed with Belo's papers in MM-DLC.

5. The resume listed above credits this journey with "arousing [her] interest in anthropology," MM-DLC.

6. George Biddle, *Green Island* (New York: Coward-McCann, 1930). More about Biddle can be found in his autobiography, *An American Artist's Story* (Boston: Little, Brown & Co., 1939), and in two summaries of his life and work: Martha Pennigar, *The Graphic Work of George Biddle with Catalogue Raisonné* [exhibition catalogue] (Washington D.C.: The Corcoran Gallery of Art, 1979), 42–43; and Marcia M. Mathews, "George Biddle's Contribution to Federal Art," *Records of the Columbia Historical Society 1973–74* (Charlottesville: University of Virginia Press, 1976): 493–520.

7. George Biddle and Jane Belo, "Foot-Hills of Cuba: A Cross-Section of Spanish-American Civilization," *Scribner's* 79 (February 1926): 128–36.

8. Belo to Biddle, postmarked May 8, 1928; also May 17[?], 1928; both GB-DLC.

9. Belo to Biddle, postmarked May 25, 1928, GB-DLC.

10. Belo to Biddle, postmarked June 23, 1928, GB-DLC.

11. Belo to Biddle, postmarked December 1928 [no day given], GB-DLC.

12. Marriage license, May 6, 1930, Department of Health, State of Connecticut.

13. McPhee to Carl Van Vechten, postmarked June 30, 1930, Cassis-sur-Mer.

14. McPhee to Van Vechten, [1930], Cassis-sur-Mer.

15. McPhee, "Orage," *Canadian Magazine* 62 (December 1923): 148. Belo, "Assimilation," *Forum* 76 (July 1926): 98, and "Protest," *Bookman* 64 (January 1927):

550. Jane discussed their drawings in a letter to Biddle, postmarked July 1, 1928, GB-DLC.

16. McPhee gave both Sidney Cowell and Victor Carl a print he made in the 1920s that shows a cat peering coyly at a mouse.

17. Following are selected citations for Van Vechten's writing in *Vanity Fair:* "Erik Satie: Master of the Rigolo (A French Extremist in Modernist Music)" (March 1918): 57, 92; "The Great American Composer: His Grandfathers Are the Present Writers of Our Popular Ragtime Songs" (April 1917): 75, 140; "George Gershwin: An American Composer Who Is Writing Notable Music in the Jazz Idiom" (March 1925): 40, 78, 84; "The Folksongs of the American Negro: The Importance of the Negro Spirituals in the Music of America" (July 1925): 52, 92; "Negro 'Blues' Singers: An Appreciation of Three Coloured Artists Who Excel in an Unusual and Native Medium" (March 1926): 67, 106, 108.

18. Carl Van Vechten, *Nigger Heaven* (New York: Alfred A. Knopf, 1926). Background information about Van Vechten is found in Bruce Kellner, *Carl Van Vechten and the Irreverent Decades* (Norman: University of Oklahoma Press, 1968), and in "The Reminiscences of Carl Van Vechten" (transcript, Oral History Research Office, Columbia University, 1960).

19. Langston Hughes, *The Big Sea* (New York: Hill and Wang, 1940), 251–52. Hughes went on to recall a slate of memorable parties from the 1920s, including "a dinner for Claire Spencer at Colin McPhee's and Jane Belo's in the village, where Claire Spencer told about a thrilling night flight over Manhattan Island in a monoplane" (p. 250). Colin and Jane were probably living in the Varèse apartment at 188 Sullivan Street in Greenwich Village.

20. McPhee to Van Vechten, postmarked March 24, 1930.

21. Zora Neale Hurston, *Dust Tracks on a Road: An Autobiography* (London: Hutchinson & Co., 1944), 89, 126.

22. Robert E. Hemenway, *Zora Neale Hurston: A Literary Biography* (Urbana: University of Illinois Press, 1977), 274.

23. Frank Crowninshield, introduction to Miguel Covarrubias's *Negro Drawings,* preface by Ralph Barton (New York: Alfred A. Knopf, 1927); W. C. Handy, *Blues: An Anthology,* introduction by Abbe Niles (New York: A & C Boni, 1926).

24. Miguel Covarrubias, *Island of Bali* (New York: Alfred A. Knopf, 1937), xvii.

25. Jane Belo, introduction to *Traditional Balinese Culture,* xix.

26. McPhee to Sidney Cowell, August 25 [1945] (B38/F611).

27. Malcolm Cowley, *Exile's Return: A Literary Odyssey of the 1920s* (New York: The Viking Press, 1934, 1951), 235.

28. McPhee to Sidney Cowell, July 28 [1946] (B38/F611).

29. Morley Callaghan, *That Summer in Paris: Memories of Tangled Friendships with Hemingway, Fitzgerald, and Some Others* (New York: Coward-McCann, 1963), 229.

30. Waldo Frank, *The Re-Discovery of America* (New York: Charles Scribner's Sons, 1929), 110.

31. "New York Polyhymnia Opening Program on April 12," *Musical Courier* (March 12, 1931).

32. Among the Saminsky letters at DLC is one written November 19, 1931, on Polyhymnia letterhead, giving officers of the organization.

33. Lazare Saminsky, *Music of Our Day: Essentials and Prophecies* (New York: Thomas Y. Crowell Co., 1932), 81–83.

34. The history of these recordings is given in Andrew Toth, *Recordings of the Traditional Music of Bali and Lombok* (n.p.: Society for Ethnomusicology, 1980), 16–17.

35. Belo, introduction to *TBC*, xviii. There is another version of this story. Sidney Cowell remembers McPhee saying he heard the recordings through Eric Clarke, who in the late 1920s was in the process of assembling a collection of records that would be distributed to colleges by the Carnegie Foundation (interview with author, Shady, New York, October 10, 1981). McPhee himself later recalled that he first heard about Indonesian music as a student in Toronto, when Leopold Godowsky, a friend of McPhee's teacher Arthur Friedheim, returned from Java (interview following a Composers' Forum concert in 1954 at Columbia University; tape at Princeton Electronic Music Center Library).

36. McPhee to Dr. William Mayer, Monday [postmarked September 2, 1942]. The quotations that follow are drawn from this letter.

CHAPTER 4: THE FIRST TRIPS TO BALI

1. Belo recalls going to the International Colonial Exposition in Paris (*Traditional Balinese Culture,* xix). Both Mandera and Lebah talked about the exposition in interviews with me. Mandera has a photograph of himself and the other gamelan members who performed there, and Lebah recalls with horror a big explosion and fire in the Dutch pavilion (Anak Agung Gedé Mandera, interview with author, Peliatan, Bali, April 11, 1984; I Madé Lebah, interview with author, Peliatan, Bali,

April 9, 1984). All subsequent quotations from Lebah are taken from this same interview.

2. Promotional pamphlet about the Rotterdam Lloyd Royal Mail Line, 1932, CM-CLU.

3. Malay has formed the basis for the language currently spoken throughout Indonesia, which is called Bahasa Indonesia. The formal adoption of Bahasa Indonesia took place in 1928, but its process of evolution and acceptance was slow.

4. Mead, February 2, 1936 (published in *Letters from the Field: 1925–1975*, 156). In this volume Mead does not tell to whom the letters were addressed.

5. Belo, *TBC*, xxi.

6. McPhee, "The Green Earth Scorched," *Modern Music* 19 (March-April 1942): 163.

7. McPhee, *A House in Bali*, 10.

8. Ibid., 15.

9. *TBC*, xv.

10. *HB*, 15.

11. Walter Spies wrote to Jane from Bali on January 7, 1932, MM-DLC. She was in India, en route to Paris.

12. McPhee to Carl Van Vechten, postmarked 4 [blurred] 1932, Paris.

13. *HB*, 78.

14. McPhee, "Musical Exploration in Bali," *Musical America* (February 10, 1940), 263.

15. McPhee to Van Vechten, postmarked May 17, 1932, Rotterdam Lloyd.

16. *HB*, 81.

17. McPhee to Van Vechten, postmarked May 17, 1933, Hong Kong.

18. Mead, *Blackberry Winter: My Earlier Years* (New York: Simon and Schuster, 1972), 230.

19. Mead, September 1, 1937 (*Letters*, 211).

20. "Inventory McPhee House, Sajan" [typescript, 5 pp.], MM-DLC. Most likely Jane prepared this document just before leaving Bali in June 1939.

21. McPhee to Van Vechten, postmarked May 17, 1933, Hong Kong. In a

letter to his mother, dated October 4, 1932, Walter Spies said the house also had a horse stable and dog house (*Schönheit und Reichtum des Lebens Walter Spies: Maler und Musiker auf Bali 1895–1942,* ed. Hans Rhodius [Den Haag: L. J. C. Boucher, 1964], 308).

22. *HB,* 118–19.

23. McPhee, undated field notes (F32), CM-CLU.

24. "Ihr Haus wird wunderschön, wir haben all die Pläne zusammen entworfen" (Spies to his mother, October 4, 1932, in *Schönheit und Reichtum,* 308). Jane, in a tribute to Spies, wrote, "Walter helped very considerably in drawing the plans for the house and in finding us skilled workmen, beautiful wood carvers and workers in bamboo" ("An Appreciation of the Artist Walter Spies," *Schönheit und Reichtum,* 317).

25. Translation of Spies to his mother, October 4, 1932, in *Schönheit und Reichtum,* 308. The German reads as follows: "Wir leben sehr ruhig und frölich beieinander, McPhees und ich. Er hat sich einen Steinwayflügel gekauft, und so spielen wir viel auf zwei Klavieren. Vielleicht, doch sehr unwarhscheinlich, werden wir eine kleine Concerttournee durch Java machen! Wir haben viel Spass beim Haushalt."

26. *HB,* 83–84. Foreigners could not purchase land in Bali, so Colin and Jane leased the property. Jane was the legal owner of the house; most likely, she provided all the capital for the project. Two documents prepared on June 15, 1939, declare that the house and property in Sayan belonged to Jane Belo. Both were drawn up so that Godfried Abraham Schotel would manage the property while Jane was in the United States (MM-DLC). Another sheet among Belo's papers in MM-DLC is in longhand: "Contract dated, 12/7/32, signed by Jacobs Controlleur, I Njadet, Colin McPhee, good till July 12, 1942, given to Mr. Schotel c/o Afscheep & Commissiezaak, Den Pasar." In *HB* McPhee mentions that they leased the land for ten years (p. 83).

27. *HB,* 138 and following. Other Westerners on the island had similar problems. Margaret Mead, for example, walked through her village's cemetery on one of her first days there only to find out that it was taboo for a woman to do so; the village assessed a fine against her (Mead, June 21, 1936 [*Letters,* 164–65]).

28. *HB,* 96.

29. McPhee to Van Vechten, postmarked May 17, 1933, Hong Kong.

30. Ni Murni, interview with author, Ubud, Bali, April 14, 1984.

31. Zora Neale Hurston to Belo, December 3, 1938, MM-DLC. Belo financed some of Hurston's fieldwork in the South (see Robert E. Hemenway, *Zora Neale Hurston: A Literary Biography* [Urbana: University of Illinois Press, 1977], 274). Rhoda Métraux, "Jane Belo Tannenbaum, 1904–1968," *American Anthropologist* 70 (1968): 1169.

32. Mead, *Blackberry Winter,* 230.

33. Mead, July 1, 1937 (*Letters,* 200).

34. McPhee to Van Vechten, postmarked May 17, 1933, Hong Kong.

35. Sidney Cowell, interview with author, Shady, New York, October 10, 1981. Interview with I Madé Lebah.

36. Hugo Adolf Bernatzik, *South Seas,* trans. Vivian Ogilvie (New York: Henry Holt and Company, 1935), 157, 165. Belo describes Bernatzik briefly in *TBC,* xxi.

37. For complete citations of the books described in the ensuing paragraphs, see the bibliography.

38. Mead, April 29, 1936 (*Letters,* 160).

39. *TBC,* xvi–xvii.

40. Ibid., xxvii.

41. Mead, *Blackberry Winter,* 234–35.

42. Ibid., 231.

43. Mead, preface to Belo, *Trance in Bali* (New York: Columbia University Press, 1960), v.

44. *TBC,* xxi; also discussed in *HB,* 72–73.

45. Most of McPhee's photographs and films, both prints and negatives, are at the Ethnomusicology Archive at CLU. Many contact prints are contained in MM-DLC.

46. McPhee to Carleton Sprague Smith, April 3, 1941, copy in Chávez Collection, Mexico City.

47. *TBC,* xx–xxi.

48. McPhee to Van Vechten, postmarked 4 [blurred] 1932, Paris. Two letters from Henry Cowell to Nicolas Slonimsky discuss the possible performance of McPhee's concerto in Paris on a concert of the Pan American Association of Composers

(January 14 and February 25 [1932]; both citations are included in Sidney Cowell to author, April 24, 1984). McPhee's concerto finally received a performance by the Pan American Association at a Town Hall Concert in New York on April 15, 1934; Mabel Schneider was the pianist (program in Deane L. Root, "The Pan American Association of Composers (1928–1934)," *Yearbook for Inter-American Musical Research* 8 [1972]: 65–66). In a *Modern Music* review Theodore Chanler called the concerto "the most substantial offering of the evening" ("New York, Spring 1934," 11 [May–June]: 207).

49. *HB,* 78.

50. Mantle Hood, interview with author, Catonsville, Maryland, January 10, 1984.

51. *HB,* 171.

52. Ibid.

53. McPhee, *Music in Bali,* xiii.

54. *HB,* 72–73.

55. See the glossary in Appendix C for definitions of these and other Balinese terms.

56. *HB,* 22.

57. Ibid., 37.

58. Ibid., 42.

59. Ibid., 69.

60. McPhee, undated field notes (F30), CM-CLU; *HB,* 175.

61. *HB,* 23.

62. McPhee, undated field notes (F30), CM-CLU.

63. *HB,* 174.

64. Ibid., 176.

65. Ibid., 177.

66. Ibid., 179–80.

67. *MB,* 308–9.

68. *HB,* 181.

NOTES TO PAGES 88–93

69. Sampih is said to have been "adopted" by McPhee in the *New York Times*'s obituary of the dancer (May 4, 1954) and in McPhee's own *New York Times* obituary (January 8, 1964). McPhee's dealings with Sampih's parents are described in *HB*, 126–27, 131–32.

70. Katharane Mershon, interview with author, Tarzana, California, June 13, 1982.

71. *HB*, 128.

72. Ibid., 123.

73. McPhee, field notes, dated April 4, 7 P.M. (F31), CM-CLU.

74. *HB*, 196.

75. Ibid., 137.

76. Ibid., 155. Lebah remembers Sampih also studying with Mario, a famous dancer of the time. Mario's performance style is described by Covarrubias in *Island of Bali* (New York: Alfred A. Knopf, 1937), 232–35.

77. Lebah, however, recalls meeting McPhee somewhat later—in 1934, when McPhee became a full member of the Gong Peliatan so that Sampih would have a good *kebyar* group with which to perform regularly.

78. *HB*, 156.

79. McPhee, "Lebah," undated field notes (F36), CM-CLU.

80. I met Lebah in Peliatan in April 1984 and heard him perform with both the Peliatan *gamelan kebyar* and *gamelan semar pegulingan*. I also had the privilege of sitting in on a drum lesson he was giving to his grandson.

81. *HB*, 157–58.

82. I Madé Lebah, interview with author.

CHAPTER 5: A WESTERN INTERLUDE

1. McPhee to Henry Cowell, written from "New York Central Lines—En Route" [spring 1935] (B16/F264).

2. The McPhees' trip can be traced through visa stamps in his passport (British passport no. 10756, issued in Shanghai, May 9, 1934), CM-CLU.

3. McPhee to Carl Van Vechten, postmarked November 17, 1934, Bali. A 1933 tax bill for the McPhees' Bali house is included among Jane Belo's papers, MM-DLC.

4. McPhee, *A House in Bali,* 194.

5. Janet McPhee, interview with author, Toronto, May 1, 1983. The quotations at the end of this paragraph come from the same interview. In a letter to Jane Belo (January 26, 1948), Douglas McPhee said he had met her twice (MM-DLC).

6. Augustus Bridle, "Former Toronto Musician Lives Three Years in Bali," *Toronto Daily Star* [undated clipping, summer 1935], CM-CLU.

7. McPhee partly fit the characterization Virgil Thomson later made of composers supported by their wives: "Sometimes nothing changes at all [after marriage], especially if there isn't too much wealth around. If there is a lot of it, class pressure is pretty strong. The composer subjected to this is likely to turn toward capitalistic proletarianism. There are two common forms of this. One is the exploitation of ornamental folklore (somebody else's folklore). The other is a cult of urban populistic theatrical jazz (jazz by evocation) and of pseudo-Viennese waltzes" ("Why Composers Write How," *The State of Music,* 2d ed. [New York: Vintage Books, 1962], 87).

8. "League of Composers Commissions Six Works," *Musical America* 55 (October 25, 1935): 4; and "Progress Seen in Plan of Composers' League," *Musical America* 56 (March 25, 1936): 12. Although the details of McPhee's commission are not known, those for one to Nicolai Berezowsky in 1934 are found in a letter to him from Claire Reis. The fee was $250; the League had rights to first performance of the work and promised to arrange it; the composer was to pay for copying; and a score was to be given to the League library (Claire Reis to Nicolai Berezowsky, February 23, 1934, NN).

9. McPhee, "The Absolute Music of Bali," *Modern Music* (May-June 1935): 163-69. McPhee's sentiments reveal a general concern of the day. Ironically enough, given McPhee's seeming political neutrality, a similar message is found in an article by Hanns Eisler, published in the same issue of *Modern Music:* "The crisis in music has been created by the general crisis in society. In music it appears definitely as a crisis in the technic of composition, which has succeeded in completely isolating modern music from life" ("Reflections on the Future of the Composer," *Modern Music* 12 [May-June 1935]: 181).

10. Program for McPhee's presentation on Bali, the Cosmopolitan Club, November 6, 1935. Other information comes from Wynne Fooshee, archivist for the Cosmopolitan Club, to author, June 1, 1984.

11. Flier, "The WEVD University of the Air Presents Modern American Music Series," Colin McPhee, commentator, C-NN.

12. A list of the programs is given in McPhee to Cowell, [late January 1936] (B16/F267).

13. Ibid.

14. Arthur W. Locke, "Festival at Hartford," *Modern Music* 13 (March-April 1936): 56; "Controversial New Music Gives Zest to Events of Hartford Festival," *Musical America* 56 (February 25, 1936): 1, 22.

15. Minna Lederman, interview with author, New York City, October 12, 1981. In *Traditional Balinese Culture* Belo tells of another dinner party that would affect their work during the next few years. Margaret Mead invited them to meet Gregory Bateson (to whom she was not yet married), and as a result of this event Mead and Bateson decided to head for Bali in 1936 (pp. xxiv–xxv).

16. Program, Princeton University Glee Club and Wellesley College Choir, The Waldorf Astoria, March 27, 1936, CM-CLU.

17. Israel Citkowitz, "Biblical Texts Set to Music," *Modern Music* 13 (May-June 1936): 43.

18. McPhee to Van Vechten, postmarked 4 [blurred] 1932, Paris.

19. McPhee to David Diamond, postmarked March 24, 1936.

20. McPhee to Elizabeth Mayer [early 1940s].

21. The length is given on a typescript list entitled "Commissioned Works of the League of Composers 1922–1952" in the Claire Reis Collection, NN.

22. Diamond, interview with author, New York City, March 27, 1986.

23. McPhee to Elizabeth Mayer [early 1940s].

24. William Strickland, interview with author, Westport, Connecticut, December 5, 1981.

25. McPhee must not have complied with one stipulation of the commission—that a score be deposited in the League's library. No score has been located there, at CM-CLU, or at Princeton University (in either the music library or glee club files) (letters to author from Paula Morgan, music librarian, Princeton University, December 3, 1982, and September 22, 1983).

26. McPhee, "Forecast and Review: New York—January, February, 1936," *Modern Music* 13 (March-April 1936): 46.

27. Ibid., 45.

28. McPhee, "New York's Spring Season, 1936," *Modern Music* 13 (May-June 1936): 40. In 1931 Josten had been along with McPhee a board member of the New York Polyhymnia, the group dedicated to fostering international musical exchange.

29. Ibid., 42.

30. McPhee to Cowell [January 1936] (B16/F267).

31. McPhee, "Forecast and Review," 42.

32. McPhee to Cowell [spring 1935].

33. "Contributors to This Issue," *Modern Music* 12 (May-June 1935).

34. "Contributors to This Issue," *Modern Music* 13 (May-June 1936).

35. McPhee to Cowell, written from New York City [spring 1936] (B16/F264).

36. McPhee, "The Sounds of Bali," *Hi-Fi Review* (December 1958): 30.

37. McPhee talked about the first part of his summer in a letter to Madeleine [Friedheim], August 5, 1936, collection of Oliver Daniel.

38. McPhee to Chávez, "Friday" [early June 1936].

39.. "Mexico City to Hear Orchestral Series," *Musical America* 56 (July 1936): 17; and Helen L. Kaufmann, "Carlos Chávez: Decidedly No *Mañana* Mexican," *Musical America* 56 (September 1936): 11, 26.

40. Season program booklet, "Orquesta Sinfónica de México, 1936," CM-CLU.

41. McPhee to Eva Gauthier, written from the San Angel Inn, September 1 [1936], Gauthier Collection, NN.

42. Program, Orquesta Sinfónica de México, September 4, 1936, CM-CLU.

43. McPhee to Madeleine [Friedheim], August 30 [1936].

44. Program, "La musica de Bali, por Colin McPhee" [no date], CM-CLU. The program is a Spanish translation of the one used at the Cosmopolitan Club.

45. McPhee to Madeleine [Friedheim], August 30 [1936].

46. McPhee, "Note," *Tabuh-Tabuhan: Toccata for Orchestra and 2 Pianos* (New York: Associated Music Publishers, 1960).

47. McPhee, "The Sounds of Bali," 30.

48. McPhee, quoted in Wallingford Riegger, "Adolph Weiss and Colin Mc-Phee," *American Composers on American Music: A Symposium,* ed. Henry Cowell (Palo Alto: Stanford University Press, 1933; reprint, New York: Frederick Ungar, 1962), 40.

49. McPhee, "The Absolute Music of Bali," 165.

50. Richard Mueller, "Imitation and Stylization in the Balinese Music of Colin McPhee" (Ph.D. diss., University of Chicago, 1983), 204. Mueller includes a table of the "Major Borrowings" in *Tabuh-Tabuhan* on pp. 193–95. His dissertation is the only thorough analytic study of McPhee's music.

51. McPhee, "An American Composer in Bali," part 3 of the script for a five-part Voice of America radio series, ca. 1958, CM-CLU.

52. McPhee, "An American Composer in Bali," part 2.

53. McPhee, *Music in Bali,* 328.

54. Ibid., 254.

55. *HB,* 38.

56. McPhee, undated field notes (F32), CM-CLU.

57. McPhee to Cowell [spring 1935] (B16/F264).

58. McPhee, "The Absolute Music of Bali," 166.

59. Belo to Chávez, September 18, 1936.

60. McPhee to Madeleine [Friedheim], August 30 [1936].

61. McPhee to Eva Gauthier, September 1, [1936].

62. Aaron Copland to Serge Koussevitzky, October 5, 1936, SK-DLC. Used by permission.

63. Carlos Chávez, carbons of letters to conductors, all dated November 12, 1936.

64. Chávez to McPhee, November 12, 1936.

65. Chávez relayed their responses in two letters to McPhee: November 25 and December 17, 1936.

66. In a letter to Henry Cowell, Colin said, "Jane sails this week by way of Tahiti" (October 13 [1936]) (B16/F266).

67. McPhee to Chávez, written on the S.S. *Jan Pieterszoon Coen,* December 24, 1936. Perhaps Stokowski's reaction to *Tabuh-Tabuhan* was affected by a review that

McPhee published in *Modern Music* in the fall of 1936. McPhee complimented Stokowski on his recent arrangement of *Boris Godunov*, which employed Javanese gongs, but looked less favorably on Stokowski's performance of Rachmaninov's Third Symphony: "There is nothing to be said about this work from our point of view, except that admirers of Rachmaninov's music seemed definitely disappointed on hearing it" ("New York, Autumn of 1936," *Modern Music* 14 [November-December 1936]: 31).

68. Virgil Thomson to Gertrude Stein, December 29, 1928, from Boston. Reproduced in Tim Page and Vanessa Weeks Page, *Selected Letters of Virgil Thomson* (New York: Summit Books, 1988), 92.

69. Henry Cowell, "Current Chronicle," *Musical Quarterly* 34 (July 1948): 412.

CHAPTER 6: THE LAST YEARS IN BALI

1. McPhee to Ann Hull, March 16 [1937], AH-DLC. The following two quotations are from the same letter.

2. The visitors included Cole Porter, his wife Linda, and Vicki Baum (Walter Spies to Belo and McPhee, June 12, 1935 [date added in pencil], and to Belo, November 4 [1936], MM-DLC).

3. Vicki Baum, *A Tale from Bali,* trans. Basil Creighton (Garden City, N.Y.: Doubleday, Doran & Co., 1937), xi.

4. Al Sherman, Jack Meskill, and Abner Silver, *On the Beach at Bali-Bali* (New York: Edwin H. Morris & Company, 1936). In 1936 the song was recorded by Tommy Dorsey (Victor 25349) and Jimmie Lunceford (Decca 915), among others.

5. McPhee to Carl Van Vechten, postmarked February 13, 1938.

6. This and the following quotation are from undated field notes (F32), CM-CLU.

7. McPhee to Aaron Copland, February 16 [1938].

8. McPhee to Van Vechten, postmarked February 13, 1938. McPhee to Carlos Chávez, December 24, 1936.

9. McPhee, undated field notes (F30), CM-CLU.

10. Spies to his mother, July 26, 1937, in *Schönheit und Reichtum des Lebens Walter Spies: Maler und Musiker auf Bali 1895–1942,* ed. Hans Rhodius (Den Haag: L. J. C. Boucher, 1964), 350. Original text: "Im Oktober haben wir hier einen Kon-

gress vom Java-Institut. Dreihundert Menschen kommen aus aller Welt. . . . Mit McPhee gebe ich ein Konzert auf zwei Klavieren von balinesischer Musik als Beweis, dass sie auch auf Pianos zu spielen ist und aufzuschrieben, und überhaupt weil sie schön ist, auch ohne Gamelan."

11. McPhee, *A House in Bali,* 222–23.

12. Jaap Kunst to Erich von Hornbostel, May 8, 1926, in *Schönheit und Reichtum,* 240–41.

13. See Chapter 9 for a discussion of McPhee's transcriptions.

14. *HB,* 25, and McPhee, *Music in Bali,* xiv. McPhee describes the founding of this gamelan in *HB,* 203–12.

15. *HB,* 121.

16. *MB,* xvi. McPhee describes the founding of this first group in the introduction to his "Children and Music in Bali," *Djåwå* 18, no. 6 (1938): 309–10. The article was revised in 1954 and reprinted twice, first in Margaret Mead and Martha Wolfenstein, eds., *Childhood in Contemporary Cultures* (Chicago: University of Chicago Press, 1955), 70–95, and later in Belo, *Traditional Balinese Culture,* 212–39.

17. *HB,* 204.

18. Anak Agung Gedé Mandera, interview with author, Peliatan, Bali, April 11, 1984. Lebah claims that McPhee paid approximately five *ringgit* to rent the instruments (I Madé Lebah, interview with Carol Warren, Peliatan, Bali, n.d.).

19. McPhee, "Children and Music in Bali," 1; and *HB,* 205.

20. McPhee, "I Loenjoeh," undated field notes (F30), CM-CLU.

21. Both quotations are from McPhee, undated field notes (F32), CM-CLU.

22. *HB,* 209.

23. Ibid., 210–11. This is an example of the frequent (and often minor) discrepancies in McPhee's accounts of life in Bali. In *MB* (p. xvii) he says that Lunyuh came to Sayan twice a week.

24. I heard the *gamelan semar pegulingan* perform in full costume at an outdoor amphitheater in Peliatan in April 1984. They played one composition by Lotring and two by Lebah. Lebah performed with them that day, even though he is now retired from the group.

25. An *angklung* could also have four tubes. "Two larger tubes of equal length produce the basic tone, while two smaller tubes sound the tone an octave higher" (*MB,* 235).

26. In a footnote in "Children and Music in Bali" (p. 8) McPhee writes: "Drawings by these children are reproduced in the paper by Jane Belo (Mrs. McPhee), 'Balinese Children's Drawing' (*Djåwå*, September-December 1937), which fills in another side of the picture I am attempting to create." Belo's article has been reprinted in Mead and Wolfenstein, eds., *Childhood in Contemporary Cultures*, 52–69, and in *TBC*, 240–59. Mead's "Children and Ritual in Bali" was published in *Childhood in Contemporary Cultures*, 40–51, and reprinted in *TBC*, 198–211.

27. McPhee, "Children and Music in Bali," 7.

28. Ibid., 7–8.

29. In April 1984 I heard this ensemble play and talked to some of the original members. I Wayan Rima, who is not of the original ensemble but whose mother was a cook for McPhee, told me that the group's *angklung* were given to them by McPhee (interview with I Wayan Rima, Sayan, Bali, April 7, 1984). To the 1954 revision of "Children and Music in Bali" McPhee added a postscript telling what he had heard in 1952 of the gamelan's progress. Lebah, who was then in New York with the Peliatan group, told him that they had added many instruments to the original ensemble given to them by McPhee and that they "'play everywhere. . . . The club,' he added, 'still like to remember and laugh about the time you first asked them to play those old-fashioned things'" (*TBC*, 236).

30. McPhee, undated field notes (F32), CM-CLU.

31. Ibid.

32. I Madé Bandem, interview with author, Den Pasar, Bali, April 11, 1984.

33. McPhee, "Tenganan," undated field notes (F32), CM-CLU.

34. This is one of the few pages of field notes that is dated: "16 August 1938, North Bali" (F31), CM-CLU.

35. This and the following quotation come from separate sheets in undated field notes (F30), CM-CLU.

36. McPhee, undated field notes (F32), CM-CLU.

37. McPhee, field notes, August 15, 1937 (F32), CM-CLU. I have changed the verb tenses in the first and third sentences.

38. *MB*, xiii.

39. *HB*, 105, 215. McPhee, letters to Van Vechten, November 10, 1934, and February 13, 1938.

40. McPhee (F22), CM-CLU.

41. McPhee tried to get a Guggenheim award in the fall of 1936 but failed. McPhee to Henry Cowell, October 13 [1936] (B16/F266).

42. McPhee to Ruth [Benedict], November 18 [1938]. Quotations in the following paragraph come from this same letter. Other information is contained in McPhee to Margaret Mead, January 3 [1939]. Both in MM-DLC.

43. Willem F. Stutterheim, *Indian Influences in Old-Javanese Art* (London: The India Society, 1935).

44. Spies to Belo [in English], September 1938, MM-DLC.

45. In a letter of February 10, 1939, to "Johnny" [no last name], Jane says she and Colin were divorced "last July," MM-DLC.

46. While at work on *A House in Bali,* Colin wrote to Chávez: "Jane is furious, for her name is not mentioned once in the book, and indeed I give no indication of having been married—au contraire" (November 5 [1945]).

47. *MB,* vii.

48. Madé Peghi, interview with author, Sanur, Bali, April 8, 1984.

49. McPhee to Mead, January 3 [1939].

50. McPhee to Sidney Cowell, June 22 [mid-1940s] (B38/F610).

51. McPhee to Sidney Cowell, October 31 [after 1947] (B38/F612).

52. McPhee to Sidney Cowell, "Tuesday" [after 1945] (B38/F613).

53. McPhee to Diamond, "Tuesday" ["21 November 1940" in pencil].

54. They include Virgil Thomson, interview with author, Chicago, Illinois, January 6, 1982; and Shirley Hawkins, interview with author, Los Angeles, California, June 16, 1982.

55. McPhee to Sidney Cowell, May 23 [after 1945] (B38/F610).

56. Belo to Mead, May 26, 1940, MM-DLC.

57. Belo to Willem Stutterheim, March 9, 1939, MM-DLC.

58. *HB,* 225.

59. Mead, *Letters from the Field: 1925–1975,* 155.

60. Belo states this in several letters written in 1939, especially one to "Johnny" [no last name], February 10, 1939, MM-DLC.

61. McPhee wrote to Van Vechten on board ship and gave his route and anticipated arrival date (letter postmarked January 9, 1939).

62. McPhee, "The Green Earth Scorched," *Modern Music* 19 (March-April 1942): 166.

63. Belo to Stutterheim, March 9, 1939.

64. This research culminated in *Trance in Bali,* preface by Margaret Mead (New York: Columbia University Press, 1960).

65. Mead describes their decision to return to Bali in *Letters,* 155. Dates for the trip are given in Mead's "Diary Covering Period from Rabaul, November 26, to January 20, on board SS Marella" (typescript). The cover of this diary gives the dates "Nov 1935–Sept 1936," but the dates specified inside, beginning with January 4 (no year), appear to relate to 1939, not 1936 (MM-DLC).

66. Belo to her mother, February 10 [1939], MM-DLC.

67. Ironically enough, Spies wrote to his mother about his new responsibilities with the gamelans on December 31, 1938, the day of his arrest (in *Schönheit und Reichtum,* 378–79).

68. Spies to Belo, January 23, 1939, MM-DLC.

69. Belo to Stutterheim, March 9, 1939.

70. Belo to "Johnny," February 10, 1939. Ibid. for the remaining quotations in this paragraph.

71. Belo to "Gerald" [no last name], April 7, 1939, MM-DLC.

72. Belo to Stutterheim, March 9, 1939.

73. Belo, typescript notes, March 18, 1939, MM-DLC. Hans Rhodius and John Darling give a parallel example in their discussion of Spies's side of the case: "In Bali, friendships between members of the same sex have always been allowed more open and intense expression than is the case in most western societies, caught in the maze of their own taboos. This attitude was clearly shown by the father of Spies's young friend [evidently the "minor" involved in the case]. When the lawyer asked if he was angry at Mr. Spies's conduct, he replied: '*Kenapa?* (But why?) He is after all our best friend, and it was an honour for my son to be in his company, and if both are in agreement, why fuss?'" (*Walter Spies and Balinese Art,* ed. John Stowell [Zutphen: Terra, 1980], 45).

74. Belo to her mother, February 10 [1939]. In MM-DLC are a number of papers prepared before Jane left Bali in 1939. Two documents drawn up on June 15,

1939, declare that the house and property in Sayan belong to Jane Belo and that Godfried Abraham Schotel would manage the property while Jane was in the United States. A four-page inventory of the house's contents also exists.

75. Rudolf Bonnet to Belo, June 17, 1940, MM-DLC.

76. Interview with I Wayan Rima, Sayan, Bali, April 7, 1984.

CHAPTER 7: HARD TIMES IN NEW YORK

1. McPhee to Carl Van Vechten, postmarked January 9, 1939; written "between Sumatra and Colombo; heavy seas."

2. McPhee, "The Decline of the East," *Modern Music* 16 (March-April 1939): 160–67. The next quotation comes from p. 164.

3. McPhee to Carlos Chávez, October 16 [1952], and McPhee to Sidney Cowell, April 28 [1946] (B38/F609).

4. See the appended list of McPhee's writings for full citations of the publications mentioned in this paragraph and elsewhere.

5. Minna Lederman, interview with author, New York City, October 12, 1981.

6. Henry Cowell, "Towards Neo-Primitivism," *Modern Music* 10 (1933): 150–51.

7. *Modern Music* articles: Raymond Petit, "Exotic and Contemporary Music," *MM* 11 (1934): 200–203. Paul Nettl, "The West Faces East," *MM* 20 (1943): 90–94. John Cage, "The East in the West," *MM* 23 (1946): 111–15.

8. Henry Cowell, "Current Chronicle," *Musical Quarterly* 39 (January 1953): 98.

9. McPhee to Lederman, May 15 [1943 or 1944], MoMu-DLC.

10. The Archives of Traditional Music at Indiana University has a fifteen-minute recording made by McPhee and Herzog at the World's Fair in 1939 (telephone conversation with Louise Spear, librarian, July 19, 1984).

11. *Balinese Ceremonial Music* was reviewed in the *New York Times* ("Three Bali Pieces Transcribed," July 14, 1940); *Music of Bali* was reviewed in the same paper by Ross Parmenter ("Records: From Bali," June 15, 1941).

12. McPhee to Ann Hull, March 16 [1937], AH-DLC. Dates for each are given in the score.

13. "Records: From Bali/An Album of Works prepared by Colin McPhee—Other Recent Releases," *New York Times* (June 15, 1941).

14. McPhee to Aaron Copland, March 27 [1941].

15. The cover and first page of Britten's copy of *Pemoengkah* are reproduced as illustration no. 176 in Donald Mitchell and John Evans, *Benjamin Britten: Pictures from a Life 1913–1976* (New York: Charles Scribner's Sons, 1978).

16. Only one letter from McPhee to Van Vechten survives from after the Bali period. It was written on October 11, 1944: "It seems too bad, to me at least, that we must glare like that at each other, as last night at the ballet."

17. Few of McPhee's letters to Lederman are extant.

18. Sidney Cowell, interview with author, Shady, New York, October 10, 1981.

19. McPhee to Sidney Cowell, July 24 [1946] (B38/F611).

20. The Mayers' guest books show that McPhee visited them frequently between 1939 and 1943 (collection of Beata Sauerlander). A photograph of McPhee and Britten on the lawn at the Mayers' home is reproduced as illustration no. 125 in Mitchell and Evans, *Benjamin Britten: Pictures from a Life 1913–1976*. Mitchell says that McPhee's name first turns up in Britten's "pocket diary" in 1939 (letter to author, November 22, 1982).

21. Elizabeth Mayer to Britten, July 1, 1942 (transcribed by Beata Sauerlander).

22. McPhee to Margaret Mead, October 4 [1944].

23. McPhee to Sidney Cowell, July 24 [1946] (B38/F611).

24. McPhee lived at 129 East Tenth Street from March 1939 to May 1941 and from October 1942 to September 1943.

25. Records at Yaddo show that McPhee was there from June 15 to July 31 and from August 11 to December 2 of 1941. The Yaddo archive has no other information about him (Kjersti Board, letter to author, Yaddo, June 24, 1984).

26. McPhee to David Diamond, "Yaddo, Saturday" [1941]. He told Diamond he was working in the "Pine Tree" studio.

27. McPhee to Diamond, November 15 ["1945" added in pencil].

28. Truman Capote, "Brooklyn Heights: A Personal Memoir," *Holiday* (February 1959): 65.

29. Paul Bowles, *Without Stopping* (New York: G. P. Putnam's Sons, 1972), 233.

30. McPhee lived in the Chelsea off and on in 1949 and 1950.

31. McPhee to Sidney Cowell, no date ["1948?" added at top], written from the Hotel Chelsea (B38/F607).

32. McPhee to Marc Blitzstein, "Thursday" [1935–36], Blitzstein Collection, State Historical Society of Wisconsin, Madison.

33. McPhee to Mead, January 3 [1939], Sumatra. McPhee had mentioned a book as his goal already in 1932, when he had returned to Paris after six months in Bali (McPhee to Van Vechten, 4 [blurred] 1932).

34. McPhee to Copland, July 20 [1941].

35. McPhee to William Mayer, October 30 [1941].

36. McPhee to Diamond, "Thursday" [1941].

37. In a letter to Benjamin Britten, Elizabeth Mayer said that "Colin has nearly finished his Travel Book on Bali" (July 8, 1944; transcribed by Beata Sauerlander).

38. McPhee to Sidney Cowell, September 11 [1945] (B38/F612).

39. McPhee to Mead, July 16 [1946].

40. Henry Cowell compares the two in his review of *A House in Bali,* in *Notes* 4 (December 1946): 85.

41. McPhee to Mead, October 4 [1945]. Review of Du Bois by McPhee in *New York Times Book Review* (September 17, 1944). The full title of Du Bois's book is *The People of Alor: A Social-Psychological Study of an East-Indian Island* (Minneapolis: University of Minnesota Press, 1944).

42. McPhee to Sidney Cowell, "Friday" [1946] (B38/F614).

43. On November 29 [1945] McPhee wrote Sidney Cowell that the book was "announced for April. Text—finished! Slight changes in process, to meet deadline of Dec. 5" (B38/F612). Then on April 5 [1946] he wrote, "My book is delayed— paper shortage for the photographs" (B38/F609).

44. Reviews of *A House in Bali:* Henry Cowell in *Notes;* unsigned in *Musical Courier* (November 15, 1946): 26; Minna Lederman in *Saturday Review* (November 23, 1946): 19; Beryl de Zoete in *The New Statesman and Nation* (April 3, 1948): 279; Ruth Benedict in *New York Herald Tribune Weekly Book Review* (October 6, 1946).

45. McPhee to Sidney Cowell, "Saturday" [fall 1946] (B38/F615).

46. McPhee to Mead, December 17 [1946].

47. The archive of Harold Ober Associates is in the Princeton University Library but contains no information about McPhee (Mardel Pacheco, assistant to the curator of manuscripts, to author, October 22, 1981).

48. Some idea of the size of these press runs is given in a letter from McPhee to Carlos Chávez: "Editions of some 3000 sold out in England and Italy in a few months" (October 16 [1952]).

49. McPhee to Copland, August 31 [1949 or 1950].

50. McPhee to Sidney Cowell, April 28 [1946] (B38/F609).

51. McPhee to Mead, "Tuesday" [1949 or 1950].

52. McPhee to Sidney Cowell, July 12 [1946] (B38/F611). McPhee referred to the categorization of instruments by Sachs and Hornbostel into four basic groups: aerophones (wind), idiophones (self-sounding), membranophones (percussion instruments with a membrane), and chordophones (string).

53. Lederman, interview with author.

54. McPhee to Sidney Cowell, August 3, 1949 [date added in ink] (B38/F607).

55. McPhee to Chávez, June 19 [1941].

56. McPhee to Chávez, October 17 [1941].

57. McPhee to Mead, August 21 [1944].

58. McPhee to Chávez, September 29, 1945.

59. Ibid.

60. McPhee to Diamond, November 15 ["1945" added in pencil].

61. McPhee to Sidney Cowell, postmarked December 27, 1946 (B38/F607).

62. McPhee to Copland, August 31 [1949 or 1950].

63. McPhee to Sidney Cowell, postmarked December 20, 1949 (B38/F607).

64. McPhee to Mead, "Monday" [clipped with letters dated 1950–52].

65. Lederman, interview with author.

66. Ives: *Modern Music* 17 (October-November 1939): 53. McBride: *Modern Music* 17 (March-April 1940): 180. McPhee wrote to David Diamond about his

criticism of Ives: "Be sure to read my article in this coming issue, out next week, just for a chuckle, for I say Ives is simply a *mess,* yes they even print the word mess, and I think it about time someone recognized this fact publicly" ("Saturday" [1939]). McPhee also wrote about Ives in "Winter Chronicle New York," *Modern Music* 8 (March-April 1931): 43. And in 1941 he had something favorable to say, citing Ives among those "who have done something significant in piano music" (*Modern Music* 18 [May-June 1941]: 268).

67. *Modern Music* 21 (March-April 1944): 183.

68. *Music for the Theatre: Modern Music* 18 (May-June 1941): 267. *Lincoln Portrait: Modern Music* 20 (May-June 1943): 277.

69. *Modern Music* 22 (November-December 1944): 58.

70. McPhee to Copland, August 23 [1943].

71. McPhee to Copland, March 27 [1941]. A brief (and favorable) review of Engel's *Triptych* appeared in *Modern Music* 18 (March-April 1941): 189. McPhee seems to have decided not to discuss Ruth Crawford's music in print.

72. McPhee to Sidney Cowell, June 3 [1946] (B38/F610). McPhee once confessed the same desire to Elizabeth Mayer: "I have a great longing to live for a while in Harlem, amidst the warmth and hustle of Negroes" (letter, August 31 [1941]).

73. McPhee, "The Torrid Zone," *Modern Music* 22 (January-February 1945): 140.

74. Ibid., 140–41.

75. McPhee, "Shadows in Bali," *Mademoiselle* (October 1946): 190–91, 306–8; McPhee reviewed records for *Mademoiselle* in 1943.

76. Lou Harrison, interview with author, Aptos, California, June 23, 1982.

77. McPhee to Diamond, "Saturday" [fall 1939].

78. A copy of the promotional pamphlet is in CM-CLU. The earliest known notice of one of his lectures was published in the *Hartford Courant* (October 8, 1940), CM-CLU.

79. McPhee to Mead, October 1 [1941]. Mead addressed a letter "To Whom It May Concern," recommending McPhee as a lecturer (July 9, 1940, MM-DLC).

80. Mead to McPhee, October 3, 1941, MM-DLC.

81. McPhee's lecture dates are nearly impossible to trace. He mentions a lecture at Sarah Lawrence College in the spring of 1941 (letter to Copland, March

27 [1941]). Elizabeth Mayer's diary for 1942 cites McPhee lectures in Chicago on April 22 and Urbana on April 23. His letters to her from that spring also mention a Boston lecture on April 27 (McPhee to Mayer, postmarked April 27, 1942).

82. McPhee to Carleton Sprague Smith, April 3, 1941, copy in Chávez Collection.

83. McPhee to Chávez, May 16 [1941].

84. Ibid.

85. McPhee to Copland, June 7 [1941].

86. McPhee to Mead, June 15 [1941].

87. As quoted in McPhee to Mead, "Sunday" [1941]. The ellipses are taken directly from McPhee's original.

88. McPhee to Chávez, June 19 [1941].

89. Telephone conversation with Eileen Holden, Research Office of the Guggenheim Foundation, January 31, 1983. The Guggenheim Foundation will not release the amount of its grants.

90. Mead to Guggenheim Foundation, undated draft [1942?], MM-DLC.

91. A copy of McPhee's proposal to the Guggenheim Foundation is in MM-DLC, together with a draft of Mead's letter of recommendation for him. Both are undated. But an attached letter from Henry Allen Moe of the Guggenheim Foundation was written on November 13, 1947.

92. McPhee to Sidney Cowell, "Sunday" [fall 1946] (B38/F615).

93. Harold Spivacke to McPhee (February 5, 1947), DLC.

94. Information about McPhee's grant is found in the Bollingen Archives in the Manuscript Division, DLC.

95. McPhee to Sidney Cowell, "Thursday" [1950?] (B38/F614).

96. McPhee to Howard Backus, chief, Fulbright Programs Exchange, September 18, 1950, copy in MM-DLC.

97. McPhee mentions these plans in letters to Copland (January 25 [1949]) and Chávez (January 15 [1949]).

98. McPhee to Sidney Cowell, March 12 [1946] (B38/F609). John Houseman talks about the New York branch in Studs Terkel, "The Good War: An Oral History of World War II," *Atlantic Monthly* (July 1984): 67–68.

99. Timothy R. Crotty, chief, Workforce Records Management Division, United States Office of Personnel Management, to author, September 20, 1984. On June 22 [1946] McPhee wrote Sidney Cowell that his salary might go up to the "middle of the 4000 bracket" (B38/F610).

100. McPhee to Sidney Cowell, May 15 [1946] (B38/F610).

101. McPhee to Sidney Cowell, June 18 [1946] (B38/F611).

102. McPhee to Sidney Cowell, June 3 [1946] (B38/F610) and July 24 [1946] (B38/F611).

103. McPhee to Sidney Cowell, "Friday" [1946] (B38/F614). No titles are given for specific transcriptions, and I have not been able to locate these recordings, either in the OWI's archives or with Maro Ajemian. George Avakian, who is married to Anahid Ajemian, Maro's sister, knows of no copy of the recording (George Avakian to author, August 6, 1982). Ajemian's Cage recordings were made in 1951.

104. McPhee to Sidney Cowell, July 31 [1945] (B38/F611).

105. McPhee to Chávez, October 5 [1946].

106. This date is approximate. In a letter written on November 7, 1946, McPhee told Chávez that he was "giving up the State Dept job end of year."

107. Chávez to McPhee, December 9, 1940, carbon in the Chávez Collection.

108. Program, "The Emperor Jones," starring Paul Robeson, Westport County Playhouse, week of August 5, 1940, CM-CLU. Program, "The Emperor Jones," starring Paul Robeson, Princeton Summer Theatre Season, McCarter Theatre, week of August 12, 1940 (collection of Alan Hewitt, New York City).

109. Oliver Daniel possesses several pages of manuscript, in McPhee's hand, for *Emperor Jones*. "Scene V—Entrance of Planters" is written at the top, and numbers for Hammond organ registrations have been indicated. This section of the score includes a series of ostinato patterns written at different pitch levels.

110. Alan Hewitt, "Colin McPhee and 'The Emperor Jones,'" typescript appended to a letter to the author, November 7, 1982.

111. Robert Lawrence, "New Theater Music," *New York Herald Tribune* (August 18, 1940). The following quotations are all drawn from this review.

112. Tennessee Williams, *Memoirs* (New York: Doubleday and Company, 1975), 61–62.

113. McPhee to Henry Cowell, January 9 [1941 added at the top] (B16/F264).

114. McPhee to Chávez, May 1 [1950].

115. Although the manuscripts to *Nun komm der heiden Heiland* and *Ciacona* have no date, two letters from 1941 reveal that McPhee was working on the transcriptions then. Both were written by McPhee from Yaddo to Elizabeth Mayer: August 20 and October 27.

116. McPhee, "Scores and Records," *Modern Music* 17 (October-November 1939): 52.

117. McPhee to Copland, June 3 [1941] and "Wednesday" [1941].

118. Clipping files, NN.

119. McPhee's score is part of the Britten-Pears collection at The Red House in Aldeburgh, Great Britain. It is dated "Feb-March 1942." Eric Walter White, in *Benjamin Britten: His Life and Operas* (Berkeley: University of California Press, 1970), 34, states that Britten "allowed" his Variations "to be used by Dance Players."

120. McPhee to Copland, June 3 [1942].

121. McPhee to Chávez, April 11 [1942].

122. McPhee mentions writing a "boogie-woogie" in letters to Chávez, June 14 [1943], and Copland, August 23 [1943].

123. According to McPhee's application to the American Composers Alliance of 1955 or 1956, the *Dances* were recorded in 1945 for broadcast by a student orchestra in Washington, D.C. (ACA). He wrote Sidney Cowell in October 1945 that Charles Seeger was making the recording and that he was using "only *part* of the . . . Dances" (October 22 [1945], B38/F612). No such recording seems to be extant. On January 2 [1946?] McPhee again wrote Sidney Cowell, "Seeger never sent me my promised copy of the recording. He does not answer my letters. I do feel sore" (B38/F609).

124. "Records and Scores," *Modern Music* 18 (March-April 1941): 188.

125. McPhee to Chávez, September 29, 1945.

126. McPhee to Sidney Cowell, November 17 [1947] (B38/F612).

127. McPhee to Nicholas J. Elsier, Jr., August 16, 1962, CM-CLU.

128. Program, Ballet Society, directed by George Balanchine, Hunter Playhouse, January 13 and 14, 1947, CM-CLU.

129. Described in McPhee to Copland, March 27 [1941].

130. "The Ballet Society, 1946–47, Vol. I" (New York: Ballet Society, Inc., 1947), 25.

131. The producer of "Arrows in the Dust" was Sig Mickelson and the co-producer Dr. Philip Eisenberg. The program originated in Minneapolis (telephone conversation with Carol Parne, CBS industry librarian, January 31, 1983).

132. Oliver Daniel, interview with author, Ardsley, New York, October 3, 1981.

133. McPhee to Mead, "Saturday" [1948].

134. McPhee discusses his negotiations with Luce in two letters to Chávez, before April 26, 1950, and on May 1 [1950]. Chávez responded on April 26, 1950.

135. McPhee to Chávez, May 1 [1950].

136. Otto Luening, interview with author, November 26, 1982.

137. Part of Minna Lederman's toast to Aaron Copland at a party on August 16, 1984.

138. McPhee to Sidney Cowell, May 23 [after 1945] (B38/F610).

139. The files of the American Composers Alliance contain an application for membership from McPhee dated May 7, 1939. Apparently he did not become a member until June 27, 1944 (the date on his contract with ACA). McPhee's resignation from ACA took effect January 1, 1946 (letter, Harrison Kerr to McPhee, October 19, 1945, ACA).

140. Chávez to McPhee, September 20, 1941.

141. McPhee to Chávez, October 1 [1941].

142. "Records and Scores," *Modern Music* 18 (March-April 1941): 189.

143. Daniel, interview with author.

144. McPhee to Chávez, November 15 [1947].

145. Mitchell and Evans, *Benjamin Britten: Pictures from a Life 1913–1976*, illustration no. 174.

146. Henry G. Mishkin, "Bartók at Amherst," *Amherst* (Winter 1978): 14–15.

147. McPhee to Elizabeth Mayer, August 20, 1941.

148. McPhee to Sidney Cowell, from the Rhinecliffe Hotel, [mid-1940s] (B38/F615).

149. McPhee to Sidney Cowell, May 13 [1946] (B38/F610).

150. McPhee to Elizabeth Mayer, postmarked January 12, 1943.

151. McPhee to Sidney Cowell, no date (B38/F613). Written while McPhee was staying at the Cowells' house in Shady, New York, sometime during the 1940s.

152. McPhee to Dr. William Mayer, "Monday" [postmarked September 2, 1942].

153. McPhee to Sidney Cowell, August 25 [1945] (B38/F611).

154. *HB*, 71, 114.

155. Clifford Geertz, "Person, Time, and Conduct in Bali," *The Interpretation of Cultures* (New York: Basic Books, 1973), 403–4.

156. McPhee to Dr. William Mayer, "Monday" [postmarked September 2, 1942].

157. McPhee mentions the WNYC job in a letter to Mead, "Friday" [1947 or 1948?]. McPhee sold "four Balinese pieces to that Blanche Evans for that hundred" (letter to Sidney Cowell, [April 1946?] B38/F609).

158. McPhee to Sidney Cowell, "Thursday" [1950 or 1951], CM-CLU. McPhee talks about the film project in several letters to her.

159. McPhee to Sidney Cowell, July 19 [1946] (B38/F611); and McPhee to Mead, "Friday" [1948].

160. There are many places in McPhee's correspondence where he either asks for money or thanks someone for having sent it. Following are two examples: letters to Mead, April 24 [1949] ("I never thanked you for those checks, really. . . . I never felt such a heel in my life as the last time I asked you to help me"), and to Copland, September 20 [1948] (McPhee asked for money from the "Arts and Letters emergency fund"; on other occasions he appealed to Copland himself).

161. McPhee discussed the problems with his mother in a letter to Mead ("Friday" [1948]), where he thanked her for lending him money: "The set-up with Jane was this. I wrote, asking if she would lend me $2000 against English royalties on the two books, which are slow in coming but certain. . . . I told her the situation regarding my mother—that it would take at least $750 from me as my share for the year, and would leave a balance for emergencies. . . . She wrote a thirty word note, asking for my brother's address. . . . She answered my brother's letter with a promise of $75 a month for four months, which 'we could consider did not have to be

repaid.'" Douglas McPhee wrote at least two letters to Belo asking her for money (January 26 and March 8, 1948, MM-DLC).

162. I Madé Lebah, interview with author, Peliatan, Bali, April 9, 1984.

163. McPhee to Sidney Cowell, "Wednesday" ["Aug. 3, 1949" added] (B38/F607).

CHAPTER 8: CHANGING FORTUNES

1. Coast traces this tour in his *Dancers of Bali* (New York: G. P. Putnam's Sons, 1953). The troupe arrived on September 16, 1952.

2. McPhee to Oliver Daniel, September 5 [1952], ACA.

3. McPhee to Virgil Thomson, no date [early September 1952]; September 30 [1952]; and "Tuesday" [September 1952].

4. Interviews with I Madé Lebah (Peliatan, Bali, April 9, 1984) and Anak Agung Gedé Mandera (Peliatan, Bali, April 11, 1984). Mandera has a plaque on his wall that includes the names of all the instrumentalists and dancers who made this trip to New York.

5. McPhee describes the room in a letter to Carlos Chávez, November 8 [1953].

6. McPhee to Sidney Cowell, "Thursday" [early 1950s] (B38/F614).

7. Daniel, interview with author, Ardsley, New York, October 3, 1981.

8. McPhee to Sidney Cowell, "Saturday" [early 1950s] (B38/F615).

9. Interviews with Sidney Cowell (Shady, New York, October 10, 1981) and Oliver Daniel. The remaining quotations in this and the following paragraph are from the interview with Cowell.

10. McPhee to Sidney Cowell, June 11 [1946] (B38/F610).

11. McPhee to Sidney Cowell [early 1950s], CM-CLU.

12. Paul Bowles to author, October 29, 1981.

13. Minna Lederman, interview with author, New York City, October 12, 1981. The ensuing quotations are from the same interview.

14. Program, CM-CLU.

15. McPhee to Aaron Copland, October 8 [1953].

16. Leopold Stokowski wrote McPhee on September 30, 1953, discussing details of the performance and inviting him to rehearsal (collection of Oliver Daniel).

17. McPhee to Copland, October 14 [1953].

18. This is among a number of references to McPhee that Ott, a longtime friend of Oliver Daniel, has culled from his diary. The entry is dated October 16, 1953.

19. Virgil Thomson, "Canadian Music," *New York Herald Tribune* (October 17, 1953).

20. Olin Downes, "Stokowski Offers 5 Canadian Works," *New York Times* (October 17, 1953).

21. McPhee to Thomson, "Saturday" [October 17, 1953], VT-CtY. McPhee to Downes, October 17 [1953], OD-GU.

22. McPhee to Chávez, October 18 [1953]. McPhee's phrase "at long last" refers not only to Chávez's attempt to interest Stokowski in *Tabuh-Tabuhan* in 1936 but also to McPhee's own effort, right after returning from Bali three years later, to line up a performance by Stokowski (as described in a letter from Walter Spies to Jane Belo, June 8, 1939, MM-DLC).

23. Information about publishing in McPhee to Thomson, October 22 [1953]. McPhee mentioned the advance in a letter to Copland, November 16 [1954]. About Rodzinsky: McPhee to Copland, October 19 [1953]. About commissions: McPhee to Copland, June 23 [1954]; Chávez and McPhee discussed these commissions in several letters, beginning with one from Chávez, November 3, 1953. Also, interview with Oliver Daniel.

24. McPhee to Chávez, October 18 [1953].

25. McPhee to Sidney Cowell, November 17 [1947] (B38/F612).

26. McPhee told about the offer in a letter to Chávez, June 3 [1954].

27. Details of the commission and the composition of *Transitions* are given in McPhee to Copland, June 23 [1954], and in McPhee's typescript program notes, CM-CLU.

28. McPhee to Chávez, October 11 [1954].

29. McPhee to Copland, November 4, 1954.

30. Ibid.

31. McPhee wrote to Chávez about the broadcast on March 21, 1955. Oliver Daniel has a tape of the radio broadcast.

32. McPhee to Chávez, October 22 [1954].

33. McPhee to Copland, "Thursday" [1954].

34. Typescript, CM-CLU.

35. Arthur Friedheim, *Life and Liszt: Recollections of a Concert Pianist* (New York: Taplinger Publishing, 1961), 254.

36. McPhee to Chávez, January 16 [1955].

37. "Colin McPhee, Hugo Weisgall and Ingolf Dahl received $1,000 grants presented to composers last year by the National Institute of Arts and Letters. Late yesterday afternoon the institute honored them further by presenting a program of their music at Carnegie Hall" (*New York Times,* February 19, 1955).

38. Program, collection of Oliver Daniel. Ross conducted the New York Philharmonic-Symphony Orchestra.

39. ACA subsidy of the recording is discussed in a letter from Carol Truax, coordinating manager of ACA, to Charles Wall, president, Associated Music Publishers, October 5, 1955, ACA.

40. McPhee to Chávez, May 26 ["1956" added].

41. Alfred Frankenstein, [review of *Tabuh-Tabuhan*], *High Fidelity* 6 (July 1956): 44. P. H. R. [Peter Hugh Reed], "Notes and Reviews," *American Record Guide* (July 1956): 177.

42. Program, Chávez Collection. McPhee shared the program with the composer Russell Smith. Both were available afterwards to answer questions. A tape of both the concert and the discussion session is in the Princeton Electronic Music Center Library. Don Ott noted in his diary that there was a party after the concert at Irving Drutman's apartment. Present were McPhee, Oliver Daniel, Peggy Glanville-Hicks, Margaret Mead and her daughter Catherine Bateson, George Davis, Lotte Lenya (to whom Davis was then married), Hermione Gingold, Aaron Copland, Arthur Berger and his wife, and Otto Luening.

43. These composers were listed in the *New York Times* review by R[oss] P[armenter], "Forum Presents Modern Program" (November 8, 1954).

44. Peggy Glanville-Hicks, "Composers Forum," *New York Herald-Tribune* (November 8, 1954).

45. Edward T. Cone, review of McPhee's Concerto for Piano with Wind Octette Accompaniment, *Musical Quarterly* 43 (January 1957): 141–42.

46. A number of letters from McPhee to Copland discuss loans: March 7, 1955, "Thursday" [1954?], "Friday" [1955?], "Thursday" [1956?], November 29 [1956].

47. A letter from McPhee to Oliver Daniel dated "Friday" [1955?] discusses a loan, and Daniel has two canceled checks totaling $250 that were issued to McPhee on July 15, 1958. McPhee received word of the Benedict Grant through a letter from Margaret Mead (April 3, 1956). McPhee asked the National Institute of Arts and Letters for a $300 loan (he had received a previous loan, too) against his $1,000 commission from the Louisville Orchestra (McPhee to Felicia Geffen, National Institute of Arts and Letters, June 27, 1957; copy in VT-CtY). Marian Eames discussed McPhee's work with *Life* (for which she was an employee) in an interview with the author, London, August 27, 1983.

48. McPhee to Sidney Cowell, "Thursday" [1950 or 1951] (B38/F614).

49. McPhee told Margaret Mead he had heard about the murder from Bobby Bruyns, his former travel agent in Java (McPhee to Mead, "Monday" [1954]). Sampih's obituary was published in the *New York Times* (May 4, 1954).

50. McPhee to Chávez, October 21 [1952].

51. McPhee to Belo, February 24, 1954, MM-DLC.

52. McPhee to Sidney Cowell, "Thursday" [1950 or 1951] (B38/F614).

53. Letters to Chávez (June 16, 1952) and Copland (February 23, 1954).

54. On May 26 [1956] McPhee wrote Chávez, "Just a line to say hello, and also to announce the safe delivery of complete book to Bollingen Foundation."

55. McPhee to Chávez, July 4 [1956].

56. Bollingen Archives, DLC.

57. McPhee to Daniel [June 1956].

58. McPhee to Copland, "Sunday" [1956].

59. McPhee to Daniel, June 8 [1956]. John Vincent, director of the Huntington Hartford, was concerned about McPhee's finances, because he would have to pay for his own laundry and postage: "We furnish all food, transportation, and

reasonable local telephone calls." An amount of $150 had also been budgeted for music supplies (Vincent to Oliver Daniel, June 26, 1956).

60. Mantle Hood, interview with author, Catonsville, Maryland, January 10, 1984.

61. McPhee to Chávez, September 10 [1956].

62. McPhee to Copland, October 9 [1956].

63. McPhee to Daniel, October 28, 1956.

64. Ibid.

65. According to Don Ott's diary, McPhee was back in New York by January 1957.

66. McPhee to Chávez, January 1, 1958.

67. Reviews were published by Eugene Lees, *Louisville Times* (January 16, 1958) and William Mootz, [Louisville] *Courier-Journal* (January 16, 1958), CM-CLU and collection of Oliver Daniel.

68. McPhee to Copland, "Tuesday" [January 1958].

69. McPhee to Daniel, "Thursday" [1957].

70. Interview with Virgil Thomson, Chicago, January 6, 1982. In addition to McPhee, Thomson recommended Peggy Glanville-Hicks and Marc Blitzstein.

71. McPhee to Thomson, January 31 [1957].

72. Marion Meadows, National Film Board of Canada, to author, November 8, 1982.

73. Program, collection of Oliver Daniel. The program included a number of Asian or Asia-inspired works—*Fantasia-Tahmeel,* by Halim El-Dabh; *Persian Set,* by Henry Cowell; *Yiskor,* by Odeon Partos; *Ten Haikus by Basho,* by Shukichi Mitsukuri; *October Mountain,* by Alan Hovhaness; and *To a Wayfarer,* by Chou Wen-chung—as well as *Divertimento for Nine Instruments,* by Walter Piston.

74. Stokowski to McPhee, October 19, 1953, collection of Oliver Daniel.

75. Diary of Don Ott, October 23, 1958.

76. Chou Wen-chung, telephone interview with author, May 18, 1989. All the quotations in this paragraph come from the same interview. Chou also recalls that McPhee's letter to Varèse, recommending Chou, suggested: "Even if you cannot or will not teach him, please do not send him to Henry Cowell."

77. McPhee to Chávez, January 1, 1960.

78. McPhee to Daniel, "Wednesday" ["March 6, 1959" added in pencil].

79. McPhee to Daniel, "Friday" [fall 1959].

80. In the letter cited above, McPhee mentions having already received a commission from Boudreau. In another letter to Daniel, dated only "Wednesday," McPhee reports, "contract with Boudreau signed today" ["1959?" added].

81. McPhee to Daniel, "Sunday" ["Nov '59?" added in pencil].

82. McPhee mentioned the possibility of a Joffrey commission in a letter to Oliver Daniel, "Wednesday" ["July 1, 1959" added].

83. McPhee to Thomson, "Friday" [1959?].

84. McPhee to Robert Boudreau, March 6, 1960, collection of Oliver Daniel.

85. McPhee to Daniel, "Monday" [March 1960].

86. Belo to Mead, February 24, 1960, MM-DLC. Perhaps the "advance" referred to *Music in Bali*.

87. McPhee to Carl Haverlin (of BMI), June 5, 1960, collection of Daniel.

CHAPTER 9: COMPOSITIONS AFTER 1940

1. Virgil Thomson, "George Gershwin," *Modern Music* 13 (1935–36): 17.

2. McPhee, field notes, "August 15" (F29), CM-CLU.

3. For a complete listing, see the catalogue of McPhee's transcriptions (Appendix B). Much work remains to·be done on McPhee's transcriptions. When it is, others for Western instruments will probably surface within the many volumes of gamelan transcriptions at CM-CLU.

4. McPhee, "An American Composer in Bali," part 2 of the script for a five-part Voice of America radio series, ca. 1958, CM-CLU.

5. Ibid.

6. From McPhee's opening sentence in his chapter "The Gendèr Wayang Ensemble" in *Music in Bali,* 201. He also wrote an article on the topic "The Balinese Wajang Koelit and Its Music," *Djåwå* 16 (1936): 322–66.

7. The old spelling, *Pemoengkah,* appears in *Balinese Ceremonial Music* (New York: G. Schirmer, 1940); in the suite of gamelan transcriptions and in *Music in Bali* it

appears in the modern equivalent as *Pemungkah.* My spelling will follow McPhee's, varying according to which piece is under discussion.

8. McPhee, introduction to *Pemoengkah,* in *Balinese Ceremonial Music.*

9. McPhee, *Music in Bali,* 204.

10. Transcriptions of *Pemungkah* (according to its later spelling) are found in *Music in Bali,* examples 181–212.

11. *MB,* 220–21.

12. McPhee, "An American Composer in Bali," part 2.

13. *MB,* 294.

14. McPhee, "An American Composer in Bali," part 3.

15. McPhee to Margaret Mead, October 1 [1941]. Mead responded with, "The authoritative edition of Wissler's American Indian is the THIRD edition, 1938" (Mead to McPhee, October 3, 1941, MM-DLC).

16. Fenton's recording was first published as *Songs from the Iroquois Longhouse* (Washington, D.C.: Smithsonian Institution, 1942).

17. McPhee, typescript program notes for *Transitions,* CM-CLU.

18. Ibid.

19. McPhee to Aaron Copland, November 4, 1954.

20. Ibid.

21. McPhee, typescript program notes for Symphony No. 2 (slightly different from the printed notes), CM-CLU.

22. Ibid.

23. McPhee, notes from printed program for Symphony No. 2, January 15–16, 1958, CM-CLU.

24. Richard Mueller, "Imitation and Stylization in the Balinese Music of Colin McPhee" (Ph.D. diss., University of Chicago, 1983), 353–63. *Jobog* is a type of dance composition played by the *gamelan pelégongan.*

25. For examples of these techniques, see *MB,* examples 127 and 134.

26. McPhee, typescript program notes for Concerto for Wind Orchestra, CM-CLU.

CHAPTER 10: THE YEARS IN CALIFORNIA

1. Mantle Hood, interview with author, Catonsville, Maryland, January 10, 1984.

2. McPhee to Sidney Cowell, "Monday," postmarked September 6, 1960 (B38/F608).

3. McPhee to Sidney Cowell, "Tuesday" [1960] (B38/F613). McPhee gave away many of his possessions before he moved. He also rented a storage room somewhere in Manhattan. Shirley Hawkins remembers seeing the storage ticket sometime before McPhee's death but afterwards it was lost (interview with author, Los Angeles, June 16, 1982).

4. McPhee to Oliver Daniel, no date [December 1960].

5. McPhee to Daniel, February 18, 1961.

6. McPhee to Sidney Cowell, June 9 [1961] (B38/F610).

7. Ibid. At about the same time he wrote Oliver Daniel, "I'm happy to stay on here, but very very lonely, having no friends here beyond John V[incent] and Mantle. My Ethno students of the past year are all very friendly and hospitable, and keep asking me to dinner or parties. But the time-gap is too great, and I find such an evening very exhausting. Miss you and other New York friends very much" ["June '61" added].

8. Rhoda Métraux to author, November 18, 1982.

9. A clipping at CM-CLU (no newspaper name or date) cites the conference participants (Eloise Cunningham, "Music Encounter in Japan").

10. A typescript of the paper is in CM-CLU.

11. McPhee to Henry and Sidney Cowell, March 4 [1962] (B16/F266).

12. Margaret Mead to Sidney Cowell, December 5, 1962, C-NN.

13. McPhee to Virgil Thomson, January 29, 1963. The next day Thomson replied, suggesting that McPhee write to Nicolas Nabokov in Paris (both letters in VT-CtY). McPhee did so on February 8, 1963, and Nabokov responded that he could be of little help (February 25, 1963; the latter two letters are at CM-CLU).

14. Unfortunately, little else is known about McPhee's plans for this new book (McPhee to Marian Eames, April 20 [1963], collection of Marian Eames).

15. Mead to McPhee, June 3, 1963, MM-DLC.

16. McPhee to Mead, September 10, 1963, CM-CLU.

17. McPhee to Daniel, "Saturday" [" '60?" added]. Haverlin wrote to McPhee on June 3, 1960, offering him the commission (CM-CLU).

18. McPhee to Daniel, September 2, 1962. This represented a change from his original plan. In response to Haverlin's letter offering him the commission, McPhee had written, "I feel I perhaps should do a work in a single movement, since I already have a number of orchestral works in several movements, then again, I have long wanted to write a piano concerto, and wonder if this is the time" (June 5, 1960, CM-CLU). On September 6, 1960, he wrote Sidney Cowell, "I also have a commissioned piano concerto which is due this fall" (B38/F608).

19. McPhee to Carl Haverlin, June 5, 1960, CM-CLU.

20. Walter Hinrichsen sent McPhee a contract on September 5, 1962, together with an advance royalty check of one hundred dollars, CM-CLU.

21. McPhee to Marian Eames, "Thursday" [spring 1963], collection of Marian Eames. In a letter written to Shirley Hawkins on January 20, 1964, after McPhee's death, Oliver Daniel said he thought the symphony "was in some way to be connected with Thoreau" (copy in Oliver Daniel collection).

22. McPhee to Minna Lederman, October 11, 1963, MoMu-DLC. UCLA kept him on the payroll until the end of 1963 (McPhee to William Melnitz, no date, CM-CLU; and Stephen M. Fry, music librarian, CLU, to author, September 5, 1984).

23. McPhee to Sidney and Henry Cowell, March 4 [1962] (B16/F266).

24. Shirley Hood Hawkins, interview with author, Los Angeles, June 16, 1982; and McPhee to Oliver Daniel, March 25 ["1962" added].

25. McPhee to Carlos Chávez, January 1, 1960.

26. McPhee to Sidney Cowell, postmarked September 6, 1960 (B38/F608).

27. McPhee to Daniel, June 18 ["1961" added].

28. McPhee to Daniel ["July 9, 1962" added].

29. McPhee to Daniel, December 9, 1962.

30. Jane Olson to Sidney Cowell, October 31, 1963, C-NN (B38/F608).

31. Métraux to author.

32. Colin McPhee, certificate of death, State of California, No. 7053/309, January 7, 1964, CM-CLU. While McPhee's death certificate confirms March 15,

1900, as his birthdate, his obituary cited the incorrect date of 1901: "Colin McPhee, Composer, Dies; Authority on Balinese Music, 62," *New York Times,* January 8, 1964.

33. A program for the service is in C-NN (B16/F265).

34. Oliver Daniel to Shirley Hawkins, February 5, 1964, collection of Oliver Daniel.

35. In the acknowledgments to *Music in Bali* (p. vii), McPhee says that the book was begun during a residency at Yaddo in 1942, but Yaddo records and his own correspondence give the year as 1941.

36. Judith Becker, review of *Music in Bali, Journal of the American Musicological Society* 21 (Fall 1968): 404.

37. McPhee, *MB,* p. vi. Hood's foreword is dated January 1964.

38. I Madé Bandem, interview with author, Den Pasar, Bali, April 11, 1984.

39. Henry Cowell, undated statement, collection of Oliver Daniel.

40. Steve Reich, "Postscript to a Brief Study of Balinese and African Music, 1973," in *Writings About Music* (Halifax: The Press of the Nova Scotia College of Art and Design, 1974), 38.

BIBLIOGRAPHY

BOOKS AND ARTICLES

Adaskin, Harry. *A Fiddler's World: Memoirs to 1938.* Vancouver: November House, 1977.

Austin, William. *Music in the Twentieth Century.* New York: W. W. Norton, 1966.

Baum, Vicki. *A Tale from Bali.* Translated by Basil Creighton. London: Geoffrey Bles, 1937; Garden City, N.Y.: Doubleday, Doran & Co., 1937.

Becker, Judith. [Review of *Music in Bali*], *Journal of the American Musicological Society* 21 (Fall 1968): 404–6.

Bellamann, Henry. "Isidor Philipp," *Musical Quarterly* 29 (October 1943): 417–25.

Belo, Jane. *Bali: Rangda and Barong.* American Ethnological Society Monographs, 16. New York: J. J. Augustin, 1949.

———. *Bali: Temple Festival.* American Ethnological Society Monographs, 22. Locust Valley, N.Y.: J. J. Augustin, 1953.

———. "Balinese Children's Drawing," *Djåwå* 17 (September–December 1937): 248–59. Reprinted in *Childhood in Contemporary Cultures.* Edited by Margaret Mead and Martha Wolfenstein. Chicago: University of Chicago Press, 1955, 52–69; reprint *TBC.*

———. "The Balinese Temper," *Character and Personality* 4 (December 1935): 120–46; reprint *TBC.*

———. "A Study of a Balinese Family," *American Anthropologist,* new ser., 38 (1936): 12–31; reprint *TBC.*

————. "A Study of Customs Pertaining to Twins in Bali," *Tijdschrift voor Indische Taal-, Land-, en Volkenkunde* 75 (1935), 483–549; reprint *TBC*.

————. *Trance in Bali*. Preface by Margaret Mead. New York: Columbia University Press, 1960.

Belo, Jane, ed. *Traditional Balinese Culture*. New York: Columbia University Press, 1970.

Bernatzik, Hugo Adolf. *South Seas*. Translated by Vivian Ogilvie. New York: Henry Holt and Company, 1935.

Biddle, George. *An American Artist's Story*. Boston: Little, Brown, & Co., 1939.

————. *Green Island*. New York: Coward-McCann, Inc., 1930.

Biddle, George, and Jane Belo. "Foot-Hills of Cuba: A Cross-Section of Spanish-American Civilization," *Scribners* 79 (February 1926): 128–36.

Bowles, Paul. *Without Stopping*. New York: G. P. Putnam's Sons, 1972.

Bridle, Augustus. "Composers Among Us." In *Yearbook of the Arts in Canada (1928–1929)*. Edited by Bertram Booker. Toronto: Macmillan, 1929.

————. "Who Writes Our Music? A Survey of Canadian Composers," *Maclean's* (December 15, 1929): 20, 30, 32.

Broder, Nathan. "Colin McPhee." In *Die Musik in Geschichte und Gegenwart*. Edited by Friedrich Blume. Kassel: Bärenreiter Verlag, 1949–67.

Callaghan, Morley. *That Summer in Paris: Memories of Tangled Friendships with Hemingway, Fitzgerald, and Some Others*. New York: Coward-McCann, 1963.

Capote, Truman. "Brooklyn Heights: A Personal Memoir," *Holiday* (February 1959): 64–68, 112–113.

Charlesworth, Hector. "Colin McPhee's Career," *Toronto Globe and Mail,* June 21, 1941.

Chou Wen-chung. "Varèse: A Sketch of the Man and His Music," *Musical Quarterly* 52 (April 1966): 151–70.

Citkowitz, Israel. "Biblical Texts Set to Music," *Modern Music* 13 (May-June 1936): 43–44.

Coast, John. *Dancers of Bali*. New York: G. P. Putnam's Sons, 1953.

"Colin McPhee." In *Baker's Biographical Dictionary of Musicians,* 4th ed. New York: G. Schirmer, 1940.

"Colin McPhee, Composer, Dies; Authority on Balinese Music, 62," *New York Times,* January 8, 1964.

Copland, Aaron. "The Composer in America, 1923–1933," *Modern Music* 10 (January-February 1933): 87–92.

Copland, Aaron, and Vivian Perlis. *Copland: 1900 through 1942*. New York: St. Martin's/Marek, 1984.

Covarrubias, Miguel. *Island of Bali*. New York: Alfred A. Knopf, 1937.

————. *Negro Drawings*. Preface by Ralph Barton; introduction by Frank Crowninshield. New York: Alfred A. Knopf, 1927.

Cowell, Henry. "Current Chronicle [review of CBS radio performance of *Tabuh-
Tabuhan*]," *Musical Quarterly* 34 (July 1948): 410–12.

————. [Review of *A House in Bali*], Music Library Association *Notes* 4 (December
1946): 84–85.

Cowell, Henry, ed. *American Composers on American Music: A Symposium.* Palo Alto:
Stanford University Press, 1933; reprint, New York: Frederick Ungar, 1962.

Cowley, Malcolm. *Exile's Return: A Literary Odyssey of the 1920s.* New York: The Viking
Press, 1934, 1951.

Douglas, Winifred. *Twenty Years of the Schola Cantorum.* n.p., [1929].

Davies, Robertson. *A Mixture of Frailties.* Ontario: Penguin Books, 1958.

Duke, Vernon. *Passport to Paris.* Boston: Little, Brown, & Co., 1955.

Farmer, Ernest. "Evolution and the Teaching of Composition." *Canadian Journal of
Music* 2 (February 1916): 183.

Fenton, William. "Songs from the Iroquois Longhouse" [booklet and recording].
Washington, D.C.: Smithsonian Institution, 1942.

Frank, Waldo. *The Rediscovery of America.* New York: Charles Scribner's Sons, 1929.

Frankenstein, Alfred. [Review of recording of *Tabuh-Tabuhan*], *High Fidelity* 6 (July
1956): 44.

Friedheim, Arthur. *Life and Liszt: Recollections of a Concert Pianist.* Introduction by
Theodore L. Bullock. New York: Taplinger Publishing, 1961.

Geertz, Clifford. "Person, Time, and Conduct in Bali." In *The Interpretation of Cultures.*
New York: Basic Books, 1973, 360–411.

Glanville-Hicks, Peggy. "Colin McPhee." In *Grove's Dictionary of Music and Musicians.*
Edited by Eric Blom. 5th ed. New York: St. Martin's Press, 1954.

Glazebrook, George Parkin de Twenebroker. *The Story of Toronto.* Toronto: University of Toronto Press, 1971.

Handy, W. C. *Blues: An Anthology.* Introduction by Abbe Niles; illustrations by Miguel
Covarrubias. New York: A. & C. Boni, 1926.

Hemenway, Robert E. *Zora Neale Hurston: A Literary Biography.* Urbana: University of
Illinois Press, 1977.

Holt, Claire. *Art in Indonesia: Continuities and Change.* Ithaca, N.Y.: Cornell University
Press, 1967.

Howard, John Tasker. *Our American Music.* 3d rev. ed. New York: Thomas Y. Crowell,
1954.

Howarth, Thomas. "Toronto." In *The New Encyclopaedia Britannica.* 30 vols. Chicago:
Encyclopaedia Britannica, Inc., 1979.

Hughes, Langston. *The Big Sea.* New York: Hill and Wang, 1940.

BIBLIOGRAPHY

Hugill, Stan. *Shanties and Sailors' Songs.* New York: Frederick A. Praeger, 1969.

Hurston, Zora Neale. *Dust Tracks on a Road: An Autobiography.* London: Hutchinson & Co., 1944.

The Jazz Age as Seen Through the Eyes of Ralph Barton, Miguel Covarrubias, and John Held, Jr. [catalogue]. Providence, R.I.: Museum of Art, School of Design, 1968.

Kallmann, Helmut, Gilles Potvin, and Kenneth Winters, eds. *Encyclopedia of Music in Canada.* Toronto: University of Toronto Press, 1981.

Kellner, Bruce. *Carl Van Vechten and the Irreverent Decades.* Norman: University of Oklahoma Press, 1968.

Klemm, Gustav. "Gustav Strube: The Man and the Musician," *Musical Quarterly* 28 (July 1942): 288–301.

Kraus, Gregor, and Karl With. *Bali: Volk, Land, Tänze, Feste, Temple.* Hagen: Folkwang Verlag, 1913.

Leedy, Denoe. "Harold Randolph: The Man and the Musician," *Musical Quarterly* 30 (April 1944): 198–204.

Leuders, Edward. *Carl Van Vechten and the Twenties.* Albuquerque: University of New Mexico Press, 1955.

Lott, R. Allen. "'New Music for New Ears': The International Composers' Guild," *Journal of the American Musicological Society* 36 (Summer 1983): 266–86.

McVey, Ruth T., ed. *Indonesia.* 2d ed. New Haven: Human Relations Area Files, Inc., 1967.

Marrocco, W. Thomas. "Colin McPhee." In *The New Grove Dictionary of Music.* Edited by Stanley Sadie. London: Macmillan, 1982.

Mathews, Marcia M. "George Biddle's Contribution to Federal Art," *Records of the Columbia Historical Society, 1973–74.* Charlottesville: University of Virginia Press, 1976.

Mead, Margaret. *Blackberry Winter: My Earlier Years.* New York: Simon and Schuster, 1972.

———. *Letters from the Field: 1925–1975.* World Perspectives. Edited by Ruth Nanda Anshen. Vol. 52. New York: Harper and Row, 1977.

Mead, Margaret, and Gregory Bateson. *Balinese Character: A Photographic Analysis.* Special Publications of the New York Academy of Sciences. Vol. 2. New York: The Academy, 1942.

Mead, Margaret, and Frances Cooke Macgregor. *Growth and Culture: A Photographic Study of Balinese Childhood.* New York: Putnam, 1951.

Mead, Margaret, and Martha Wolfenstein, eds. *Childhood in Contemporary Cultures.* Chicago: University of Chicago Press, 1955.

Mead, Rita. *Henry Cowell's New Music 1925–1936: The Society, the Music Editions, and the Recordings.* Ann Arbor: UMI Research Press, 1981.

Mershon, Katharane. *Seven Plus Seven: Mysterious Life-Rituals in Bali.* New York: Vantage Press, 1971.

Métraux, Rhoda. "Jane Belo Tannenbaum, 1904–1968," *American Anthropologist* 70 (1968): 1168–69.

Mishkin, Henry G. "Bartók at Amherst." *Amherst* (Winter 1978): 14–15.

Mitchell, Donald, and John Evans. *Benjamin Britten: Pictures from a Life 1913–1976.* New York: Charles Scribner's Sons, 1978.

Morey, Carl. "Toronto." In *The New Grove Dictionary of Music.* Edited by Stanley Sadie. London: Macmillan, 1981.

Mueller, Richard. "Imitation and Stylization in the Balinese Music of Colin McPhee." Ph.D. diss., University of Chicago, 1983.

Nassagaweya: A History of Campbellville and Surrounding Area. Campbellville, Ontario: Campbellville Historical Society, 1982.

Natoli, Joseph. "Colin McPhee." Unpublished undergraduate essay, University of Toronto, ca. 1976.

Nettl, Bruno. "From the Editor [obituary for McPhee]," *Ethnomusicology* 8 (May 1964): iv.

Oja, Carol. "Colin McPhee." In *The New Grove Dictionary of American Music.* Edited by H. Wiley Hitchcock and Stanley Sadie. London: Macmillan, 1986.

———. "Colin McPhee, A Composer Turned Explorer," *Tempo* (March 1984): 2–6.

———. "Colin McPhee: A Composer Who Visited Paradise," *New York Times,* November 7, 1982.

———. "Colin McPhee (1900–1964): A Composer in Two Worlds." Ph.D. diss., Graduate School of the City University of New York, 1985.

———. "The Copland-Sessions Concerts and Their Reception in the Contemporary Press," *Musical Quarterly* 65 (April 1979): 212–29.

———. "Cos Cob Press and the American Composer," Music Library Association *Notes* 45 (December 1988): 227–52.

———. *Distant Tones: Excerpts from the Bali Field Notes of Colin McPhee.* Toronto: Aliquando Press, 1990.

Pennigar, Martha. *The Graphic Work of George Biddle with Catalogue Raisonné.* Exhibition catalogue. Washington, D.C.: The Corcoran Gallery of Art, 1979.

Potvin, Gilles. "Colin McPhee." In *Encyclopedia of Music in Canada.* Edited by Helmut Kallmann, Gilles Potvin, and Kenneth Winters. Toronto: University of Toronto Press, 1981.

Powell, Hickman. *The Last Paradise.* Illustrations by Alexander King; photographs by André Roosevelt. New York: J. Cape and H. Smith, 1930.

[Reed, Peter Hugh.] "Notes and Reviews" [Review of recording of *Tabuh-Tabuhan*], *American Record Guide* (July 1956): 177.

Reich, Steve. *Writings About Music.* Halifax: The Press of the Nova Scotia College of
Art and Design, 1974.

Reis, Claire. *American Composers of Today.* New York: The United States Section of the
International Society for Contemporary Music, 1930.

Rhodius, Hans, ed. *Schönheit und Reichtum des Lebens Walter Spies: Maler und Musiker auf
Bali 1895–1942.* Den Haag: L. J. C. Boucher, [1964].

Rhodius, Hans, and John Darling. *Walter Spies and Balinese Art.* Edited by John Stowell.
Zutphen: Terra, 1980.

Robinson, Ray Edwin. "A History of the Peabody Conservatory of Music." D.M.E.
diss., Indiana University, 1969.

Root, Deane L. "The Pan American Association of Composers (1928–1934),"
Yearbook for Inter-American Musical Research 8 (1972): 49–70.

Saminsky, Lazare. *Music of Our Day: Essentials and Prophecies.* New York: Thomas Y.
Crowell Co., 1932.

Sigmon, Carl. "Colin McPhee," *ACA Bulletin* 12 (Spring 1964): 15–16.

Steiner, Ralph. *A Point of View.* Middletown, Conn.: Wesleyan University Press, 1978.

Stutterheim, Willem F. *Indian Influences in Old-Javanese Art.* London: The India Society,
1935.

Terkel, Studs. "The Good War: An Oral History of World War II," *Atlantic Monthly*
(July 1984): 45–75.

Terry, Sir Richard Runcian. *The Shanty Book.* Part 1. London: J. Curwen & Sons,
1921.

Toth, Andrew. *Recordings of Traditional Music of Bali and Lombok.* n.p.: Society for
Ethnomusicology, 1980.

Van Vechten, Carl. *Nigger Heaven.* New York: Alfred A. Knopf, 1926.

Varèse, Louise. *Varèse: A Looking-Glass Diary, Vol. I: 1883–1928.* New York: W. W.
Norton, 1972.

Whall, Captain W. B. *Ships, Sea Songs and Shanties.* Glasgow: J. Brown & Son, 1927.

White, Eric Walter. *Benjamin Britten: His Life and Operas.* Berkeley: University of
California Press, 1970.

Whitesitt, Linda. *The Life and Music of George Antheil (1900–1959).* Ann Arbor: UMI
Research Press, 1983.

Williams, Tennessee. *Memoirs.* New York: Doubleday and Company, 1975.

Wilson, Edmund. *O Canada: An American's Notes on Canadian Culture.* New York:
Farrar, Straus and Giroux, 1965.

Young, Douglas. "Colin McPhee's Music: (I) From West to East," *Tempo* 150 (September 1984): 11–17.

———. "Colin McPhee (II): 'Tabuh-Tabuhan,'" *Tempo* 159 (December 1986):
16–19.

Zoete, Beryl de, and Walter Spies. *Dance and Drama in Bali*. Preface by Arthur Waley. London: Faber and Faber, 1938.

INTERVIEWS

Unless otherwise specified, all of the following interviews were conducted by the author.

Bandem, I Madé. Den Pasar, Bali. April 11, 1984.

Carl, Victor. New York City. January 26, 1982.

Chou Wen-chung. New York City (telephone). May 18, 1989.

Copland, Aaron. New York City. November 17, 1981.

Cowell, Sidney. Shady, New York. October 10, 1981.

Daniel, Oliver. Ardsley, New York. October 3, 1981.

Diamond, David. New York City. March 27, 1986.

Eames, Marian. London, England. August 24, 1982.

Friedheim, Eric. New York City. February 21, 1984.

Harrison, Lou. Aptos, California. June 23, 1982.

Hawkins, Shirley. Los Angeles, California. June 16, 1982.

Hood, Ki Mantle. Catonsville, Maryland. January 10, 1984.

Hull, Ann. Westport, Connecticut. December 5, 1981.

Lawson, Stuart. Toronto, Canada. May 1, 1983.

Lebah, I Madé. Peliatan, Bali. April 9, 1984.

Lebah, I Madé. Peliatan, Bali. n.d. Interview by Carol Warren.

Lederman, Minna. New York City. October 12, 1981.

Levin, Sylvan. New York City. September 25, 1981.

Luening, Otto. New York City. November 26, 1982.

McPhee, Janet. Toronto, Canada. May 1, 1983.

Mandera, Anak Agung Gedé. Peliatan, Bali. April 11, 1984.

Mershon, Katharane. Tarzana, California. June 13, 1982.

Peghi, Madé. Sanur, Bali. April 8, 1984.

Rima, I Wayan. Sayan, Bali. April 7, 1984.

Ross, Hugh. New York City. October 4, 1982.

BIBLIOGRAPHY

Sauerlander, Beata. New York City. October 16, 1982.

Strickland, William. Westport, Connecticut. December 5, 1981.

Thomson, Virgil. Chicago, Illinois. January 6, 1982.

Varèse, Louise. New York City. November 18, 1981.

White, Donald. Red Bank, New Jersey (telephone). November 8, 1982.

INDEX

Page numbers in italics indicate illustrations
Page numbers in bold indicate musical examples

INDEX

Halusa, Dr., 139
Hambourg Conservatory, 4, 7
Hambourg Trio, 4
Handy, W. C., 59–60
Hanson, Howard, 25, 37, 193, 194
Harold Ober Associates, 160
Harris, Roy, 24, 26, 37, 53, 99, 116, 255
Harrison, Lou, ix, 166, 205, 251
Hart House, 16
Harvard University Glee Club, 299n.41
Haverlin, Carl, 18, 253, 335nn.17
Hawkins, Shirley, xiii
Haydn, Franz Joseph, 101
Heifetz, Jascha, 4, 22, 29
Hemingway, Ernest, 19–20, 24
Henderson, W. J., 28
Herman, Woody, 171
Herzog, George, 152, 168, 219–20, 317n.10
Hindemith, Paul, 98, 99
Hinrichsen, Walter, 335n.20
Hippolytus, 17
Hitler, Adolf, 68
Hoffman, Irwin, 192
Holt, Claire, 63, 79, 255
Honegger, Arthur, 95
Hood, Ki Mantle, xiii, 82, 198, 249, 251, 252, 253, 254, 255, 256
Hood, Shirley, 253
Hopkins, Miriam, 173
Hornbostel, Erich von, 63, 124, 161
Horowitz, Joseph, xi
Houseman, John, 322n.98
Hovhaness, Alan, 331n.73
Hughes, Langston, 30, 58, 59, 160, 301n.19
Huízar, Candelario, 101
Hull, Ann, xiii, 9, 11, 121, 154
Huntington Hartford Foundation, 197, 198, 199, 253, 330n.59
Hurston, Zora Neale, 59, 75, 305n.31
Hyperprism, 27

Imperial Order of the Daughters of the Empire, Toronto, 20, 294n.63
Instituto Indigenista Inter-Americano of Mexico City, 174
International Colonial Exposition, 60, 65

International Composers' Guild, 25, 27, 99, 296nn.13, 18, 297n.28
Iturbi, José, 117, 118
Ives, Charles, 2, 26, 164, 321n.66

James, Harry, 171
Joffrey Ballet, 203, 332n.82
Johannesen, Grant, 194
John Day Company, 169
Johnson, James Weldon, 58
Josten, Werner, 99, 310n.28
Judson, Arthur, 296n.18

Kalér, Nyoman, 68, 84, 89, 91, 126, 128, 134
Kallman, Chester, 156
kebyar. See *gamelan kebyar*
Kebyar ding, 107, 109
Kedaton, Bali, 67, 68, 81
Kirstein, Lincoln, 175, 191
Knopf, Blanche, 59
Koussevitsky Foundation, 191, 195
Koussevitzky, Serge, 117, 118
Krause, Gregory, 78
Kreisler, Fritz, 10, 29
Kunits, Luigi von, 17
Kunst, Jaap, 124
Kuta, 84, 85, 86, 208, 212, 214

Lambert, Constant, 32
Lawrence, Robert, 172
Lawson, Stuart, xiii, 4
League of Composers, 25, 94, 95, 96, 308n.8, 309nn. 21, 25
Lebah, I Madé, xiii, 24, 65, 70, 74, 76, 77, 81, 87, 90–91, 123, 125, 127, 128, *129*, 129, 135, 136, 140, 144, 183, 186, 247, 302n.1, 307n.76, 307n.80, 313nn.18, 24, 314n.29
Lederman, Minna, xiii, 56, 96, 141, 151, 155, 156, 161, 163–64, 176, 186, 187, 189, 190
Lee, Gypsy Rose, 157
Leedy, Denoe, 9
Le Flem, Paul, 21, 28, 36
Léger, Fernand, 299n.47
legong gamelan, 84, 134
Lenya, Lotte, 329n.42
Levin, Sylvan, xiii, 9
Lewis, Sinclair, 59

Vishinsky, Andre, 190
Vivaldi, Antonio, 29, 102

Waters, Ethel, 58, 59, 166
Webern, Anton, 27
Wen-chung, Chou, xiii, 76, 202, 331nn.73
WEVD (New York), 95
Whaley, Royce & Co., 7, 9
Whall, Captain W. B., 44
White, Josh, 166
Whitney, Robert, 199
Williams, Tennessee, 173
Wilson, Edmund, 19
Wissler, Clark, 220, 333n.15

Women's University Glee Club, 28, 297n.21
Worcester (Massachusetts) Festival, 10
Wyldes, Victor, 7

Yaddo, 156, 158, 162, 176, 179, 318n.25, 336n.35
Yale University Glee Club, 299n.41
Yale University Press, 197, 251, 254, 255
Young, La Monte, ix

Zimbalist, Efrem, 29
Zoete, Beryl de, 77
Zorn, John, ix